D1735679

INSTRUCTIVE JOURNEY

An Essay in Autobiography

Nicholas Rescher

University Press of America, Inc.
Lanham • New York • London

Copyright © 1997 by
University Press of America,® Inc.
4720 Boston Way
Lanham, Maryland 20706

3 Henrietta Street
London, WC2E 8LU England

Library of Congress Cataloging-in-Publication Data

Rescher, Nicholas.
Instructive journey : an essay in autobiography / by Nicholas Rescher.
p.   cm.
Expanded ed. of: Ongoing journey. c 1986.
Includes index.
1. Rescher, Nicholas. 2. Philosophers--United States--Biography. I.
Rescher, Nicholas, Ongoing journey. II. Title.
B945.R454A3 1996   191--dc20   96-44938 CIP
(B)

ISBN 0-7618-0585-0 (cloth: alk. ppr.)
ISBN 0-7618-0586-9 (pbk: alk. ppr.)

FOR MY CHILDREN

CONTENTS

Preliminaries

INITIAL INTRODUCTION: 1975

I took up my first teaching post at the age of 23 at Princeton, ending the years of academic apprenticeship and embarking on a professional career. I shall—God willing—in due course be rusticated at the age of 70, the long-established retirement age at the University of Pittsburgh. Thus at the time when this biographical material is being written—in 1974-75, when I am 46/47 years of age—I stand at the exact mid-point of my professional life.

Autobiographies are generally produced by septuagenarians reviewing the course of their lives in distant and detached retrospect. It is a matter of looking back with seemly pride at one's achievements, offering plausible excuses for one's failures, and perhaps settling a few old scores. One shortcoming of this procedure is that whatever wisdom might come from such a scrutiny of one's self and one's doings can no longer be put to active use. The hour is late, the sun is setting, the work of the day is done—it is too late to do or undo. In writing the present book too early, as it were, I hope to avoid this shortcoming. This premature autobiographical exercise will, I trust, enable me to obtain whatever useful lessons of self-knowledge can be extracted at a stage when some profit can still be drawn from its deliberations.

In retrospect things always look simple: we know with the wisdom of hindsight just where the twists and turns lead. But at the time, when much in unknown and undecided, there is an uncertainty and anxiety that yields some element of suspense. And so, it seems fitting to take stock of the journey I have traveled and to peer—however myopically—down the road that lies ahead.

I believe, moreover, that some special interest attaches to such an essay written *in medias res*, before all the returns are in and one confronts settled issues with the wisdom of hindsight. For then the course is not yet run, so that it is a genuinely open question how things will eventuate—whether with fondest hopes exceeded or with reasonable aspirations blighted. Some element of suspense still hovers about the picture of a life that is yet unfinished and has to face the yet unissued rulings of the goddess Fortuna whose stern decrees permeate all human contingencies.

This autobiography began in an endeavor to record for the benefit of my children some information about their own antecedents and parentage—information which would otherwise go to the grave with me, leaving them virtually pastless. Gradually, however, a sea-change came upon the work. It took on a life of its own and became an endeavor in self-definition and self-comprehension.

The reader who looks here for "the life and times" will be disappointed in the latter regard. For one thing, I am too small a fish in too large a pond for this sort of enterprise. For another, it has been my practice to go my own way insofar as possible and let the times go hang. By temperament I am not a joiner or promoter of causes. I have generally found my own allotted share of the world's work quite enough to handle. Without hiding my head in the sand as to the great issues and developments of the day, I have concentrated on the tasks that confront me on the agenda of my personal and professional life, and have been disinclined to expend time and energy on things I deemed impervious to such feeble efforts as I could muster.

Ideally, a "life"—be it written of lived— should have a certain plan, a plot that endows it with some coherent structure. It should have a tale to tell—a rise to riches or power, a failure to realize great expectations, a story of achievement or of tragic decline and unmerited degradation, perhaps even a conquest of great obstacles by sheer force of character. In my own case, there is indeed such a plot, although one that lacks the great drama of the preceding sketches. Its story-line revolves about my finding myself in the career of a philosopher and especially as an author of philosophical books. In reviewing one of my publications, a German scholar once spoke of my *"beängstigender Autorenfleiss"*—fearsome diligence in authorship or *scriptomania*, to put it less kindly. It is this aspect of my makeup—the gradual emergence of an inveterate writer of philosophical books—that is the recurrent leitmotiv of these pages. Paradoxically, the book is my *Apologia pro libris suis*.

In the Preface to his *Autobiography*, the English philosopher R. G. Collingwood wrote that "The autobiography of a man whose business is thinking should be the story of his thought." I do not believe this for a moment—instead, I believe that the autobiography should tell the story of a *life*, and the worker generally lives neither in nor for the work alone. Moreover, an author should not have to speak for his books—they should speak for themselves. I have tried to write here the biography of a person who happens to be an "intellectual" of sorts, but not to produce an intellectual autobiography.

At this point, more than sixty thousand copies of my two dozen books are knocking about in the world. By best-seller standards this is infinitesimal, but for an academic author of professionally technical material it represent a respectable production. And it seems plausible to suppose that occasionally here or there someone who encounters one of my books should wonder about the person who brought it into being. After all, as one wanders down the library shelves among all those products of brains long stilled, one cannot wholly suppress one's curiosity about the people who produced these books—about their personalities and characteristics, their hopes and fears, their successes and failures, and their management of the business of living. Moreover, when viewed at close range no active human life can be altogether without interest for a fellow human being. This circumstance, which assures immortality to the character of the gossip, also gives the autobiographer some comfort when faced with the otherwise daunting question: "But why on earth should you presume that *your* doings are of the least interest to anybody?" After all, even the most commonplace life of one generation is destined to appear rather strange and extraordinary from the distant retrospect of its eventual successors.

No man is a hero to his valet, no man a villain to his autobiographer. Yet pretty much everyone's life involves some episodes that occasion subsequent regret—transactions from which he does not emerge as the sort of person he would wish to be. The reader can scarcely expect to find all of them chronicled and detailed in an autobiography. The amazing Pepys aside—for in human affairs every rule has its exception—the autobiographer whose candor knows no limits has a boor for a subject. This said, I think it nevertheless fair to add I have endeavored to produce and honest work, one that portrays a real and thus an imperfect person, endowed with an ample quota of human shortcomings and failings.

It is sometimes said that biography is fiction because the author molds his factual materials into a creation of his own. And this is all the more true of autobiographies. All the same, I am persuaded that a reasonably accurate picture—not necessarily of the sort of person I would ideally like to be, but of the sort of person I actually am—can be drawn from the data presented here. The watchful reader will find that I have pictured myself as Cromwell wished to be painted, "with the warts on."

Still, a biographical work is bound to wear a somewhat unrealistic aspect. Its subject is constantly at the center-stage. Such exclusive focus upon oneself suggests a false importance and centrality. Life, of course, is not like that. Almost always and everywhere we are but one among numerous others who feature no less prominently in the scheme of things. However, exactly because such distortion of emphasis is unavoidable in a work of this nature, the reader should be generous enough not to impute automatically to an autobiographer a narcissism that is not necessarily there.

Because it is a writer that is at issue, perhaps a word about the writing itself is not out of order. I must say that I have found it harder to write this book than anything else I have produced. For I am a person who is naturally reticent about his personal affairs almost to the point of secretiveness, and the idea of admitting others into the inner precincts of my life is antipathetic to me. But having embarked on the project as a matter of obligation I have pressed ahead undaunted. All the same, I have found this sort of writing possible only in very short bursts, usually lasting for only a paragraph or two, as a particular mood conducive to this sort of candor was transiently upon me. For me, this writing project was a harder-won victory over blank pages than most.

ADDENDUM: 1985

Initially written in 1974-75, the book remained tucked away as a typescript in a drawer until 1982. At that point, the University Press of America was about to launch a series of reprints of books of mine, and Jed Lyons, its excellent and enterprising editor, asked me it I might have something of a more personal nature to form part of this project to give it an "added touch" of sorts. After some thought and hesitation I concluded that there was no cogent reason for declining to "go public" with this book, which thus appeared in 1983 under the title *Mid-Journey*. For reasons explained below, I eventually decided to update the book to 1985, by adding the three additional chapters. (Apart from this, there are only a few minor emendations and additions to the earlier text.) The title now given to the book, *Ongoing Journey*, seemed an obvious choice for indicating the relationship to its predecessor.

ADDENDUM: 1995

As the saying has it, time flies. Here it is 1995—ten years further on—and the decade seems to have passed in the proverbial twinkling of an eye.

Superficially very little has changed: We still reside in the Aylesboro Avenue house in Pittsburgh's Squirrel Hill area; we still spend the summers in Cunliffe Close in Oxford; I still teach philosophy at Pitt. But beneath the surface there are big changes. Some of them are for the good. For example, at this stage, I am no longer just another philosophy professor but have somehow transmuted into a respected elder scholar whose work and person figures in encyclopedias and handbooks. But others are for the bad. My memory, especially for names, grows weaker with age, and health problems—hypertension to give just one example—come increasingly to the surface. Still, I am not only among those yet present but continue active and stirring. Many things have happened in my life during the past decade and some of these eventuations deserve to be placed alongside the preceding. Three further chapters manage to do the needful here. The title of this expanded book, *Instructive Journey*, is again designed to indicate a linkage with what has preceded.

One

FAMILY BACKGROUND

RESCHER FOREFATHERS

The general consensus of opinion and the universal practice of biographers agree that people are to be viewed against the background of their family antecedents. As a traditionalist, I find no difficulty in yielding to the pressure of this tradition. Few people are wholly self-made. For most, at least some facet of what sort of a person one is will turn on one's biological and communal heritage. And here the motley throng of people who constitute one's ancestral heritage becomes significant.

The basic name-pattern R-*scher* has many dialect variations through the multiplicity of spoken German forms. It can occur with A, or E, or O, or Ö (the is, OE). But all of these go back to *Rascher* as their common original. However, two distinct etymological routes lead to this common destination: one via the Anglo-Saxon *rasch* = swift, active, lively, hasty,[1] the other via *rasch* from Arras, the medieval tapestry center, with *r-scher* = *r-schner* = a weaver of tapestry.[2] The name would thus have two distinct English equivalents: *Rusher*, one who hastens, and an approximation to the far more common *Weaver*. I have sometimes thought fleetingly of anglicizing the name in the former way.

Raschers were active in Franconia in the 13th century?[3] The Roschers are an old Nether-Saxon family who produced several well-known scholars—in particular the important 19th

7

century economist Wilhelm Roscher.[4] One Johann Roescher (1589-1668) was court preacher for a duke of Brunswick-Luneburg, just prior to the time when Leibniz entered the service of this house.[5] Reschers have been substantial land-holders in Hesse at least since the 17th century.[6] There ere R-schers pretty well scattered throughout the German-speaking realm. However, my own ultimate ancestors were Swiss. The clan of von Rascher was an old family prominent since medieval times in the town of Chur (Coire) in the canton of Graubünden (Grisons), the most remote and per-haps the most backward region of Switzerland. Ennobled in 1550, the family divided in the troubled times of the Refor-mation. In 1580 its Catholics emigrated to Vienna, leaving the Protestants in possession of the home ground in Switzer-land.[7] By the early 1700's this emigré branch of the family had prospered and was again raised to the minor nobility —this time in Austria.[8] It was to this group that my own forefathers belonged.[9]

The first paternal ancestors whom family tradition identi-fies by name is my grandfather's great-grandfather Albrecht Heinrich von Rascher, who was born in Austria around 1750. The younger son of proud and prosperous parents, only re-cently ennobled, he outraged his family by making an "unfor-tunate" marriage which severed him altogether from his relations. The young lady he chose to make his own was Jewish, and to obtain her hand in marriage be agreed to have their children brought up in his wife's beliefs.[10] Their son, Johann Jakob, was accordingly raised in this faith, and in loyalty to his mother's memory, he eventually named his own son—my father's grandfather—Nehemias, after the Old Tes-tament hero. But this son's adherence to his grandmother's religion faded away in time, and he resumed the Christianity of his forefathers—not however as a Catholic, but in the standard German Protestantism of the Lutheran-Evangelical stripe.

His marriage having alienated him from his family, Al-brecht Heinrich von Rascher left Austria in the early 1780's and resettled in southern Germany, near Mannheim in Baden. Dropping the nobiliary prefix *von* as unsuitable to his changed circumstances in life, he also altered the name to Röscher, attuning its orthography to the local Swabian dialect.[11] I do not know just how he earned his livelihood; apparently he was never prosperous. He died around 1810. As a result of his move to southern Germany, the destiny of my ancestors unfolded in Baden and Württemberg, and the theater of their activity came to lie in the valley of the river Neckar—in Mannheim, Stuttgart, Schozberg, and their environs.

Albrecht Heinrich's fateful marriage produced one son, Johann Jakob Röscher (named, as family tradition has it, after Jean Jacques Rosseau), who was born around 1780. Eventually he came to enjoy a modest prosperity as a proprietor of a business in the small town of Hochberg, in Baden. Around 1815 he married a local girl who was about a decade younger than himself. They had several children, but all died in infancy except one boy, Nehemias, born in 1828. The father died (in his middle fifties) in June of 1835, when the son was only seven, and the mother followed her husband to the grave a year and a half later, still in her early forties.

My father's grandfather was thus orphaned as a little boy of eight. I do not know who took charge of his upbringing or just where he was raised. However, there was no financial difficulty. His father's business had prospered and adequate funds were available for the boy's immediate needs. He received a good schooling, which he concluded in 1848. During 1848-49 he discharged his military service obligation in the army of Württemberg, and then proceeded to study at the University of Tübingen. After further medical study at the University of Würzburg—at that time perhaps the best medical school in Germany—he took his M.D. examination in the summer of 1852. Later that year he settled in the rural hamlet of Schrozberg (not far from Stuttgart) with his new bride, Emilie Isar, the twenty-year-old daughter of one Leopold Isar of Sonthaim-on-the-Neckar. By then he had already simplified the spelling of his name from Röscher (= Roescher) to Rescher.

Throughout his working life Dr. med. N. Rescher practiced medicine as a *Landartzt* in Schrozberg. He was very popular in the village, and on the 30th anniversary of his service there his fellow citizens held a public celebration in his honor. Family tradition depicts him as the typical old-time country doctor, struggling to make ends meet to support his growing family. As a son of his son Alfred wrote me, "I well remember my father saying how, on cold winter nights, he often hitched the horse and buggy and would drive his father into the country to attend a patient, and of how, very often he was not paid for his services, which he gladly performed on the basis of need, or was paid small amounts, often only in kind with a few eggs or vegetables." Dr. Rescher was quite handsome —as evidence by a fine, old lithograph of him as a young man which remains in the family. (It was made in 1849, when he was a young university student of 21 years, and shows his in the characteristic tighwaisted jacket of the day.) He died of a chronic ailment in 1885, at the relatively early age of 57.

My father's grandfather had married twice. His first wife, Emilie, bore him seven children, of whom only four survived to adulthood: Otto b. 1853 (my own grandfather), Adolf b. 1856, Emma b. 1860, and Julie b. 1865. The marriage had lasted some seventeen years when Emilie died in March 1869, leaving the bereaved physician with sons aged 16 and 13 and daughters aged 8 and 4. The family evidently needed a mother, and so, after a minimally seemly period had elapsed, my father's grandfather remarried in December of 1869, then aged 41. His second wife Nanette, was the 28-year-old daughter of Alexander Gunzenhausen, a businessman from Mannheim. In the course of the next ten years she gave birth to eight children, four of whom survived to adulthood.[12] Notwithstanding the rigors of almost annual maternity throughout the decade of her 30's, she lived to a ripe old age in America, where she eventually emigrated with all her children.[13] They settled in Denver, where she died in 1925 at the age of 84. The subsequent history of this part of the family forms and independent unit, and a somewhat sad one, since the Rescher name now stands at the brink of extinction in this "American Branch" of Reschers, launched by the children of my great-grandfather and Nanette Gunzenhausen Rescher.[14]

The Schrozberg doctor's first marriage had produced two sons. The second, Adolf, was born in 1856, and in due course became a successful businessman in Stuttgart, where he resided throughout his life as a prosperous pillar-of-the-community type. (Around 1878 he married a local girl, and this union resulted in the birth in 1883 of a single child, Oskar Rescher, who was to become an eminent but eccentric Arabist.[15]) The other son—the elder—was my own grandfather Otto, born in 1853.[16]

On reaching adulthood, my grandfather, Otto Rescher, left his parental roof in Schrozberg together with his brother Adolf to make their way in the business world of Stuttgart. Their father had hard work of it to support the growing family of his second marriage on a modest medical practice of a rural village, and could not afford to send his sons to the university. However, the lads were apparently endowed with business acumen, and both ultimately prospered. Otto Rescher became an importer and wholesaler of textiles (largely woolens imported from England). By his late forties he had made a substantial fortune. He then sold his business, invested the proceeds, and went into retirement, living in a comfortable apartment in the Bad Cannstadt section of Stuttgart. He devoted himself to the maintenance of his (as he thought) delicate health, pursuing the then-common hypochondriac routines of vegetarianism, bottled waters, and extensive spa visits, and so continued pretty much hale and hearty until his death at almost eighty years in 1932. (The only occasion on which I can recall meeting him occurred in a family visit in Stuttgart in the previous year.)

Around 1880 Otto Rescher married Emilie Haarburger, the daughter of a prosperous Stuttgart manufacturer.[17] Born in 1861, this young lady born the name of his own mother, Emilie, but was nicknamed Emmy. They had five children in all, of whom only two survived infancy—my father Erwin Hans, born in 1890, and his sister Gertrude, born in 1903, whom I remember well from my childhood. She was a charming, somewhat flighty woman—married three times, with all of her marriages ending in divorce.[18] As to grandmother

Rescher, she died at the age of eighty in 1941, having outlived all of her children except for my father.

As this brief family history indicates, the Reschers of recent generations have all been solid, middle-class professional people: physicians, businessmen, lawyers, scholars. Moreover, they have usually been well-to-do, with a more than ordinary ability in matters of business. They have generally shown considerable drive and tenacity in making their way in the world. Finally, they have also often exhibited a streak of decided eccentricity, manifested in grandfather Otto's hypochondria, the peculiarities of great-uncle Oskar, and even in Aunt Gertrude's succession of marital mishaps. They have been people outside the common run, with more ability and more "character" than one ordinarily meets with.

FATHER

My father was born in Stuttgart on April 21, 1890. He grew up in the midst of a prosperous, bourgeois, Forsyte-like family circle. All I know about his early youth is that his uncle Adolf was a great favorite of father's who as a child loved to go on long rambles with him in the woods around Stuttgart. My grandfather was apparently not much given to small-talk, and so it was from Uncle Adolf that my father learned about the struggles of the Rescher brothers for business success in the Stuttgart of the 1870's and 80's.

After completing his schooling at a humanistic *Gymnasium* in Stuttgart, my father attended the local university in nearby Tübingen. During the period from 1909 to roughly 1912 he there lived the life of the typical university student of Kaiser Wilhelm's Germany: hard work, good companions, beer, and, of course, a dueling society (called the "Allemania," I think). Throughout his life, father wore across his left cheek the dueling scar that was the characteristic badge of such a fraternity. His studies at Tübingen completed, father transferred to the University of Berlin, where he enrolled in the Faculty of Law. He completed his legal studies in 1914, just in time to join the ill-fated throng of young men being herded over the precipice of World War I.

In the fall of 1914 my father received a commission as a lieutenant in the army corps which the King of Württemberg contributed to the military cause of the German Reich.[19] He trained initially for the cavalry, and after mastering such splendidly obsolete skills as the use of a lance on horseback, spent four years in the trenches of the Western Front. Amazingly, he survived the war, emerging from four years of trench warfare as a senior grade lieutenant, the holder of the Iron Cross (second class) and some lesser decorations. I remember well the tale of father's Iron Cross. One day the commanding general of his division inspected his unit. He commented on father's lack of decorations and father replied that he had no deeds of special valor to his credit. The GOC asked how long the young lieutenant had been in service at the front and father said he had been there for some two years. "That's valiant enough," said the GOC, and ordered the award of an Iron Cross.

The majority of my father's friends and classmates were devoured in the senseless slaughters of the Western Front. When I was a boy of five or six years, we visited Stuttgart and walked in the cemetery where my father's own father had recently been buried. There father showed me the great cenotaph for local victims of the war, many of them the companions of his youth. (Fewer than one in ten in father's Gymnasium class survived the war and father almost never talked of his wartime service.)

After the demobilization, father returned to the law, serving as "assessor" with a law firm in Frankfurt an der Oder. With this training completed, he settled down in 1922 to practice law in Hagen, in Wesphalia. Initially he was in partnership with another attorney (one August Fischer), and they maintained an office in the "Hagener Zeitung" Building. However, after a couple of years he set up on his own. No doubt he had a strugglesome time of it at first, but by the later 1920's he had built up a flourishing practice.

My mother entered this picture in 1924 when she came to work in my father's office as his secretary. She was a young woman of great beauty and charm, and it is little wonder that they soon fell in love. They were married in September of 1925, when father was 35 and mother just under 20.

At first they lived in a small flat in the Hohenzollernstrasse (at the corner of the Körnerstrasse), but shortly before I was born in 1928 they removed to a larger apartment in the Ruhrstrasse, which then became my birthplace. Not long afterwards they purchased a family-sized house in the more suburban Leibnizstrasse.

The early 1930's must have been "the years of wine and roses" for my parents. Father was building up a thriving law practice. Mother busied herself not only with child and home, but also an active social life, and, above all, with athletics. At this stage mother was an enthusiastic gymnast and sports-woman, who, weather permitting, spent part of each day at the local sporting ground.

My parents' good fortune came crashing down in flames with the onset of the Nazi regime in 1933. Father never troubled to conceal his dislike of the Nazis and what they stood for—imprudently, for a practicing attorney. As the Nazification of the judicial system proceeded, lawyers known to be unsympathetic toward the Nazi cause simply stopped winning cases.[20] In consequence, clients, of course, went else-where. By the middle 30's my father's law practice was *kaput*. Economic hardship, dismay at political developments, and the approach of the day when, on reaching the age of ten, I would soon have had to join in the compulsory activities of the "Hitler Youth," combined to set my parents to think of emigration. In 1936 they sold the house on the Leibnizstrasse. That summer father went to the U.S.A. for an exploratory visit, and he returned permanently the next year to arrange for a place to live and a means of livelihood. After a circuit of farewell visits to our relations, Mother and I crossed the Atlantic to join him in 1938.

The transatlantic migration was financially ruinous for my parents. One could bring only a modicum of personal posses-sions, and the Nazi regulations prohibited emigrants from taking more than 100 marks apiece in cash (then some $25). Fortunately, father was able to transfer a modest sum of around $1,500 surreptitiously through Switzerland.

The most immediate problem facing my father was clearly that of earning a living for himself and his family. He was unable to resume his career as a lawyer, the difference between the German and the Anglo-American systems being so substantial that this would have required several years of preparation in a law school, which was out of the question for financial reasons. In an American still caught up in the slump of an unconquered depression, the obstacles to the useful employment of an immigrant aged almost fifty were formidable. So father turned for a career to his hobby, photography. With the money salvaged via Switzerland, he started a small photographic business.

After 1939, he shared a small storefront at 161-11 Northern Boulevard in north Flushing with a friend who operated a sporting goods shop—a somewhat curious arrangement! This business went on in a modestly adequate way. (By 1940 we were even able to afford our first car, a 1936 vintage Studebaker, whose acquisition for some $300 impressed me greatly, since in Germany we had never owned—nor indeed needed —an automobile.) Mother would sometimes help out in the studio, and father brought home to her all pictures for coloring, which in those days was done by hand-painting.

Catastrophe struck in the wake of America's entry into the war upon Japan's attack on Pearl Harbor in December of 1941. As part of the military security precautions launched after America's entry into World War II—measures which most notably included the internment of many Japanese-Americans—a regulation was instituted prohibiting all "enemy aliens" who lived within 300 miles of the seacoast from owning cameras. The point, it seems, was to prevent their taking pictures of military installations, war plants, shipping, troop movements, and the like. At this time, however, father was still a German national—he did not acquire U.S. citizenship until late in 1942. Overnight, his photographic business was finished, and he had to sell his stock at a substantial loss. For the second time in a decade father's vocation had been pulled out from under his feet and his livelihood destroyed by the rude intrusion of political developments. Over fifty years old, he once again stared economic disaster in the face—this time in a still unfamiliar and unaccustomed environment.

What to do? Father met with courage and good humor the difficulties of a man no longer confronting the task of making his living in his new homeland. He turned to being a self-taught bookkeeper and accountant—first at Bloomingdale's large department store in Manhattan, and then as the war-economy expanded in a small shipyard in Whitestone. After 1946—when it became clear that the shipyard, a wartime product now transformed into the "Whitestone Woodworking Co." could not survive in peacetime conditions—father's place of employment shifted to the head office of Drake's Bakery in Long Island City. The work was doubtless tedious, but it provided a modest and secure income.

Father's spare time was always devoted to reading and writing. Amidst the routine and largely uninteresting occupation which had replaced his shattered career, he turned to the development of inner resources. Gradually my father made himself over into something he had never had the time to be in Germany—an intellectual. He spent his leisure hours (and very little money) building up a small but solid library of German and English literature—especially his favorite Goethe. And he even turned out a couple of rather amusing short stories. His reading covered a wide range of English literature, with 18th century authors among his favorites—Sterne, Goldsmith, and, above all, Boswell's *Johnson*.

The late 1940's were a time of much financial stringency for our family, but they were also a time of security and stability—a comparatively happy period after a decade of turmoil. Around 1950 circumstances were eased slightly by the onset of a modest monthly compensation payment to those who had lost their professions in Germany during the Nazi era. Now finally—when he was some sixty years old—the family's finances were once more relatively comfortable.

But is was too late. In 1951 father began to show the signs of a distressing and dangerous heart condition (*angina pectoris*). Though occasionally painful, it did not stop him from getting about—on a visit to Washington in the summer of 1952 (where I was then stationed on military service) or on a final visit to Germany that August—the first and last time father revisited his native land after emigrating in 1937. Suddenly one evening in late October of 1952 he died of a heart attack just after turning in for the night. His body was cremated a few days afterwards, as he had instructed. Not until a decade later did his ashes find their final resting place—in the peaceful little cemetery by the newer Quaker meeting house on Middleton Road at Lima, PA near Philadelphia (where my mother's ashes were eventually to join his, more than a quarter century after his death).

Father lives in my memory as a man who, though strict, was warmhearted, kind, and endowed with a sense of humor. When my interests turned to mathematics and technical philosophy, they diverged increasingly from his, but we nevertheless were always close—especially during the latter 1940's. Father was unquestionably an officer and a gentleman, and in various ways a rather admirable person. I still find it surprising and impressive that he was able to keep up his good spirits and even temper throughout all those upheavals, an any rate as far as all external appearances went: his resilience of spirit must indeed have been substantial! He was rather "unflappable," as the English put it. The experiences of World War I had impressed his personality with a degree of Stoicism. "*Kommt Zeit, kommt Rat*" (roughly, "We'll cross that bridge when we get there") was one of his favorite sayings, and another was the Roman legal maxim *Ultra posse nemo obligatur* ("No one is obligated to do more than is possible"). The strength not to lose heart in the face of adversity is among the most difficult of human accomplishments. It is to my father's great credit that he managed to achieve this.

MY MOTHER'S FAMILY

My mother's father, Wilhelm Heinrich Ludwig Landau, was born in 1869 in Kreis Waldeck in Hesse. In my recollection he stands out as a characteristic German burgher type—a fine, bluff, somewhat irascible old gentleman who forms one of the vivid memories of my childhood. He was among the younger sons of Karl Landau (1825-1898), a flourishing farmer in the rural hamlet of Goddelsheim. The Landaus had been settled in Waldeck since time immemorial, taking their name from the village of Landau (near Arolsen). However, by the 17th century the family no longer lived there, but had removed first to Neukirchen and later to Goddelsheim. The Lutheran parish register at Sachsenberg traces our line continuously from Johannes Landau (1665-1735), a miller of Neukirchen; in fact, the Landaus owned and operated the mill at Neukirchen throughout the 17th and 18th centuries.

Subsequently the Landau family owned a large farmstead in Goddelsheim through succeeding generations, maintaining the property intact by the old expedient of letting it pass always to the oldest son.[21]   And so young Wilhelm—as a younger son—went off around 1890 to seek his fortune in a nearby city, and somehow found a niche in the sales office of the Andreas Brewery in Hagen, Westfalen. He worked in this office for some fifty years until his retirement at the age of seventy—rising gradually to become manager of the sales department. I remember the tale that in his earlier days he carried a large rubber syringe on his public relations rounds of the *Bierstuben* that featured Andreas beer ("Edelpils"), so that he could secretly empty the *Kleines Helles* pressed on him by a convivial innkeeper, accepting hospitality without impairment to his working efficiency. He died in 1943 on the ancestral lands in Goddelsheim, where he and grandmother had moved "for the duration" to escape the bombings of industrial Hagen, so that I never saw him again after we left Germany in 1938.

My maternal grandmother, Adele Landau née Kämper, was born in 1878. The Kämpers lived in Gevelsberg, near Hagen, but also had some family connection in Goddelsheim. (Family tradition has it that these Kämpers came originally from the Netherlands—and that one of their ancestors was a pirate named Hans Störtebekker (?).) On the morning when Adele was born, her father returned home in such a condition from revels celebrating the anniversary of the German victory at Sedan in the Franco-Prussian War that he did not learn of his new daughter's arrival until several days after the event.

Wilhelm and Adele Landau had two daughters, my maternal aunt Luise (b. 1903)[22] and Meta Anna, my mother, born on December 14, 1905. Grandfather Landau very much wanted a son and was so furious that mother was a girl that for a time he would not speak with grandmother! Grandfather had a choleric strain, and did not lead his wife and easy life. During my childhood in Hagen they lived in a small apartment house (of perhaps five units) at 69 Bergstrasse. The building was owned by grandfather himself, and it was an open secret in the family that if any tenant was financially embarrassed when the rent fell due on the first of the month, grandmother would dip into her carefully nursed savings to make the rent-payment possible on time. For whenever someone's rent was overdue, grandfather Landau with each passing day became increasingly irritable and hard to live with, so that grandmother's apparent altruism was very much a matter of self-interest.

I remember the Bergstrasse house well from childhood, for mother and I lived there with my grandparents during 1936-38, after my father's departure for the U.S.A. The building was burned out in the incendiary bombing raids of World War II, and grandmother sold the land to the city after the war for reconstruction. Another small apartment-house was erected on the site and grandmother continued to reside there by special arrangement for the rest of her life.[23] On visiting her in September of 1963, I recognized in the immediate neighborhood only one old building across the street which housed a shop whose two old-maid shopkeepers remembered me from a quarter-century before. Among local houses, it alone survived the incendiary raids, thanks to the efforts of the two brave old ladies who manned their roof during air-raids with buckets of sand to extinguish the firebombs.

Grandmother Landau was my only grandparent to survive into my adulthood. (She died in 1966, so that I was—happily—able to see her again during visits to Germany after the war.) It was, I suppose, the fact that I was her first grandchild that created a special bond between us. As any rate, during my German boyhood she was the adult with whom, parents aside, I was the closest, and we spent a good deal of time together.

MOTHER

My mother was born in Gevelsberg near Hagen, Westfalen on 14 December, 1905, her parents' second daughter (and last child). Mother and her sister Luise ("Ise") had a typical German childhood of the period, unhappily including the deprivations of World War I and the very difficult immediate post-war period. Upon completing her schooling in the early 1920's, she first spent a year in a finishing school for girls that principally trained them in "home economics," including the mysteries of Hausfraudom. Then she spent some time in secretarial school. At the age of 18, in early 1924, she finished her training and was ready for her first employment, which she found in my father's law-office. She must have made a deep impression, for she was a strikingly beautiful young woman, as the photographs of this period attest.[24] A little more than a year later my parents were married (in September of 1925). Some three years after that came the birth of their only child, myself.

The period up to 1933 must have been a time of ease and happiness for my mother. But the next twenty-five years were a period of constant difficulty and anxiety for her. She had to support her husband through a steady stream of catastrophes: the collapse of his career in 1934-35, the transatlantic migration in 1937-38, the struggles to gain a foothold in a strange country during 1938-40, the collapse of father's photographic business in 1942, the economic stringency of the early war years (when mother held down one makeshift job after another to help keep us afloat), the war's severance of all contact with her parents and relations, a time of ill health around 1944-46, my father's period of (ultimately fatal) illness during 1951-52, and then the difficult readjustment to living on her own. One after another the hammer blows of ill fortune came down on mother. Yet, nothing daunted, she carried on throughout it all cheerfully and constructively. Her own inner spirit somehow equipped her with resources to cope with difficulties for which her early years of secure girlhood and affluent matronhood must have left her utterly unprepared.

After 1942, until her "retirement" in 1971 at the age of sixty-five, mother held a varied succession of jobs. During World War II she worked for a time as a saleslady at Macy's Department Store in Manhattan. From 1944 until the time of my father's death she worked in the same capacity at Henri Bendel, a fashionable ladies-wear shop on West 57th Street. After moving to California in late 1954, she continued in this line of work for some months in a similar establishment in the 400 block of Wilshire Boulevard in Santa Monica.[25] But then she changed gears. In 1955 she became assistant to the director of the Friends (Quaker) International Center at UCLA. Then from 1957 to 1958 she directed a Quaker work-camp for young people at Tlaxcala in Mexico, and then spent another year there helping to run the Quaker hostelry, Casa de los Amigos, in Mexico City before returning again to Santa Monica. Thereafter, from 1962 until her retirement in 1971, she served as the "Official Hostess" of Westtown School, the Quaker boarding school near Philadelphia. After her retirement she stayed for another year at Westtown, living until the Fall of 1972 at "The Farmhouse" on the school campus. Then mother moved to Illetas near Palma in Mallorca, where she lived for almost two years. (Her time in Mexico had given her a liking for Hispanic culture.) At the present writing (August 1974) she lives in our house at No. 6 Cunliffe Close, Oxford. She enjoys Oxford where she keeps busy with activities in the North Oxford community center (The Ferry Center), with volunteer work—especially for the little Oxfam Shop on Oakthorpe Road in Summertown—and with active participation in the Quaker Meeting.

As this brief account show, my mother is a versatile and resourceful woman, with great powers of adjustment to varied settings, and equally at home in a German, English, or Spanish environment. She is a warm, enthusiastic, outgoing person who makes friends easily—gregarious on the surface, though not without some reserve and attachment to privacy underneath. She is a lady of enormous charm and great practical good sense. I have always loved her dearly and with the passage of years I have come to admire her as well.

NOTES

1. See H. Bahlow, *Deutsches Namenlexikon* (München, 1961), under the entry "Resch" = "Rosch." The word occurs in Middle English in precisely the same sense, and the modern English verb *to rush* and adjective *rash* (= overhasty) are its direct descendants. The verb form is *raesen* = *to rush*, whence also the English *race*.

2. See the entry "Resch(n)er" in J. K. Brechenmacher, *Etymologisches Wörterbuch der deutschen Familiennamen*, 2 vols. (Limburg a.d. Lahn, 1957). The name indicates a weaver of *Rasch* = *arr-sch*, derived from the city Arras—that is, a maker of tapestry wall hangings, known as "arras" throughout Europe, and highly popular as a wall-covering in the houses of the affluent in medieval and renaissance times. (Shakespearean villains are frequently found hiding "behind the arras.") On *rasch* = *arras* cf. Grimm's *Deutsches Wörterbuch*, where various data are also given for the equivalence *resch* = *rasch*.

3. Bahlow, *op. cit.*, under the entry "Rascher."

4. See T. Roscher, *Zur Geschichte der Familie Roscher in Niedersachsen* (Hannover, 1891).

5. Data from *Universal-Lexicon aller Wissenschafter und Künste*, vol. 32 (Leipzig and Halle, 1742).

6. There is still one remaining topographic trace of their presence there in the name of an old country road, "Resachersfield Lane" (*Reschersacker Schnitt*) a few kilometers north of Zwingenberg, not far south of Darmstadt. See the *Gazetteer to the Army Map service: 1:25,000 Maps of West Germany*, vol. III (Washington DC, 1954; Army Map Service).

7. See the *Dictionnaire historique et biographique de la Suisse*, vol. V (Neuchatel, 1930), p. 394.

8. See the entries *Rascher* and *Raschar* in vol. III of J. B. Rietstap *Amorial Général* (Lyon, n.d.). The Rachar's of Chur in Switzerland were ennobled in the 16th century. The Austrian Rascher's were made chevaliers in the early years of the 18th century. Their coats of arms are illustrated under the same entries in J. B. Rietstap, *General Illustrated Armorial*, ed. by Victor and Henri Rolland (Lyon, n.d.), vol. V (the French original appeared in Paris and The Hague in six volumes during 1903-1926).

9. The family is now extinct in Chur, but collateral branches are still extant in Zuoz and elsewhere in Switzerland. Rascher & Cie A. G. was once a major bookseller and publishing firm in Zurich (the bookshop having been founded in 1758 and the publishing

house in the 1880s). However, the Austrian branch appears to have died out.

10. A devoté of Lessing and admirer of *Nathan der Weise*, he did not see this step in the same light as his relations.

11. In the 18th and 19th centuries, people throughout Europe changed the styling of their names readily. The grandfather of John Stuart Mill was born a Milne, for example, and the Duke of Wellington's family exchanged Wesley for the more distinguished Wellesley.

12. These four half-siblings of my father's were Lina (1870-1943), Alfred (1871-1950), Ernest (1873-1951), and Martha (1879-1962).

13. She emigrated around 1890 to Denver, Colorado (where one of her brothers lived), apparently to extricate her sons Alfred and Ernest from the system of compulsory military service that had been established throughout recently unified Germany. She died at age 84 in 1925.

14. Its epitaph is written on the headstones of the family plot in Denver's Fairmont Cemetery:

Emil A. Gunsen	Joseph A. Gunsen	Lina Gunsen	Nanette Rescher
1842-1890	1845-1910	1856-1938	1841-1925
Lina Rescher	Alfred Rescher	Ernest Rescher	Martha Rescher
1870-1943	1871-1950	1873-1951	1876-1969

In moving to Denver, Nanette joined her two brothers, who had simplified the family name to Gunsen (from GUNZENhausen). A third brother who changed the name to Hansen (from Gunzen-HAUSEN) settled in New Jersey. (One of his sons became a supreme court justice there.) Of her sons, only Alfred had sons; but both of these are now (1974) childless septuagenarians, and so the Rescher name stands on the verge of extinction in this branch.

15. See pp. 132-133 below.

16. There were also two daughters, Emma (b. 1860), and Julia (b. 1865). Of Emma I know little. A childhood illness left her in broken health; she never married and died in 1901. Julia married one Johann Fröhlich in 1885. They had four daughters, none of whom survived childhood save one, Irma, who was born some four months after her father's death in 1891. She eventually married but had no children.

17. Her brother Ludwig Haarburger touched my life more closely than most of my other distant relatives, because in 1958 I came into a small legacy of about $3,000 under a will he made in 1889. It struck me as amazing that anything at all should be left by 1958 to be inherited under a will made long ago by someone who died in

1903—notwithstanding the passage of several generations, two world wars, and the catastrophic inflation of the 1920's. The father of Ludwig Haarburger's wife Flora was Jewish, a circumstance that was to bring home the most despicable aspects of the Hitler period. For while Ludwig himself had died in 1903, Flora survived long enough to end her days at great age in 1942 in the "concentration camp" at Theresienstadt.

18. Apparently thinking that the "roaring 20's" were designed for her benefit, Aunt Gertrude took three husbands in rapid succession in the course of the decade. Her first husband, who she must have married at around 1921, at age 18, was Franz Siegele of Starnberg, a then well-known landscape painter. (See Hans Vollmer, *Allgemeines Lexikon der Bildenden Künstler des XX. Jahrhunderts*, vol. 4 (Leipzig, 1958), p. 177.) He was, I take it, a charming but undomesticable man—a typical artistic bohemian. After divorcing him around 1926, Gertrude married again with a Herr Keuffele in Gersthofen, but this marriage ended in divorce after a matter of months. Gertrude's third husband, whom she married in the late 1920's, was a physician, Dr. Hermann Neussell of Gersthofen. He was a rather authoritarian type, and became and ardent Nazi. Gertrude divorced him around 1937—no doubt a sensible move—but she did not live to enjoy her restored independence for long. Becoming melancholy and despondent over the collapse of her personal and public worlds, she died a year or two later in 1939 (according to reports, of an overdose of sleeping pills made conveniently available by her hired lady companion, who had gained ascendancy over her, and had talked Gertrude into making a will naming herself as sole beneficiary).

19. By the terms of the convention of 1871, the troops of Württemberg constituted a distinct element that formed the XIII corps of the imperial German army.

20. The Nazis has been particularly incensed by the acquittal of five defendants in the Reichstag fire trial in 1934. The crackdown on the judiciary proceeded apace thereafter.

21. To this present day (1974) there are still Landau relations in Goddelsheim, farming some much-reduced portion of the ancestral lands.

22. I can only recall my mother's sister, Luise, as the aunt of my young childhood, and so do not really know her well as a person. Around 1928 she married Erich Sander—a salesman or manufacturer's representative for some sort of metal-products. Their one child, Wilm, born in 1935, is the only first cousin I have. In 1964, Wilm married Karin Schröter whose family also hailed from God-

delsheim. They produced two children, Eric and Karin. Wilm has always remained in Hagen and works as a mechanical engineer in a metal-fabricating firm in Schwelm. His father Erich—and outgoing, personable, easygoing man of who I have fond childhood memories—died in 1943 or 1944 as a German infantryman fighting on the Russian front.

23. Aunt Luise, my mother's sister, still lives in grandmother's old flat at this writing (1974). [She died there at the age of ninety in 1993.]

24. She long kept her youthful good looks. Throughout my boyhood, people took her for my "big sister"—somewhat to father's chagrin.

25. I had moved to Santa Monica in 1954. Mother came for a visit, and liked the place so well she decided to stay.

Two

A GERMAN CHILDHOOD
Hagen: 1928-1939
(Age 0-9)

After their marriage in the spring of 1925, my parents lived in an apartment on the first floor of a large house on the Ruhrstrasse, in a pleasant residential district of Hagen in Westphalia. It was there that I was born on Sunday, July 15, 1928. I am the only person I know of among my contemporary acquaintances who was born at home rather than in a hospital. My mother's obstetrician believed in this if the parents could arrange to hire the necessary help—an idea nowadays sporadically returning to favor in Europe. I was christened Klaus Helmut Erwin Rescher, becoming Nicholas only in 1938, after our emigration to the U.S.A. (The Germans shortened NICKOLAUS = NICHOLAS to KLAUS from the second half of the word, the English to NICK from the first.)

When I was about a year old, our family moved to a two-story family-sized house with a many-gabled roof of brown tiles, "standing in its own grounds," as the English say, at the top of the Leibnizstrasse (No. 3). I remember the pleasant, gray-green stucco covered house well, for we resided there until I was seven years old. The entire neighborhood was then an attractive suburban area, and I enjoyed roaming over it on exploratory rambles with my friends or relations.

This period of my early childhood was the era of my parents' greatest prosperity. My mother was at this stage very energetic and greatly devoted to sports and gymnastics. She spent much time at such activities, and until I was four years old or so I was mostly committed to the care of a nanny. Thereafter, mother did many more things with me, and for a time I became her steady companion. Father was generally away at his law office, and so remained somewhat on the periphery of my life. Until 1934, his legal practice thrived and he joined an active social life to his busy professional one.

As a small child I spent much time with my Grandmother Landau who lived in a spacious apartment in the Bergstrasse at the other end of town. Grandmother and I would often make long excursions across the fields and meadows of the nearby countryside. I adored "found objects" and invariably brought home various treasures—bits of rusty old iron and the like. I was, of course, less close to my paternal grandparents, who lived in far-off Stuttgart. I recall only very dimly a visit to them in 1931, the last time I saw my grandfather Rescher, who died the next year. (I remember somewhat better a later visit to Stuttgart in 1934, when we left flowers at his grave.)

My memories of early childhood are for the most part happy ones. Much of my time was spent in the large, sloping garden of the Leibnizstrasse house, digging in some unused corner, building rock constructions, playing games with my little friends, and the like. I was basically a good child but also mischievous. On one occasion in 1933 or 1934 a friend and I came upon some catechism books left by some pupils from the neighborhood Catholic girls' school who, their classes over, were playing near a pond in a local park. We promptly threw the books into the water while the girls were busy at their games. On another occasion around this time, while mother and I were on holiday at Bad Honnef on the Rhine, I released the numerous occupants of a rather large rabbit-hutch, and appeared in our hotel room with my apron full of little bunnies.

In the fall of 1933, at the age of five, I was enrolled in a kindergarten—a small, privately run affair under the care of Fraulein Irmgart Ritter, a pleasant young lady who struggled

three of four mornings a week to channel our youthful energies in such constructive directions as drawing and paper
cutting. At this time, I also began to read—apparently quite
spontaneously. I had learned the alphabet when four and a
half years old from an alphabet picture-book that my parents
had given me. (It still remains in my possession!) After this
I would amuse myself by spotting letters on store-signs, plac-
ards, and the like, having taught myself how to put letters
together into words. One day, aged just over five, I surprised
my mother by reading her all the signs along the trolley-route
into town.

In the fall of 1934 I began the first grade of school at the
public (state) elementary school in the neighborhood. Little
about my initial school year now remains in my memory apart
from two things: that I rather liked school itself, but that
during playtime in the schoolyard I was regularly oppressed
by the class bully—an obnoxious little boy a year or so older
than I, who had somehow managed to lose the first joint of
one of his thumbs. I was not displeased when we moved away
at the end of the school year and I was transferred to another
school.

Increasingly after 1933, the shadow of National Socialism
lengthened across Germany—and across my father's career.
The Nazi movement made itself felt on every side. No opportunity was lost for holding a parade or rally or comparable
demonstration of physical presence. Uniforms sprouted
forth everywhere—and makers of brown shirts and leather
straps and jackboots must have made a fortune. It was known
in legal circles that father was decidedly not a Nazi. One small
but symbolic episode sticks in my mind. In 1933-34 many
boys—even the little one of my own age—started to sport
swastika armbands in imitation of the members of the Brown-
Shirt brigades who were always strutting about. I launched
an agitation with my parents to be allowed to have an arm-
band like the other boys. Finally they gave in and let me have
one—but with a difference. Instead of the Swastika, the
arm-band mother made me displayed a small-scale version of
the old three-striped black-white-red German flag. I was

disappointed and felt that this was "just not the same thing." And I'm sure that that's exactly what other people thought.

Though my parents kept their worries about political developments to themselves, I could not help learning that something was amiss. I still recall various signs of this. The summer of 1934 we were to take a holiday in Switzerland. We started out with a visit *en route* to my grandmother in Stuttgart, where we were also to pick up some travel documents. These were denied to us, and so we went for a (very pleasant) visit to Baden-Baden instead. Again, later that year my father was called in for the extra-thorough tax audit—a device used to annoy persons deemed unfriendly towards the Nazi regime. I recall his spending several days at home worriedly compiling his records and documents. On another occasion, my father received a summons to attend a meeting in the Town Hall, and he and mother were greatly concerned about this. It transpired—to my parents' great relief—that the occasion was merely one of distributing some medal being awarded routinely to those who had served as officers during World War I.

Behind all this loomed one crucial and crushing fact. After 1933, my father's law practice was increasingly moribund as members of the bar who were known to be cool to the regime found fewer and fewer clients. (After the Nazification of the judiciary in the wake of the aquittals in the Reichstag fire trial, it was difficult for non party-member attorneys to win cases before the party-enthusiast judges.) And so the spring of 1935 saw a development that was truly momentous for my parents and for me—the decision to emigrate to the U.S.A.

As the first preparatory step, my parents sold the house in the Leibnizstrasse during that summer. Thereupon we went to live in two rooms of my grandmothers' flat in their house in the Bergstrasse. I attended the local elementary boys' school (*Volksschule*) in the fall of 1935, and continued there until early 1938, with various interruptions for travel on farewell visits to relations. As best I recall the system, the class kept its same teacher from year to year. I remember my teacher well—a kind, intelligent, and sensible Herr Feist, who was eventually killed as a soldier on the Russian Front. Only a handful of school incidents of this period remain in my mind, most prominently my first caning in the office of the school principal for some trivial offense. At the time, I regarded this punishment as unmerited by the minor transgression that occasioned it. Only later did I learn that it had actually been instigated by my own mother, who suggested to Herr Feist that the experience "might be good for me." We spent many hours playing games in the schoolyard, and I recall that at the time—like my classmates—I was very enthusiastic about soccer.

My various playmates of this period are now dim in my memory. They included Dieter Nölle whose father was, like mine, an attorney; Günther Alles whose parents owned a leather-goods shop, and Günther Grote whose father owned a photography shop. One boy in particular remains vividly in my mind because of an amusing incident often retold in my family. Wolfgang Maier, a friend of my own age (then 8) whose father was an agent for a pharmaceutical company, in my presence once asked mother in a very serious grown-up sort of way, just making polite conversation, "Haben Sie viel Last mit dem Lümmel?" (Does the good-for-nothing give you much trouble?). I cannot say whether I was more shocked by his nerve or impressed by his maturity.

The things I principally enjoyed doing as a small child were the usual ones—play with my friends, outings with my parents, games with adults at my grandparents' place. Perhaps only two of my interests were developed beyond the level of the ordinary at this stage: woodworking, which I soon gave up altogether, and reading, which has remained my prime avocation to the present day. The stories of Wilhelm Hauff were among my favorites. And I still have in my possession the copies of *Robinson Crusoe, Dr. Doolittle*, and *Little Lord Fauntleroy* in the German versions in which I first read them at age seven or eight.

In early 1936 my father made a short exploratory visit to New York. And the next year he crossed the Atlantic for good, mother and I traveling to Hamburg to see him off. Hamburg impressed me greatly as a beautiful, prosperous seaside city, liberally sprinkled with greened copper roofs.

The year 1937-1938 was largely given to preparations for emigration. I attended school rather intermittently at this stage, though various attempts were made to assure that I did not stop doing school work altogether. My mother arranged with a young nun from a local convent, who had lived in England for a time, to tutor me in English. She used *Mother Goose* as a text and for some reason thought it well to begin with "Humpty Dumpty." I found it most strange that the English would use the word for egg (German *Ei* pronounced just like the letter I) as a term meaning *myself* (I).

One vivid recollection of that last year in Germany relates to the plebiscite of 1938. In April of that year, a month after the *Anschluss* of Austria, Hitler appealed to the citizenry of the new Gross-Deutschland for a renewed 4-year mandate of power. (He won it by over 99%.) Among the last memories of my childhood in Germany is my going with mother to the voting place on this occasion. Since the two different styles of ballots (yea of nea) were preprinted, with only the affirmative ballots made available at the polling stations, the whole thing struck me as silly. What, I thought, could be the point of holding an election when there were no alternatives for a choice? Young innocent that I was, the deeper ramifications of the political process were quite beyond me!

The two years between father's first exploratory trip to the U.S.A. in the spring of 1936 and the summer of 1938 when mother and I joined him there were spent in a sort of limbo as far as our own family life was concerned. Mother and I became planets orbiting the family of my grandfather and grandmother. I am now surprised that this did not seem strange to me, but as I think back to my early years, I am struck again and again by a child's ability to take things in stride and adapt to drastic changes without thinking anything amiss.

After our emigration to the U.S.A. became a settled issue, it transpired that a development of significance for our lives had taken place more than a decade before. In the 1920's my father's father had made plans to emigrate to ancestral Switzerland. Among the preparatory steps, he had transferred the bulk of his fortune to the care of the Schweizerscher Bankverein in Basel. However, my grandmother dug in her heels. She had lived in Stuttgart all her life, and most of her friends and relations lived there. Understandably enough, she was reluctant to move away to a new and strange city. Though natural, this was also unfortunate. For the Nazis eventually forced the repatriation of these assets and ultimately confiscated them as the property of a refugee when my father inherited them after grandmother's death. (But for grandmother's stubbornness, I might today be a wealthy man—and perhaps a Swiss one as well.) Yet even a black cloud can have a silver lining, for grandfather's Swiss fund made it possible for father to have a modest sum slip past the fiscal controls imposed by the Nazis.

One day in early July in 1938 mother and I made the trip by train to Bremen, accompanied by grandmother Landau. There we boarded the U.S.S. President Roosevelt for the transatlantic voyage. I left my native land without much sorrow or regret. My thoughts dwelt wholly on the adventures that lay ahead—the reunion with father and life in a new country about which I knew little more than what I had seen in the Keystone Kops movies, which were popular in the Germany of my childhood.

What sort of boy, now nearing ten years of age, was crossing the Atlantic? I was (I do believe) good natured, and of a friendly, outgoing disposition, reasonably alert and intelligent, rather fond of reading, and fond also of sports and physical activities. (I made the error of taking my never-to-be-used soccer equipment along.) But there was nothing whatever to indicate special ability in any particular direction, such as art of music, which children so often manifest at a tender age. My work at school had been mediocre—not egregiously bad, but by no means outstandingly good. I was an altogether ordinary youngster—good of heart, but quite average in abilities. And I certainly lacked any crystallized ambitions or aspirations—all that came along years later.

Was our leaving Germany for a fresh start in a new and foreign land a wise step or a foolish one? I have never hesitated for a moment to regard it as eminently wise. Conceivably, our lives might in some ways have run smoother course in "the old country," for there is no doubt that a time of very real hardship lay ahead for my parents. But the actual likelihood is that things would have been far worse. The Nazi pestilence was a present and worsening reality, and a major war lay in the foreseeable future—a war in which, young though I was, I might well have been caught up, as many of my contemporaries actually were.

Over the years my thoughts have often dwelt on that force in human affairs to which the Romans gave the name of *fortuna* and that we call fortune, luck, chance, or the like. Its role becomes paramount in extraordinary circumstances such as war, disaster, or revolution, when the "normal" circumstances of normal life are ruthlessly abolished. The whole experience of emigrating from Germany and placing an ocean between ourselves and the Nazi catastrophe and its concomitant war left me with the strong conviction that it is safer and wiser to sidestep rather than grapple with world-historical disasters. The sensible course in such circumstances is not, alas, that of valor and heroic confrontation, but that of prudence and discretion. When the cattle stampede or the avalanche thunders down, there is no point in standing pat. It is wiser to follow the course of prudence and get out of the way than to undertake a hopeless struggle against potent and malign forces that are wholly beyond one's control.

Dr. Nehemias Rescher
(Great-grandfather as a medical
student in 1849, age 21)

Otto Rescher
(Grandfather ca. 1885, age 32)

Erwin Hans Rescher
(Father as a student in his
dueling fraternity outfit,
Tübingen 1912, age 22)

Meta Landau Rescher
(Mother at the time of her
marriage in 1925, age 19)

**Nr. 3 Leibnizstrasse, Hagen,
Westphalia (Boyhood home ca. 1934)**

**Klaus Helmut Erwin Rescher
(The author in 1936, age 8)**

Oskar Rescher (Osman Reser)
("Uncle Oskar" in 1965, age 82)

Nicholas Rescher
(1971, age 43)

A Family Portrait (1991)
(Owen, Dorothy, Elizabeth, Nicholas, Catherine, Mark)

Three

AN IMMIGRANT BOY
Beechhurst: 1938-1942
(Age 10-13)

Mother and I sailed on the U.S.S. President Roosevelt from Bremerhaven on the 8th of July, 1938. After brief stops at Le Harve in France and Cobh in Ireland, the ship crossed the Atlantic on a smooth voyage of which I still have various pleasant recollections. As any boy would, I loved roaming about the large vessel, breathing the sea air, sensing the unaccustomed motion of the ship, and being awed by loud blasts of its great horn.

At the synthetic "horse races" in the ship's lounge one evening, a kind elderly gentleman placed a 25¢ bet for me and I won a dollar of two, which I saw as a good omen. I recall the thrill of first sighting the Statue of Liberty and the impressive view of the New York skyline. We landed in the early morning of July 16th, the day after my tenth birthday. This new year of my life was to see a new start in an altogether strange place.

It felt exciting—and somewhat odd—to be in a foreign country with a different language. But I was happy to be reunited with my father, whom I had not seen for over a year. We soon cleared through customs and made our way by taxi out to Long Island. I was glad to leave Manhattan behind. It seemed over-powering to me: intimidatingly massive, over-crowded, and—after the tidiness of German towns—rather dirty. Still, an aura of excitement hung over the hustle and bustle of the place, and a mixture of wonder, apprehension, and hopefulness filled my mind.

Our first residence in the U.S.A.—where we lived for some six months after our arrival—was a small apartment upstairs in a recently built duplex which father had rented in a newish, red-brick, residential suburb somewhere on the outskirts of Flushing. My recollections of that summer form a kaleidoscopic series. I particularly remember working in the garage to make various things out of orange crates including a small boat which, hauled to a distant beach by public transportation on a very hot August day, sank instantly upon launching.) Then too I recall the excitement occasioned by a succession of hold-ups at a local bar. Proximate criminality was a new phenomenon for me.

1938 saw the opening of the New York World's Fair, which took place virtually in our own back yard, so that we often went there. By and large, the national exhibitions made relatively little impression upon me. The industrial ones were a different matter, however. Several of them had a futuristic orientation, and I was fascinated by the robots, the fanciful automobiles, and ultra-modern houses, and other accouterments of twenty-first century cities as seen from the vantage point of 1938. This vista of a different world reinforced the sense of new horizons and challenging possibilities opened up by our transatlantic move.

That fall I took my place as a student at the local public elementary school conveniently located a few blocks away from home. The first day of the new school year came on a hot day in early September and I reported with an open shirt—without a tie. The school rules required boys to wear ties, and I still remember vividly how the teacher's vain attempts at explanation were followed by the vista of a surrounding sea of boys and girls, pointing at their necks or mine, tugging their ties, some enthusiasts even taking theirs off to wave in the air. I got the idea, and henceforth appeared duly tie-equipped.

The school made a special effort to help me—a foreigner virtually bereft of English—to adapt to the grade into which

I had been place according to age. I was excused from some of the usual classes to have special lessons with one of the reading teachers. Though she knew no German, she helped me to work my way through the whole curriculum of readers, beginning with the "baby-books" used in the first grade. After a time she left me pretty well to my own devices, just giving me books and doing what she could to resolve any questions I might have. I made good progress—heaven knows how— and at the end of ten or twelve weeks was getting pretty well caught up in reading. And so, gradually, I began to settle into the routine of the school.

But another change was in the offing. Early in 1939 we made a further move—this time to the village of Beechhurst on Long Island Sound. Here father had found a larger and more pleasant apartment, not far removed from the house of Dr. Egon Wolff, a refugee physician who, with his family, had been friends of my parents in Hagen.

Located a bit further out than Whitestone on Long Island Sound, Beechhurst in those days was a small, virtually rural hamlet of some six thousand souls, with only a few shops—a grocery, a drug store, a dry cleaning establishment, and perhaps one or two others. The only residential structure of larger than domestic size was our new home—a large apartment complex known as "The Beechhurst Towers," located at 160-65 Seventh Avenue. The building itself was a somewhat pretentious brick pile, with stone trim-work here and there. It had been erected in the economic euphoria of the mid-1920's and had offered a good deal in its prime, but had soon fallen on hard times with the Depression. Even so, it still afforded an amazing range of amenities, albeit now in a state of ongoing decline. There was a pair of tennis courts, a beach with a pier extending into Long Island Sound (as well as a dilapidated and already virtually useless beach-pavilion), a recreation room equipped with ping-pong tables, and a private bus service which linked the Towers to the subway rail-head in Flushing and also took the children back and forth to the local school. All this erstwhile grandeur of the place was slowly decaying from lack of upkeep in the new era of financial stringency. But my playmates and I did not require the splendors of well-maintained facilities—the old tennis-courts, the ping-pong tables, and the beach provided us with endless hours of pleasure, notwithstanding their increasing decrepitude.

The Towers was important to me not just as a dwelling, but as the *social* unit on which I drew for most of my friends and which provided the stage-setting of our communal activities (tennis, ping-pong, swimming, etc.). Being an inhabitant of the Beechhurst Towers provided the first bit of community identification that I achieved since our American migration.

When we arrived in Beechhurst, my knowledge of spoken English, although progressing, was still rather imperfect. I distinctly recall being somewhat hampered by language dif-ficulties that spring during a birthday party for Jack Beddell, one of my Towers playmates—my very first peer-group social occasion in the U.S.A. But my English now improved with leaps and bounds, and I soon managed "to pass for native."

After we settled in the Beechhurst Towers I began to attend P.S. 30, the local elementary school. Housed in a little red brick schoolhouse that accommodated only the first six grades, if afforded a rather modest physical plant, and an unkempt, minimally equipped schoolyard. The human ele-ment was, happily, more auspicious, for the staff was both dedicated and competent. Miss Jones, the principal, was a petite, red-haired lady who, despite an inclination to school-marmish imperiousness, looked kindly on the red-haired im-migrant boy being committed to her charge. She placed me in Miss Sabbathé's class, the fifth grade, which suited my age, though not quite yet my language-skills. This class was just one year from the top of the school, since only one further class, Miss Ferber's sixth grade, followed within this school itself. Our home-room teacher taught us all subjects except for penmanship. This was Miss Ferber's specialty, and I fear I must have taxed her patience sorely when trying—never with full success—to convert my Germanic hen-scratches into the smooth loops and whirls of Palmer penmanship.

The thing that impressed me very much about P.S. 30 can be summarized in the word *good will*, for a great deal of it prevailed throughout this small and modest school. It seemed to govern the relationship of all concerned, of teachers to students, students to teachers, and teachers to one another. Miss Sabbathé was a most kindly and helpful person. She began each morning with a reading from the psalms (the 23rd was her favorite), and the majestic verses of the King James Bible were the first piece of English prose I learned by heart. One of my favorite times each day was the brief period allotted to free creative activity. (I was particularly fond of modeling with clay.) The fastidious Miss Ferber—who taught the sixth grade—seemed to me rather severe at first, but I came to like her immensely once she became my regular teacher in the sixth grade. It was her custom to spend that last 15 or so minutes of each day reading us a story on the installment plan, and listening to her do this was always one of the highlights on my day. The entire period I spent in this school from early 1939 to June of 1940 was a thoroughly happy time for me.

One Beechhurst friend who made a deep impression on me was Thomas Floyd Buckley, whose family lived in a large detached house around the corner from the Towers. Our friendship deepened only gradually, for Tom was some two years older than I, and in boyhood even two years makes a big difference. With his two somewhat younger sisters, his charming mother, and his bluff and imposing father (a professional actor whose gruff voice served for the radio-characterization of Popeye the Sailor), the Buckleys formed an attractive group which I have always regarded as the archetypically American family. Tom was a very bright and gifted lad, with a remarkable gift as a public speaker and as a writer. (He eventually would end up on the staff of the *New York Times*.) Tom was something of a hero to me because there was about him an aura of easy assurance, of secure place in the fabric of the society, which I myself certainly lacked. (The experiences of my family had instilled in me a trace of uneasiness that no matter how well things seem to stand, circumstances beyond one's control can always intervene with disaster.)

My other close companions of this period were three occupants of the Towers, the two Merwin brothers, Donald and Philip, and John Beddell. Jack was the only one of my boyhood friends with strong scientific inclinations. He was a dabbler in chemistry and biology, tinkerer with electric gear, and devotee of science fiction, and eventually went on to study engineering in college. A blond, lanky, and somewhat moody lad, he tended to be more of a "loner" than my other friends. Of the Merwin brothers, Donald, a year of so older than I, was the intellectual, while Philip, a year or so younger than I, was a friendly, carefree, happy go lucky youngster. They were my constant companions and true friends. To my regret, I have long ago lost track of them. (Both, I believe, eventually entered careers in social services of some sort.) But throughout my years in Beechhurst these lads loomed large in my life and we whiled away endless hours in one another's company. Boys of ten through twelve are naturally gregarious creatures. They flock together, and the center of their world is populated by their fellows—adults live very much on the outskirts.

What did we do? We walked and talked. We took long aimless rambles along the East River shoreline. In bad weather we played Monopoly or ever roulette (on a home-made wheel). On Saturday afternoons we would sometimes go to the 25¢ matinee at a movie house in nearby Whitestone. Ping-pong in the Towers' erstwhile clubroom was another indoor favorite. In good weather we swam and played on Beechhurst Towers' pier on the East River or played "box-ball" on the sidewalk or in the driveway of Tom Buckley's house. Tennis was also popular with us, and much of our time was spent on the Towers' gradually decaying tennis courts.

I am keenly alive to the great debt I owe to these companions of my boyhood—for their companionship, their friendliness, and not least, their *teaching*. For the time we spent together was a precious learning experience for me: the testing of ideas and opinions in discussion, the perception of other views, the rubbing of one personality against another. One owes to one's childhood friends a debt which, unless repaid in kind at the time, can never be repaid at all.

The speed with which my acculturation was accomplished still impresses me in retrospect. I had arrived at P.S. 30 in early 1939 as a "different" boy who stuck out in the setting of an

American school like a sore thumb. But by mid-1940 I had become transformed into an indistinguishably American boy. That this was possible is a tribute to the atmosphere of the school and to that of the wider Beechhurst environment of which it was an integral part. I cannot explain the process of Americanization, it was something that just happened—like growing up itself. Imperceptibly I felt less distanced from my fellows, and came to view the American past as my own tradition. Washington and Jefferson were now part of my heritage, not Frederick the Great or Bismarck. (Now, almost four decade later, I always feel that I am among "my people" when I return to the U.S.A. from abroad. When I visit my native land, I feel among strangers.)

Upon completing the sixth grade at P.S. 30, we Beechhursters transferred to the rather larger P.S. 79 in Whitestone, where I began the seventh grade in the fall of 1940, having just turned 12. At first we still went there by the Towers' private bus, but this stopped operating in the spring of 1941, and thereafter we traveled the two miles or so on the standard yellow school bus. This new school involved an innovation: the weekly "Assembly" of all the children in the school. A white shirt was mandatory for boys on assembly day. Early on, I came to assembly several times "out of uniform"—I cannot recall whether I did not own a white shirt of just forgot to put it on. One of my classmates thereupon gave me a new white shirt as a present. I felt grateful for this gift, but distinctly sheepish at being the recipient of such a charity. Still, this act of kindness produced the desired effect. Never again did I appear on Assembly day without the appropriate garb.

Games and outdoor activities were more organized at P.S. 79 than I had been accustomed to. Mostly we played softball, which bored me because one is inactive so much of the time. But I did enjoy the "clubs" held at school for one appointed hour each week. I particularly liked the stamp club. I had started collecting stamps in Germany and continued as an enthusiastic philatelist until my latter teens. I also liked the science club and acquired from it an enthusiasm for science that was to be dampened by poor instruction in high school later on.

At this time I began to acquire some taste for "literature," including poetry. Already in P.S. 30 we had to memorize various poems. (Of these I now only remember the inevitable "Tree," which I thought rather silly—though it did lead me to take a closer and more appreciative look at this form of vegetation.) I now acquired a taste for poetry that endured until the college days (but faded away swiftly thereafter). Our literature teacher in the seventh grade at P.S. 79 was a kindly spinster who had no capacity for disciplining her class, with the result that the students had no respect for her and disorder sometimes prevailed. Her very incapacity in this regard seemed to provide my fellow-students with a challenge to produce this result. This was my first memorable encounter with the need in human affairs for that trait of character called "capacity for leadership," the ability to elicit cooperation amidst centrifugal tendencies.

At school I was not one of the cleverest children, but I always did my work competently—and always received and A in "conduct." Had I grown up in the securer ambiance of my native land, there would almost certainly have been more mischief about me. But now, being—or *feeling*—somewhat different from my fellows, I wanted to remain inconspicuous and not attract unfavorable notice. At the back of my mind there was always a vague sense of difference, even though being *German* was something that the ethos of the war era led me to de-emphasize—certainly to others, and perhaps even to myself. While this feeling did eventually lessen, it nevertheless left its effect on me. It unquestioningly provided and added stimulus to thought: it drove me more into myself, and made me more introspective and cerebral that I otherwise would have been. We borderers who dwell at the interface of different cultures tend to be more reflective about things.

Brief and limited though it was, I am glad to have had a glimpse of American life before World War II. Now more than a third of a century past, it seems like the image of another world—one that belongs to a long gone generation, though (thanks to the movies!) it will never become quite as dead as the ethos of earlier eras. Still caught up in the aftershock of the Depression, it was the day of a people tried by great hardships and not found wanting. The America of the 1930's is scarcely an era to evoke nostalgia, but there is actually much about it that deserves admiration, for it was a time of people who cared for standards of achievement and ideals of heroism, despising the merely tawdry, and eager to look upwards towards those people and actions exhibiting an element of the larger than life.

The Japanese attack on Pearl Harbor on 7 December 1941 for a time—a regrettably brief time—produced almost no viable change in our peaceful microcosm. The next day the school was a buzzing hive of chatter and speculation, but then all settled back into the normal routine—except, of course, for an occasional air-raid drill. (Who, in heavens' name, was going to bomb Whitestone?) The whole war saw periodic outbreaks of air-raid hysteria in New York: blackouts, sky-watchers, air-raid wardens, the whole silly charade (mainly calculated, one suspects, to "keep up morale" by creating a harmless outlet for patriotic enthusiasts who "just *had* to do *something*" to help the war effort).

As the weeks passed, the effects of the war made themselves felt with increasing intensity and pervasiveness. My father's business was an early casualty. It had to be sold—at a substantial loss. For the second time in less than a decade economic catastrophe struck the family.

I was too young at the time to be in a position to remember much of the collapse of my parents' social and economic world in 1933-36—too young, or perhaps too preoccupied with the travails of a boy just beginning school. But the second disaster in 1942 has a quite different effect upon me. Not that I was ever for a moment anxious of apprehensive on my own personal account. Youthful innocence, combined with a total trustfulness in parents, always led me feel that we would be provided for somehow—that I would not have to look into the face of disaster absolute. But I did feel rather acutely that we were not as others; that for other people circumstances were by and large smooth, but for us difficult.

Still, my own feelings—whatever they were—mattered little in the face of the massive problem that now arose. For

what was to be done now that my father's business had col-
lapsed and our livelihood with it? Somehow father turned up
a makeshift job at Armonk in Westchester County, New York,
and we moved there in the spring of 1942.

At Beechhurst my feet had come to be place on increasingly
familiar ground. Now, for the second time in a few years, came
another major upheaval. Fortunately, it was confined to the
now-familiar American context. In this regard, at any rate, a
great transformation had come over our lives since the
time—less than four years back—when Mother and I set sail
for "the New World."

Four

HIGH SCHOOL DAYS
1942-1946
(Age 13-17)

My primary schooling came to its end at the Armonk village school in Westchester county. I attended this establishment only for a few months in the spring of 1942 and still recall pleasantly the diminutive but impressive graduation exercise of that June, for which I had to acquire my first-ever white summer suit. There were perhaps twenty children in my class, but the only Armonk schoolmate of whom I now have any recollection is a pleasant, lanky boy named Richard Landers. He came of an old local family, and used to take all the history prizes as a matter of course until I arrived to give him some competition. As best I recall, he was my only school friend at this stage. I was thrown on my own resources a good deal during this time, for we lived in a rather isolated location several miles distant from Armonk itself. So I now became an even more avid reader than heretofore.

In September of 1942, I entered Pleasantville High School located in the nearby Westchester town of that name. We were shuttled back and forth from Armonk by bus, but this ride was often made unpleasant for us younger boys by some older bullies, a circumstance which eventually led me to feel that the child who can walk to school is fortunate.

I recall very little about Pleasantville High apart from the roomy, much bewindowed classroom in which we now began the study of Latin, a language of which I came to be very fond. As (supposedly) mature high school students, we were left to our own devices during the lunch hour, and I soon discovered the delightful small public library located near the school which I visited with great regularity. Libraries have ever since remained among my favorite haunts—I can walk into one in any corner of the globe and feel immediately at home.

Throughout my high-school years I was an enthusiastic stamp collector. I had already been an active participant in the stamp club at P.S. 79 in Whitestone, and used to extend my collection by trading there. Eventually, however, I decided to specialize in 19th century European stamps, largely because I did not want to get involved in a pursuit of unending proportions and welcomed the idea of working with a limited domain. Thereafter I could only proceed by making purchases, so I came to devote most of my (always small) "allowance" to buying stamps. Fortunately, other interests—in reading, in social contacts, and in tennis—eventually pushed stamp collecting aside.

Late in 1942 we removed to Summit, New Jersey to follow up some brighter job prospect that beckoned to my parents there. It must not have answered fully to expectation, because our stay lasted only for some six months. During that time I attended Summit High School and mildly enjoyed it. The compulsory class in mechanical drawing gave me a chance to discover my lack of artistic ability, but in general my performance is school was adequate, though I recall getting bogged down with long division of polynomials in algebra. I liked the school library, however, and used it a good deal for miscellaneous reading. Adventure stories (especially Robert Louis Stevenson) and swashbuckling historical novels (especially those of Alexander Dumas) were my favorites in those days.

While I was on casually good terms with several of my schoolmates, I did not form any close friendships in Summit and cannot now recall the name of a single one of my classmates or associates there. At home I was alone by myself a good deal and tended to live the somewhat interiorized mode of life, doing a good deal of miscellaneous reading. It was, I think, at this stage of adolescence, when I was much left to my own devices, that I first began to think of who I was and what I wanted to be. In a vague sort of way I now sensed within me the first stirrings of an aspiration to make something of myself. At this stage I was rather given to day-dreaming and the building of "castles in the air," indulging myself in this during leisurely walks to and from school through a pleasantly residential section of the town. It is just as well that an early move shifted me to a more active and sociable setting.

In the spring of 1943 we returned to the North Shore of Long Island—to Flushing. There we moved into a large, dark-brick, five or six story apartment building at 36-20 Parsons Boulevard, just off its intersection with Northern Boulevard. The site was only about three city blocks north of Flushing High School—around the corner from the attractive setting of the old Bowne House and the great Weeping Beach Tree. Our apartment here consisted of an entrance hall, a kitchen with attached dinette, a living room, a bathroom, and a single large bedroom. It was cramped quarters for a family of three. I often slept on a convertible studio-bad in the living room, but when my parents stayed up late, mother did so instead.

I still think of this small apartment as the home of my youth. When we moved to Flushing in early 1943, I was only a fourteen-year-old high-school freshman, and my mother continued to live there after my father's death until early 1954. Accordingly, this apartment house was my family's home for over a decade, a period that included most of my high school years, all of my time in college and graduate school, the beginnings of my academic career at Princeton, and the whole of my military service. (I myself lived there until leaving for graduate studies in Princeton in 1949, a period of six years; to this very day in 1974 I have never resided so long at a single address in the U.S.A.) The apartment complex lacked physical charm, but sheer familiarity bred a certain attachment. It was unquestionably convenient: only a short distance from my school, within an easy walk of the Public Library, the subway, and the local town center—and the movie houses, which I often frequented during my high-school years.

With its large and motley group of students, Flushing High was not one of the elite schools in the New York system. But there were many excellent teachers and a small core of able students who regularly met together in the more challenging courses and created a stimulating environment for one another. Here my academic inclinations first manifested themselves in a serious way. I liked Latin—though it was sometimes strugglesome going for me (in part, I now realize, because we were not really taught all that well). I always enjoyed history and social studies and still fondly remember a Mr. Harry Esterowitz who taught the latter subject in an uncommonly lively way.

I took to French from the very first. Our teacher—a middle-aged Mademoiselle whose name, alas, eludes me—was a very able teacher and great Francophile. French was the only language I ever learned really easily, and I loved every minute of it. I began to study the language in the spring of Operation Overlord, the allied cross-channel invasion of the Continent, and it was exciting to mark the progress of the allied forces across Normandy on he large map of France that hung in our classroom. As my study of French made headway, I became increasingly enthusiastic about this beautiful language and did much reading above and beyond the call of duty. On occasion I traveled to town to see French films, and I often read the French newspaper then published in New York. From time to time I attended a French-language lecture on some aspects of French thought sponsored by the *Alliance Française*, an organization of wartime expatriates concerned to promote the appreciation of Gallic culture. Gradually I acquired a reasonably good command of French—now, alas, much eroded.

Mathematics was unquestionably the subject that I made mine above all others. I have never been fond of arithmetic, nor had first-year algebra been a great success with me, but from my first exposure to geometry in the fall of 1943, I loved this subject and, through it, all of mathematics. (Just imagine —being able to dispense with the whole business of arithmetical computation!) Charlotte Knag, our unusually gifted teacher in algebra, at whose blackboard I first learned about mathematical induction, still remains fondly and vividly in my memory. The discovery of a penchant for mathematics was undoubtedly the high-point of my high school career.

Not that everything was peaches and cream. Some of the teachers at Flushing High School seemed to me very bad indeed—and strangely enough, it is their names that stick in my mind while those of their more competent colleagues have mostly vanished. A Miss (and Dr.) Mann taught me biology in my first term and did so in a way that killed forever any wish on my part for further formal instruction in the subject. Dr. Lilian Lieber was the head of the Mathematics Department and author of some strange books—works not exactly of mathematics but of a propaganda of sorts for mathematics. (The chief of these productions was entitled *The Education of T. C. Mits*—that is, "The Celebrated Man In The Street.") She made a poor impression on me because the classtime we should have devoted to learning mathematical techniques was given over to boring discussions of one or another of her books. I resented our being made a captive audience. Had my interest in mathematics not been firmly established by the time I arrived in her classroom, it too might have gone the way of biology. My contacts with chemistry were somewhat less traumatic, but also negative. It is a chastening thought that for most students a subject is made or unmade not by the intrinsic interest of its subject matter but by the personality of its teacher.

German, to be sure, was something I never studied formally at all. I did, however, read a good deal of miscellaneous classical literature on my own at this period, including Goethe's *Faust*, Schiller's *Wallenstein*, and the stories of Johann Peter Hebel, which I enjoyed immensely. It seemed to me that there was no point in wasting good courses on what came naturally. My ceasing to feel any sort of personal allegiance to Germany as a nation never diminished my appreciation of and admiration for the cultural products of German civilization.

In early 1944 I went to some Manhattan courthouse with my parents to arrange for my citizenship papers. I cannot say by what mysterious alchemy I had become transmuted into an American. Nowadays it might appear that I am something of a citizen of the world. My roots lie in Germany, the land of my youth. I am attached to England and spend a considerable period of each year there. I do much traveling and lecturing elsewhere—in Canada and in various European countries. My scholarly attention has been devoted extensively to the products of Mediterranean civilization—the intellectual products of classical antiquity and of the Arabian scholars. Yet there is no doubt whatever in my mind that America is my homeland and Americans are my people. Though I never set foot in the U.S.A. until after my tenth birthday, Franklin, Washington, Jefferson, and Lincoln are an integral part of "my" historical heritage.

Throughout my high school years in Flushing, I often took the bus to Beechhurst for Saturday visits with my friends of Beechhurst Towers days. Jack Beddell had moved away, but Donald and Phillip Merwin and Tom Buckley were still there. We would go on rambles or, more frequently, just sit around and talk—of our reading, our activities, or our various interests.

During the spring of 1944 Philip Merwin had become involved in a study-group run by a middle-aged dentist on Henry George's *Progress and Poverty*. By some mysterious process, a few cells of the "single tax" movement launched by Henry George in the 1880's had somehow survived into the New York of the 1940's, laboring to indoctrinate youngsters with the economic merits of a policy of restriction of taxation to land alone. Though the sessions had already been under way for some weeks, Philip persuaded me to accompany him and join in, and I attended this group for some half dozen weeks. I came away from it with an utter skepticism about this (or any other) socio-economic panacea and with an enhanced opinion of my mental powers. It seems to me that I was able to detect many flaws in Henry George's reasoning, which, on the other hand, seemed totally convincing to our dentist-leader.

My father too must be numbered among the friends of my high school years, for around this time we became closer than before, drawn together by a shared interest in secondhand books. We often spent Saturdays combing the second-hand bookshop on Fourth Avenue in downtown Manhattan. These Saturday excursions had the effect of confirming me in my scholarly inclinations. I gradually built up a library of several hundred miscellaneous philosophical and literary volumes. This could be done at very little cost, since many second-hand treasures were available in the 25-75¢ range. The combination of a human fondness for bargain-hunting with a high school boy's penchant for collecting made for endless pleasurable hours among the dusty shelves of the obscure little bookshops which in those days littered that part of downtown Manhattan. These Saturday outings—downtown by subway, combing the bookshops, lunch in some self-service cafeteria —provided an inexpensive, constructive, and pleasant activity. I learned a good deal from my father, not so much by way of specific facts, as by the transmission of attitudes and predilections in bookish and academic directions.

During my high-school years I spent much time reading. I regularly walked over to the Flushing Public Library (as usual, a Carnegie foundation), and did a good deal of general miscellaneous reading. At this stage P. G. Wodehouse became a great favorite. (He was already in those days a long-established author—a virtual classic—and it is startling to think of him as still alive and productive at this writing (1974), thirty years after the days of which I speak.) I also went through a Sherlock Holmes phase. But detective stories in general never held much attraction for me, nor did science fiction. I was interested in real life, and novels, biographies, and histories have always been the staple of my diet.

In summer I regularly spent much of my time on the tennis courts of the Whitestone Tennis Club. When the Beechhurst Towers stopped maintaining its tennis courts for reasons of economy in the spring of 1940, a group of three of four Towers couples had joined to purchase this very modest four-court establishment, which soon passed into the exclusive possession of John and Beatrice Hackenberg, a childless couple who had lived in the Towers until recently. The club's days of prosperity came when the Whitestone Yacht Club was closed for the duration of the war after the end of the 1942 season and many of its tennis enthusiasts came over to "our" club. Until 1947—throughout high school and on into my early college days—I was a "regular" of this establishment throughout the tennis season.

I was on friendly terms with many of the adult members of the club. But it also yielded much contact with boys my own age. One lad whom I now got to know at this time was John Frankenheimer, who later came to fame as a film director and producer. His family was one of wartime exiles from the Whitestone Yacht Club, and Johnny had enjoyed the benefit of professional coaching. He played far better tennis than the rest of us, and when I met him in the finals of one of the club's junior tournaments, he massacred me by something like 6-1, 6-2. He was a decidedly self-impressed young man, and though I respected his prowess on the courts, I was put off by this.

Jack Clarke was a very different sort of youth. He was a typical "good time Charlie," an outgoing Irish American with a consummate gift for blarney, a fellow of infinite jest and good humor, ever fast with a quip and handy with a story—one of the most glib raconteurs I have ever encountered. He was a latecomer to the tennis club, a lad somewhat older than I (he had seen service in the Navy and had been discharged on some trivial medical ground). He had an impressive mastery of the American tongue, and an immense quota of native wit. We became fast friends during the summer of 1944 while both enrolled for summer studies at the Garden County Day School. Our friendship reflected the attraction of opposites—he had no academic inclinations whatever, and could think of little but larks and girls (subjects at that point but seldom on my mind). Considering the difference between our personalities, I honestly cannot say exactly what brought us together, but we were fast friends at this stage. After I entered college we drifted apart, and lost sight of one another. Many years later I heard that he was married, settled someplace on Long Island, and had a successful law practice. This last did not surprise me at all. If anyone ever had a natural gift of plausible gab Jack Clarke did—I feel certain of his ability to convince a jury of anything.

While I was shooting pool with Jack at the Flushing YMCA one rainy evening in the fall of 1945, a call was put out for an extra person for a duplicate bridge game. I was interested and, since Clarkie had other things to do, agreed to fill in. My partner, it turned out was a Mr. Charles Diels, a fine white-haired old gentleman of seventy-some years. I must have impressed him as promising raw material—eager and teachable, even if somewhat unskilled—for he expressed an interest in playing with me again the following week. This was the beginning of a collaboration that lasted for almost two years. I don't know that we won often, but we regularly came in among the first few, save for a handful of occasional catastrophes (no doubt of my doing) which saw us finish at the bottom of the ranking.

We must have seemed a strange pair, separated by some fifty-five years, and I don't quite know what kept us together week after week. I suspect that on his side it was the appeal of dealing with someone not a septuagenarian. As to me, I felt the Mr. Diels was counting on me and that it would be wrong to let him down. Then too, I welcomed this unorthodox opportunity to interact with someone of an older generation, a surrogate for the grandparents I had left behind in Germany.

During my high school days I had little interest in girls until the last year (1945-1946). Even then I never had any one particular "sweetheart," but there were several girls in school who were my good friends, and of whom I was fond in that ill-defined, semi-romantic way that is seldom far removed in the friendship of young persons of the opposite sex. The recollection of most of these friendships has grown so dim that for the most part I cannot even now recall the names of the young ladies.

In the course of the 1944-45 academic year I was elected to Flushing High School chapter of ARISTA, the scholastic honorary society. This was important for me in two ways. For one thing, it had a marked effect on the development of my self-image: I began to think of myself for the first time not simply in atomistic terms, as one student distinguished from others by the pattern of his personal interests and activities, but as a member of an elite distinguished by academic interests—in books, ideas, and issues.[1] Moreover, by throwing me into closer contact with those of my schoolmates whose orientation was in essentials congenial to my own, membership in ARISTA had an expansive effect on my contacts and friendships. For the first time at the Flushing High School I entered into an active social life. This broke the pattern of isolation and self-sufficiency into which I had been thrown since Beechhurst day by the shift of succession of moves to Armonk to Plainfield to Flushing. Eventually, the shift to college in 1946 broke up these high school friendships, but these classmates still stick in my mind, and I remember them well and fondly.

The greater part of my high school career unfolded against the background of the Second World War, which ended only some five months before my graduation. As best I recall, we students never talked about the war with each other, though no doubt, some attention was devoted to it in the current affairs part of social studies courses. To be sure, we read the newspapers and heard the radio and were acutely aware of what was going on. But we were determined to live out lives in a "normal" way.

As the panorama of the war passed before my fascinated gaze during these impressionable teen-age years, it all seemed very far from home. And for me it never came close. I read avidly of the generals and their campaigns, eagerly studying the maps to follow the vast struggles of far-off armies. I was ever anxious to see how "our side" was doing. There was never a moment of doubt that the U.S.A. was "my country" and that it held my absolute allegiance. Although I had at this stage spent the lesser part of my life within its borders, I could not have been a more convinced and unquestioning patriot had I descended from ten generations of native Americans. This is not to say, however, that I was personally anxious to enter the fray. I signed up for the draft at age 17 as was required, but was thoroughly pleased when the war ended before I was of age to be called up. I was acutely conscious that only the lucky accident of a well-timed birthdate enabled me to view this world-catastrophe as a spectator rather than a participant.

The war undoubtedly made its greatest impact on me through films. Intended for propaganda and morale-building purposes, they managed to endow the whole process with an aura of unreality that a casual reading of newspapers could never offset. Only in later years, after reading books and, above all, myself seeing military service during wartime, did I begin to form a realistic picture of what was involved, a picture that gave me deep sympathies towards that sincere pacifism which is not a mere cover for personal convenience.

During high school days, I had two brief period of Saturday employment: one as a packer at the Loft candy factory in Long Island City, and one as a counter boy at a Bickford's diner in Elmhurst. The latter involved getting up at around 5 AM and traveling on the subway for over a half hour. It made for a miserable, drawn-out day, with little pay and next-to-nothing in tips. It was generally unpleasant and un-productive and I gave it up after two or three Saturdays. And the candy packing job was deadly-dull assembly-line labor of the most routing sort. But here one's companions were other high school kids with whom one could joke and talk. I kept this up on Saturdays for a period of some months, before concluding that I would really rather have the time than the money (probably around 40¢ an hour). However I derived lessons of great value from these two brief spells of common, unskilled labor. I learned how enervating and thought-eras-ing work of a totally routinized nature could be and so be-came reinforced in my determination to "make something of myself"—and to avoid at all costs having to toil at meaning-less work in a deeply uncongenial occupation. I was deter-mined to get a good education and put myself into the position of earning a livelihood with my head rather than my hands. Above all, the need to go to college became a settled idea with me.

Towards the middle of my high school period my thoughts regarding a career began to take some more definite shape. I now began to toy with the idea of the Diplomatic Service.

(I was fluent in German and making headway in French, with some talent for learning languages, and a strong interest in history and international affairs.) But this idea was demolished sometime in 1944 when I wrote to the State Department to get information regarding the qualifications and training for the appropriate civil service examinations. I learned to my dismay that a naturalized citizen could only enter the service after holding his U.S. citizenship for 15 years. Since I obtained my citizenship only that year, I could not see my way clear to contemplating a career that I could not enter upon until many years after completing all the necessary training. Though disappointed, I realized that it is pointless to fret over what cannot be mended.

In the spring of 1944 I had my first experience as a teacher, tutoring mathematics to a French immigrant boy a little younger than I who lived in our Flushing neighborhood. I succeeded rather well in this teaching effort and found it enjoyable and satisfying. The cumulative impression of this experience and some others of a similar nature later on implanted in my mind the idea of teaching as a vocation—an idea which took increasingly firm hold with the passage of time.

When I now look back, it strikes me a curious—and even in some degree unnatural—that my parents left me entirely to my own devices in this regard. As best I can recall, they offered no suggestions and gave me little if any advice and counsel. It is perfectly conceivable that I could have had a successful and satisfying career along lines very different from the actual ones—as a physician, say, or an architect. And I suspect I could easily have been impelled in such directions. But for better (as I now think) or for worse, no direct impetus was provided by my parents.

Indirectly their influence was crucial, however. For one day in early 1945 my father brought home a copy of Will Durant's *Story of Philosophy*. (Father had some amateur interest in philosophy and was particularly interested in Arthur Schopenhauer—to say nothing of that semi-philosopher Goethe, to whom he was greatly devoted.) I had soon devoured Durant's book and found it fascinating. This was my initial discovery of philosophy. I went on to other miscellaneous reading—some Schopenhauer, some Descartes, and quite a lot of Hume. I was altogether captivated, and came to the view that philosophy was something really worthwhile, something in the doing of which one could rewardingly spend the rest of one's days. Neither then not for some years afterwards did philosophy displace mathematics completely from the forefront of my interest. But it was clear from the first that these two fields were the really live options for me. And happily, it soon appeared that these disciplines were more complimentary than divergent—at least from one perspective. For I discovered symbolic logic.

At some point during my high school career I was enrolled in a mathematics course with Mrs. Charlotte Knag, then a recent graduate of Queens College who had just married the treasurer of that institution. On one of my book buying excursions I had acquired a copy of Andrew Paul Ushenko's *The Theory of Logic* from a second-hand bookshop. I read it with interest and I found symbolic logic utterly fascinating. Mrs. Knag—with whom I talked about this—made some other reading suggestions, and she told me about Professor Hempel at Queens who was an authority in this field and an excellent teacher. I looked forward to going to Queens and working under him. Since logic lay at the border-area between philosophy and mathematics, it afforded a perfect way of combining my two paramount interests.

In January of 1946, at seventeen and a half years, I graduated from Flushing High School with a place well up on the honors list. I now made ready to begin collegiate studies—in the middle of the academic year—at Queens College. At this stage, there was still much about me that was indeterminate and formless, but nevertheless I had begun to make some headway in the process of maturation and self-definition. To be sure, I never thought of myself as a person of outstanding talents in comparison with the ablest of my contemporaries (quite the reverse!) But it now became a settled thing, at least in my own mind, that I was to make my way in the world by means of brainwork. The idea of an academic career loomed ever larger in my thoughts. I recognized clearly that in realizing this aspiration I would be quite on my own, since my family lacked useful contacts and connections. But while I may not have had many splendid opportunities to look forward to, I was set on making the most of those that would come my way.

NOTES

1. In those days, I even wrote some poems, of which one still remains—a sonnet written in 1945. I reproduced this juvenile production here not because I think it to have the slightest shred of merit, but only because it shows something about the sort of lad I was at this stage.

On Reading Aeschylus's "Prometheus Chained"

To a high cliff Prometheus is chained,
Which neither men not hostile gods do see.
His limbs by Vulcan's well-wrought chains are pained.
And his a myriad dreadful tortures be.
This is his punishment for giving aid
To man whose doom the god-king Jove had planned.
And so by Vulcan's very able hand
Fast to a Scithian rock his chains are made.
Jove punishes with undeserved pain
Those who his iron will do dare oppose;
This harshness was unknown before his reign,
Never before had gods endured such woes;
But still great Jove might fail to reach his goal,
For they who body chain, chain not the soul.

(From *Young America Sings: 1946 Anthology of New York City High School Poetry*.)

Five

QUEENS COLLEGE
Flushing: 1946-1949
(Age 17-21)

My undergraduate studies began at Queens College in New York in January of 1946, at the midpoint of the 1945-46 academic year. Located in what was then a largely undeveloped no-man's land between Flushing and Jamaica, this institution was still in its infancy. It had commenced operations only a few years before in the converted buildings of a former boys reformatory, soon supplemented by a few wartime prefabs. By 1946, its only new building was the student union; even the library was still housed on an upper floor of the old reform school administration building. However, the austerity of the physical plant was more than offset by the excellence of the faculty at that time.

The Queens College philosophy department contained a group of men of capability and good repute: Herbert G. Bohnert (a disciple of Rudolf Carnap), William Callaghan (a charming Irish-American Catholic who was a neo-Thomist of sorts), Donald Davidson (a disciple of W. V. O. Quine, then just beginning his academic career after wartime service in the Navy), John Goheen (the chairman, who maintained interests in ancient and medieval philosophy, but devoted his main efforts to administration), Carl G. Hempel (a German emigré logician and philosopher of science), and Arnold Isenberg (an aesthetician). They were a likable group of people and always helpful to me. Moreover, they were, on the whole, dedicated teachers. To be sure, with the hubris of callow youth, I regarded them as ordinary mortals of ordinary abilities, the one outstanding exception being Hempel, a man of unusual capacity and massive intellectual power. Primarily, however, what attracted me to philosophy was not so much the example of its teachers, as the fascination of the subject itself. Once I had discovered the field in Will Durant's *Story of Philosophy* as a high school sophomore, my interest was firmly locked in place. The more I came to grapple with the issues that filled the pages of the great philosophers of the past, the more my enthusiasm for the subject grew.

To be sure, mathematics for a time exerted a temptation. The Queens College mathematics department then also afforded an impressive array of talent. T. Freeman Cope, the chairman, taught classical analysis with a clarity and precision that amounted to elegance. And his staff consisted of very able people indeed: Leon Cohen (who specialized in the theory of functions), Banesh Hoffman (applied mathematics), and Leo Zippin (topology), among others. Cope in particular had one impressive and amazing trait. In working problem upon problem at the blackboard and presenting a wide variety of proofs, he never made the slightest slip-up, not even a minor mistake in calculation. This gave a certain virtuosity to his teaching performance which was not in other ways particularly colorful, keeping us in suspenseful waiting for that error which never arrived. The other mathematics professor who most impressed me was Leon Cohen who joined the faculty at Queens in my Junior year. His course in Analysis of Real Variable was a sheer joy to me. Cohen really loved mathematics and managed to endow its presentation with excitement and warmth. He in particular among my teachers ultimately became a friend, and I continued to see him from time to time later on in Washington, when he had left Queens college to head the Mathematics Section of the National Science Foundation in the early 1950's. I am grateful to these men for making the study of mathematics an intensely exciting and rewarding experience throughout my college years. And my efforts in this filed were not unsuccessful; I was sometimes ablest student in the class, and always among the two or three best.

Not long after graduating from high school, I had learned quite accidentally from a friend that the competitive examinations for the New York State Scholarships were to be given shortly. (To their discredit, my teachers and advisors at Flushing High School had left me quite uniformed about this whole venture.) I put my name in to take the examinations only a few days before they were actually offered, and had no chance to prepare—I could not even obtain information as to the *sort* of thing at issue. I thus took the examination in a rather casual spirit, simply gambling on the off-chance that something might come of it. To my surprise and pleasure, I did succeed in winning one of these scholarships. They then paid $750 per annum, with no strings attached, to any New Yorker attending an in-state college or university. The purchasing power of the dollar was in those days such that this modest amount was far from contemptible. Since Queens College was a tuition-free, publicly supported institution, it more than sufficed for all my expenses for books, fees, transportation, lunches, etc. With the convenience of living at home, this windfall freed me of any pressure to earn money by irrelevant summer jobs, so that I could now devote my summers to recreation and study. Whenever I am minded to grumble about taxes—a not infrequent experience nowadays—I remind myself of this debt to the taxpayers of New York.

In my college work I was relatively hardworking and serious-minded. I carried a joint major in mathematics and philosophy. Philosophy never made great demands on me—it was like coasting downhill. But mathematics was a different story, and while I enjoyed it greatly, I also worked at it quite hard.

What led me to major in philosophy and mathematics? As with all too many students, I was actuated by the sheer impetus of interest. I was not much concerned to look at the matter in practical terms of a possible future career. Then too, no countervailing forces were at work—no successful uncle to beckon me into his banking house or flourishing architectural practice. Had such opportunities been at hand, I do not doubt that I could have been diverted—whether for ultimate good or bad it is impossible to say.

Classics was another area I pursued seriously, continuing with Latin and commencing Greek. I much liked and respected Konrad Gries, the professor of classics, who was a person of substantial capabilities. But, while I expended considerable effort at classical languages, I feel that I never attained that real facility at Latin (or at Greek) which the time devoted to these subjects might lead one to expect. Though the instruction we received was certainly competent, I now think my training was seriously defective in point of pedagogical strategy. It lacked that constant review of grammatical fundamentals, that well-structured plan at building vocabulary, and that systematic program aimed at developing a facility for rapid reading, which ought to be a prime aim of the teaching of dead languages.

I much enjoyed the study of literature—in French and classical languages as well as English. (I recall being particularly appreciative of Edwin Knowles in whose class I studied Chaucer's *Canterbury Tales*, and Paolo Milano with whom we read some of the *philosophes* of 18th century France.) I was very much interested in drama and read masses of plays from Shakespeare to Shaw. I also began at this time to be interested in the history of art and architecture. But I viewed all these interests in diverse cultural matters as ancillary to my philosophical concerns. Under Oswald Spengler's influence—whose *Decline of the West* made a deep impression on me—I inclined to view all cultural phenomena, philosophy included, as belonging to one over-arching and unifying (albeit evolving) intellectual tradition.

Throughout my Queens College career I lived at home with my parents in our Parsons Boulevard apartment, traveling to school by the public transport system's Jamaica bus—a trip of perhaps 20 minutes or so. But while I continued to reside at home, the old patterns changed and with them the nature of my familial and personal relationships. My ties to old Beechhurst friends grew more tenuous—they were now away at college and we only had some sporadic contact in the summers. And my relationship with my parents gradually changed too—as my horizons broadened they, as in natural enough, no longer cast quite so large a shadow over my life.

My first term at Queens College saw the burgeoning of my first relatively serious feminine interest. That spring of 1946—aged seventeen—I became attracted to my first real "girl-friend," a girl called Lorna from Hackson Heights. (Lorna what?—I cannot even recall the name, though I do know that it wasn't Lorna Doone.) I took her to various entertainments and sporadically visited with her. Howerver, my interest could not have been too serious. While she was away on vacation for that summer, I never wrote her, being too busy playing tennis. When college resumed in September, I found that she had taken this much amiss, and our friendship came to an end.

More important was my attachment to Jean H. which commenced late in 1946 and lasted throughout my college years. She too was a mathematics major, a year ahead of me in the program, who was much interested in logic, and was also an enthusiastic ping-pong player and devotee of bridge. (It was, I think, the floating bridge games in the Student Union that first brought us together.) We became good friends and relatively constant companions, sharing various common activities and interests. She was an attractive, dark-haired girl, of middling height and build, neither svelte nor plump. Her personality was pleasant and cheerful, and she was highly intelligent though perhaps a bit impassive. For years on end we spent much time together, and in due course of time an understanding evolved that we might eventually marry.

Although I had many casual friends of my own sex at college, I was not a close companion to any of them. My work certainly absorbed much of my time and energy, and my social life centered around the friends I shared with Jean, with whom we would generally do things together (especially play bridge). Only a handful of my college contemporaries made a lasting impression on me. These included Richard Myers, an intense young man who was an authentic mathematical genius, and Joan Drakert, an exceptionally bright and sharp-tongued girl who went on to a Ph.D. in physics. Another person I was in regular contact with was Cornelius Ryan Fay, a philosophy major who was some two years my senior. His parents were Catholic and had a large family of boys, so that Neil had some five of six brothers. They all lived at home, and those who were still in school held down part-time jobs. When there were any financial needs of difficulties, father Fay would go to church to pray for guidance, the result of which was generally an increase in the "rent" all of his sons were charged. They were a charming and attractive typical Irish-American Catholic family.

During the summers of my college years, the pace of my life ran a more leisurely course. One summer I worked as a factotum in the Foreign Language Department of the Jamaica Public Library. Whereas earlier my free time went almost wholly to tennis, I now became more sedentary and intellectual, enroute to becoming something of a bookworm.

It was at this stage that I was first introduced to the writings of Freud which made (dare I say it?) a very poor impression on me. Accustomed to the rigors of academic philosophy—to say nothing of those of mathematics and natural science—I viewed him a sloppy thinker, inclined to fanciful leaps from scanty data to remote conclusions. Nor did I think it plausible to view sexuality as the controlling factor in life's dealings—it has always struck me a just another of man's biological drives which, important thought they are, scarcely constitute an all-encompassing pivot of human affairs. I deemed Freud, as I had deemed Henry George before and was to deem Karl Marx later on, as just another 19th century one-track thinker who had an oversimple, monolithic solution to a complex manifold of issues. This was my view as a brash undergraduate, and I still hold it to this very day.

During my final college years I audited several mathematical classes at Columbia University. Professors never bothered to take attendance in the large classes there, so that bootlegged knowledge could be had for the taking. I enjoyed these classes and profited by them. One of these courses made a particularly vivid impression on me—Samuel Eilenberg's lively lectures on Algebraic Topology. Eilenberg was a very clear and well-organized lecturer and projected a striking, if somewhat abrasive, personality. Once, for example, he repeatedly declined to recognize a questioner, and then at a later stage interrupted his presentation to address him personally: "Now *this* point has answered your question hasn't it? I knew you were bright enough to spot the difficulty, but felt it best to let it be resolved in the natural course of things."

On one occasion during my visit to Columbia I had the chance to hear a lecture by Norbert Wiener, the eminent mathematician and father of cybernetics. Unfortunately, the presentation proceeded at so general and descriptive a level that there was nothing particularly memorable about it—it was the sort of talk that would have been given by anybody. However, Wiener delivered it quite informally, without notes and in so conversational a manner that it was easy to listen to.

The mathematics Department at Queens College required all its majors to take a comprehensive examination towards the end of their career. This served a dual purpose, both as a general proficiency examination in the major field and as a prize examination. I took this exam prematurely at the end of my Junior year (in the Spring of 1948). Nonetheless, I tied for first place. As a prize I could pick a mathematics book of my own choice, and I selected Alexandroff's *Topologie* which I still have, but to my shame have never finished reading.

For a brief time this success led me to the (probably mistaken) idea that I might succeed as a professional mathematician. Going on with mathematics in graduate school became an increasingly live prospect. But several things prevented it. One was the feeling that a real mathematician needs not just an adequate talent for his subject, but a positive genius—a truly extraordinary gift for it, and that this was something which I lacked. Though certainly competent at mathematics, I never sense the inner power of real creativity in this field, and never felt that intense commitment to it, analogous to near demonic dedication of the real chess player.

In philosophy, on the other hand, I thought I could do well. I believed (heaven knows for what reason!) that none of my classmates at Queens were more capable in this field than I.

To be sure, I did not credit myself any extraordinary gifts of intellect. But I combined dedication and willingness to work with an intense interest in the field. More than most, I had an ability to cut through to the core without irrelevancies: a capacity to get a job done. The subject appealed immensely to me, and I "felt in my bones" that I could do well at it.

Moreover, I saw my interests in philosophy as altogether compatible and congenial with others I had in mathematics, the sciences, and the humanities. Philosophy cannot do its work on a pedestal set apart, but must labor in the very midst of other concerns. The philosopher is entitled to be a jack of many trades—perhaps even required to be so. Philosophy cannot operate *de haut en bas*: it must address the materials secured by other branches of learning rather than lord it over them. In short, a philosopher can and should be a generalist, and this is how I saw myself.

What attracted me to philosophy was the chance to deal in a serious and hard-headed way with issues that are both challenging in themselves and of substantial human importance: the nature of the world, the business of acquiring knowledge, the source of value, and the like. I succumbed also—and especially—to the siren call of logic, and was keenly alive to the beauties of formal reasoning and the almost aesthetic appeal of a clear analysis of complex issues.

As my college years progressed, it somehow jelled in my mind that I was going to go on to graduate school. My professors represented a type—the professional academic—that was new to me and that I found appealing. The prospect of being able to dwell within the realm of ideas exerted an ever-increasing appeal for me. Grappling with the things of the mind struck me as a venture vastly preferable to dealing with the hurly-burly of the world's practicalities. Gradually I was captivated by the idea that "this is the life for me"—that there is nothing else I would rather be doing. At that point my professors ceased being just my teachers and became my role-models as well.

When I sent out applications for graduate school scholarships in the fall of 1948, I also applied to several programs in mathematics. But my thoughts and aspirations by now turned mainly in the direction of philosophy, and my main hopes were placed in those applications I made for graduate study in this field.

When the returns were in, I had two offers from mathematics departments—from Syracuse and some other, now forgotten university—but I was also offered scholarships in philosophy at Harvard, Yale, and Princeton. (Hempel had advised me in my applications, and the whole department had supported them—obviously a good effect.) The Princeton offer had the greatest attractions for me. The field was philosophy, the institution was of good repute, and its location was within easy visiting distance of home. Last, and not least, the financial terms were attractive since the grant covered all the tuition expenses and most of my living costs as well. Without much hesitation I decided that Princeton was to be the place for me.

On a warm and pleasant day in June of 1949 I attended the graduation exercise and listened to the usual commencement platitudes from the mouth of Judge Charles S. Colden. (I still remember him, not because of his message, but because he was a remote descendent of Cadwallader Colden, one of America's earliest philosophers.) I received my B.S. with honors in mathematics and was graduated *magna cum laude*.[1] I looked forward to the rest and relaxation of the summer—even more to the challenges of Princeton that lay beyond.

The years of adolescence and young adulthood generally see some struggle at learning about oneself, largely by toilsome trial and error, to determine just where one's potential lies and what one can and cannot do. This self-definition is certainly not a matter of simply making up one's mind —willpower as such has little to do with it—it is largely a matter of natural selection through learning by way of trial and elimination by actual failure, a painful process because it is never easy for human beings to face up to their inadequacies. The issues often take years to resolve and may well exact a heavy psychological toll. I was fortunate that in my own case my natural bent came to the fore readily, so that the period of uncertainty was reasonably painless and mercifully short. Realizing fairly clearly where I wanted to go, I could settle down and address myself to the task of getting on with it. And so, by the time of my graduation from Queens College, still at the age of 20, I knew pretty well what I would ideally want to do with myself in life: to be a teacher and student of philosophy.

Considering the formative years at issue, I naturally left Queens College in June of 1949 a very different person from the raw youth who came there in January, 1946. I had acquired a good deal of knowledge and skill, but—more importantly—an enhanced confidence in myself and in my intellectual abilities. And, above all, I had formed a determination to put these abilities to work. My college experience had provided an incentive to broaden and enlarge my interests and a stimulus to develop them. To credit this result to an educational institution is to give it high praise, and I have felt—then and ever since—greatly indebted to Queens College.

NOTES

1. I missed membership in Phi Beta Kappa because there was not yet a chapter at Queens. More than a quarter-century later (in 1977), the University of Pittsburgh chapter made me an honorary member, a thoughtful step which pleased me greatly.

Six

PRINCETON UNIVERSITY
1949-1952
(Age 21-23)

I recall clearly the balmy day in early September of 1949 when my mother saw me off at the Flushing depot of the Long Island Railroad to start the train journey to Princeton. I had never lived away from home before. Mother, of course, cried bitterly, despite my embarrassed urging that this was really quite uncalled-for, considering that I was a full-grown man of twenty-one and would, in any case, be only two hours' journey away from home. But in my heart of hearts I too was struck with the moment of the occasion, which was clearly an augury of coming changes.

After the Pennsylvania Railroad had deposited me in Princeton late that morning, I settled into my assigned room in the gray-granite, neo-Gothic pile known as the Graduate College. I had brought along the Everyman's Library edition of Fielding's *Tom Jones* and spent an hour or so reading it in an armchair by the open dormer window of my small third-floor room trying to get into the "feel" of the place. That afternoon I set off for campus. I began with a visit to the Philosophy Department offices in 1879 Hall for an orientation interview with W.T. Stace, who was in charge of graduate studies in philosophy. I let no grass grow under my feet. After completing registration for my courses, I went off straightaway and passed my French and German language-proficiency examinations that very day.

One thing still stands out in my mind about my interview with Stace. He gave me a list of courses and asked me which four I would like to take. I indicated several, including one by Jacques Maritain, the celebrated French neo-Thomist. Stace pulled a face and indicated I would do well to select something else. The situation was strange to me, and in any case I was not brash enough to demur from the views of the Director of Graduate Studies. Only later did I learn that Stace and Maritain had quarreled in print about religion and were ideologically at loggerheads. Opposed to all Christian orthodoxy, Stace was reluctant to see a student come under the influence of this eminent Catholic thinker. Though I came to like and respect Stace, this incident left a blot on his image, and whenever in after years I heard talk of the anti-Catholic animus of American academics, this episode leapt to recollection.

My first impressions of Princeton on that September day of a quarter century ago are still vivid in my mind: the little train station, tidy and clean beyond any of my acquaintance in the big city; the handsome campus, incomparably greener and more picturesque than those I knew in New York; the people—students and faculty alike—who, in comparison with those of Queens or of Columbia, impressed me as more leisurely, self-assured, and at ease with the world. The town itself, then a mere village, seemed a compact and congenial little place whose sole reason for being was catering to the needs of students. I was by now a New Yorker who had scarce left the crowded and untidy confines of the metropolis for the past six years. By comparison, Princeton struck me as a veritable heaven on earth, I thanked a kindly fate for having set this phase of my life's drama on such a splendid stage, revelling in the prettiness of the place, somewhat daunted and overawed by it all, but proud to be a little fish swimming in so noble a lake.

I registered for four courses that first term: Alonzo Church on logic (which was taught in the Department of Mathematics), Walter Terence Stace on recent philosophy (Bradley,

Whitehead, Russell), Andrew Paul Ushenko on epistemology, and Arthur Szathmary on Descartes. I also audited two courses in mathematics, one of them the very excellent lectures on algebra by Emil Artin.

Stace's course proved to be particularly interesting to me, partly on account of the material, but largely on the account of Stace himself, who had a vivid personality and an engaging style of presentation. Stace—then aged sixty-three—was certainly not a professional philosopher of the usual sort. After academic training at Trinity College, Dublin, the bulk of his professional career has been spent in the Ceylonese civil service, where he had risen to be mayor of Columbo, the capital city. A tall, impressive man with a somewhat bluff manner, it was clear that his concern for philosophy was deep and real. In a pleasantly disarming way he was not always sure he fully understood the thinkers whose ideas he was presenting, but it was clear that he credited them with importance and value. He was thus able to get us to take seriously philosophers like Bradley and Whitehead whose way of thinking and writing was altogether antithetical to the temper of the time. Stace's many years in the East had awakened in him an interest in religious mysticism, an inclination towards which I then felt no sympathy, but which did somehow augment his interest in my eyes.

Andrew Paul Ushenko was rather an enigma. Although he was a soft-spoken little Caspar Milquetoast of a man, the epitome of the shrinking violet, the concept of *power* played a central role in his philosophizing. He had a genuine dedication to philosophical ideas and inquiry. I thought his seminar on aesthetics managed to identify some points of interest in a pretty bleak terrain. He had a good sense of where the important problems lay in philosophy and was eager to come to grips with them. This, to my way of thinking, did much to offset his lack of charisma. Moreover, I felt a debt to him because of the impact that his logic-book had made on me in high-school days.

Alonzo Church, of the department of mathematics, was a unique figure. A more dull and pedestrian lecturer can hardly be imagined. But this hardly mattered, since the man was scholarship personified—accurate, painstaking, and amazingly widely informed in matters of logic, in fact, a walking encyclopedia of the subject. He made a deep impression and did so by intellect alone, unaugmented by any trace of charisma of personality. He was bulky in mind and body alike, and moved slowly and ponderously—a juggernaut weighted down by the burden of prodigious learning. A scholar of the highest standards and capabilities, he stood in a class by himself, though, to be sure, the comparison class to which he belonged, or at any rate to which I assigned him, was that of logicians and not philosophers as such.

The graduate program in philosophy at Princeton was in those days a relatively small affair—there were some seven or eight students in the entering class and altogether a total of some twenty in residence taking courses. The individual seminars had around eight members. They met in sessions of two of three hours and usually consisted of an hours' lecture followed by a somewhat longer period of discussion. Occasionally (but rarely) the participants would be asked to present seminar papers about which the group then deliberated as a whole with eager but generally constructive criticism.

I certainly had no reason to be discontented with my formal academic fare. Still, I profited as much—or more—from contacts with my fellow students, some of who were truly outstanding: Rogers Albritton, who possessed a keen albeit labyrinthine philosophical mind, and was a very good discussant with an unusual capacity for insightful criticism. Fadlou Shehadi, an enthusiastic young Lebanese, who was at this stage very much of a beginner at Western philosophy, but had an impressive deep dedication to philosophical ideas. James L. Cole, an Oberlin "faculty kid" and graduate, who had a good head and rather out-of-the-way philosophical interests—having been a psychology major as an undergraduate, he tended to look at things from a viewpoint rather different from mine. And in a more casual way I was touched with many nonphilosophers—chemists, romance linguistics, classicists—who contributed both to my intellectual and social nurture in the monastic fellowship of the Graduate College.

My routine during these days ran somewhat as follows: Arising around 7:00 A.M., I dressed and went downstairs to breakfast. Then I would work in my room until just before class-time at 9. Returning for lunch at noon, I would thereafter work—or go to class—until the middle of the afternoon. Around 5 P.M. I would go round to a friend's room for talk and a glass of sherry until dinner at 6:30. After dinner I would work until 10 o'clock—or sometimes go to a film or for a social visit off campus with a married friend. I was always back in my room by 10:30, and would then spend a final half hour or so with light reading to clear my head of philosophical cobwebs before going to bed. (I now first read the *Autobiography* of Herbert Spencer, which I liked immensely, and which began a lifelong interest in philosophical autobiography. However, my usual reading fare tended towards English novels—Fielding, Smollet, Jane Austen, Disraeli—and towards books on American history.) Generally, I must frequently have spent some ten hours of the day at work in or out of the class—8-12 noon, 1-5 P.M., and (frequently) 8-10 P.M. I never drove myself and never burned the midnight oil, maintaining a slow, steady, even pace of reasonably efficient application to the tasks at hand, with little wasted motion. I was perhaps not so much of an all-work-and-no-play sobersides as such a schematic account may suggest. For while I tended to approach the work in hand with zest, I generally did so with a bit of humor as well. It never seemed to me that philosophical concerns precluded a certain detached amusement towards the issues and a willingness to treat them with an admixture of fun.

Class-work aside, I pursued a major project of my own devising during this first year of graduate studies. Over the preceding summer, I had begun a study of the philosophy of Leibniz with a view to developing a suitable project that I could carry with me to graduate school that fall. (I already possessed my life-long tendency to "steal a march" on the future by getting a head start on the discharge of its commitments.) My Queens College friend, Cornelius Ryan Fay —who had already begun graduate work at Columbia —had drawn Bertrand Russell's *The Philosophy of Leibniz* to my notice, and Russell engaged my attention for this fascinating thinker. His many-sidedness and especially his genius for the utilization of logic and mathematics towards philosophical ends exercised a powerful appeal for me. I spent a good bit of that fall of 1949 reading whatever Leibnizian material I could lay my hands on. In particular I discovered Louis Couturat's *La Logique de Leibniz*, and this splendid book gave me much stimulation. But while it was two figures of a past generation (Russell and Couturat) who had led me to Leibniz, it was Leibniz himself who held me there. And so throughout the 1949-1950 academic year I enthusiastically pursued a study of Leibniz' cosmology, producing a substantial essay as a vehicle for my ideas.

In early May I told Professor Ledger Wood about this writing project. I asked him if he could suggest some faculty member to read it with a view to judging its potential for development into a dissertation. He replied that he had best read it himself, seeing that Leibniz was as much in his area of interest as anybody's in the department. I gave him a copy of my script. A fortnight later he called me into his office to discuss this project. He said he felt this to be a very good piece of work and eminently suitable as the first draft of a dissertation. He proposed that, as I was so far along, I would do well to try my hand at the General Examination for the Ph.D. which was due to be given in ten days time. He assured me that failure would not be held against me in these circumstances. I accepted this proposal eagerly though not without trepidation and set off on an intensive program of last-minute review of material that might be relevant.

Perhaps to everyone's surprise, and certainly to mine, I not only sustained that battery of examinations but (so I was told) performed well enough to have passed "with distinction" had not my ethics paper been relatively weak—which certainly did not surprise me, since I had never taken even so much as an undergraduate course in the subject.

Clearing the hurdle of the General Examination had important implications for me. After a single, relatively unpressured year, I had now completed all the official obligations of the doctoral program apart from the dissertation. And even here I already had in hand a first-draft version that only needed some polishing which I could attend to, in the main, over the summer months.

Thus when I returned to Flushing at the end of my first year, in June of 1950 the work for the Ph.D. lay almost completely behind me. In other ways too I had made progress, having at last been required to live on my own and be responsible for myself. By some glacial and inconspicuous process I had become a relatively self-sufficient young man.

At this stage my attitude towards my parents also underwent a significant change. Living away from home led me to view them with greater detachment—to see them as people rather than as simply a part of my family unit. I came to respect them more, to appreciate their good qualities, to take them less for granted. In sum, I became fonder of them. But I became distanced from them as well. I certainly wished them well in every way, but was now fully committed to proceeding on my own.

Then too, I now at last became fully independent in point of finances. The graduate scholarship I had held during my first year sufficed for the tuition fees and also went part-way towards defraying my room and board. But there was still a deficit to be made up—partly from a small nest-egg I had saved from my New York State Scholarship, but principally by the contribution of my parents. Now, however, I was promoted to the somewhat more elevated status of University Fellow, a post whose ampler emoluments just about covered the whole of my expenses. From this point on I was able to stand on my own financial feet. (And none too soon—considering the I was now turning twenty-two.)

This seems a proper place to record my deep sense of debt to the various strangers who helped to make my participation in higher education financially possible: the officials of New York City who set Queens College up as a public institution, the legislators of New York State who established the system of state scholarships, the benefactors of Princeton who gave funds for scholarships. To all of these I feel an immeasurable gratitude. I realize what a tragedy it would have been for me had higher education not been attainable—as it would otherwise almost surely not have been, considering the tight financial straits into which my parents had been plunged. (However, this is a debt I believe I have repaid through many years of work in the modestly compensated ranks of higher education.)

One important development occurred at this juncture. I had dated Jean H. ever since my second year at Queens College. But as the years passed the relationship gradually wore stale. Moreover, being away at Princeton had changed my perspective. I came to see my life in a different light and Jean no longer seemed a necessary part of it. Perhaps our friendship had just dragged on for too long. Perhaps the shift to graduate school and the opening of new horizons made me eager for new contacts and new experiences. As any rate, I now broke off our relationship—doing this so abruptly that it was actually cruel. Jean deserved better of me. But I felt that there had to be an ending, and did not trust myself to make it at all if this were not done in a swift and decisive way. I felt—and still feel—that the unkind manner of this inevitable breach casts no credit on me. In his *Autobiography,* Benjamin Franklin speaks of certain *errata* in the typography of his life that he wishes it were possible to correct. For me, this lack of consideration towards someone who deserved far better of me was such an erratum.

That summer of 1950 I was relatively lazy. I revised the thesis and did some desultory philosophical reading. In the main I saw friends and occupied myself with tennis and other recreational activities.

After a relaxed summer, I returned to Princeton that fall refreshed and eager. Having sustained the General Examination, I was now free of any obligation to take courses formally, but I audited a variety of offerings in various departments. Apart from some philosophical courses, I recall another session with Alonzo Church on logic and William Feller's lectures on probability in the Mathematics Department, and in Classics I attended Whitney Oate's seminar on Aristotle's *Metaphysics*. Otherwise, I polished my thesis, socialized with friends, and lived in the relative comfort that an increased fellowship stipend afforded me in the easy circumstances of the Graduate College. I particularly enjoyed interaction with some of the lively and interesting members of the newly incoming group of graduate students: Vaclav Benes, Jerome Schneewind, and Jerome Shaffer.

Unfortunately, I began to experience a succession of headaches at this stage. I thought at first that they might be occasioned by eye troubles, but this possibility was soon eliminated. What, then, might be the cause? The suggestion came that they might perhaps be of psychological origin. I found this difficult to believe—for had I not just recently put various prime sources of psychological stress and pressure behind me? Still, I thought it best to consult "the experts." Accordingly, I visited the Health Clinic's psychologist, as well as another such practitioner who was recommended to me. I was surprised and impressed at the ease with which these men proposed diagnostic etiologies that placed my problems squarely within their favored framework—be it Freudian or whatever. But I was no less surprised when the problem cleared up overnight a week of so later when a tooth with an infected root canal was extracted. This experience did nothing to alter my already low estimate of the psychiatric craft.

Now at last I started to practice the career for which I felt myself destined. My new fellowship called for instructional duties, so that for the first time I became a practicing teacher. I served as "preceptor" for various courses, meeting with groups of 8-10 students in Princeton's version of the Oxbridge tutorial system. Next to authentic individual tutorials, this process of small group colloquies has always seemed to me a near-to-ideal method of philosophical instruction. At any rate, teaching in this context was a new and highly pleasurable experience for me.

I now also began work on what was to be my first published paper, appearing in the course under the title of "Contingence in the Philosophy of Leibniz" in *The Philosophical Review* (in vol. 61 for 1952). As a matter of fact, my dissertation on Leibniz inaugurated an ongoing concern on my part with the work of this outstanding thinker. He came to play an important part in my professional life, and as the years went on, I was to be frequently preoccupied with this great man. I periodically taught seminars devoted to his work,

wrote a succession of articles about him, and in 1967 published an exposition of his philosophy, parts of which drew on my
dissertation of some 15 years before. In November of 1967
Leibniz scholars from all the world gathered in Hanover,
Germany to commemorate the 250th anniversary of his
death. Dr. Wilhelm Totok, the able and enterprising head of
the Nether-Saxon State Library, was the leading spirit behind
this celebration, and on its occasion he took the decisive steps
towards launching an international Leibniz Society. It was
founded at a meeting at which I was present, and I was chosen
a member of its Council (*Beirat*), an office I continued to hold
to the present day (1974). I also became a member of the
editorial board of its official journal, *Studia Leibnitiana*. (Indeed, it was my plea for a Latin rather than German title—made for reasons of internationalism and in homage to
Leibniz's boundary-transcending spirit—that led to the selection of this title in the place of *Leibniz-Studien*.) When the
idea of an American Leibniz Society first came to be mooted
some years later, I was also involved, helping to organize the
society and becoming a founding member of its Executive
Committee.

The inspiration of Leibniz is clearly present in some of my
books (e.g., *The Coherence Theory of Truth*), and is discernible in my general approach to the conduct of philosophical
work. I do not view myself as an adherent of his teaching or
doctrine, but rather of his mode of philosophizing. Leibniz is
to my mind the master of us all in the use of the formal
resources of symbolic thought in the interest of the clarifica-
tion and resolution of philosophical issues—role-model for
the way in which one wants to introduce exactness and rigor
into one's philosophical work. Many of my books accordingly exhibit the Leibnizian tendency to use some formal
notational or symbolic mathematical of logical or diagram-
matic, device for the elucidation of philosophical issues.
Moreover, I have always felt a certain spiritual affinity with
Leibniz, in that we have both faced a broadly common situation in a broadly common way. We both came to philosophy
after a generation of iconoclasm—represented by Cartesian-
ism in his case, and logical positivism in mine. In each in-

stance, there had been a prior phase of annihilation of traditions and search for a fresh start, for building up everything
anew on a novel foundation erected on the ruins of the older
structures. This created a common mission of our philosophical generations: to build a bridge across the rubble left by our
demolitionist predecessors—a bridge able to reach the far
bank of the rich philosophical heritage that lay beyond. In
any case, my Princeton dissertation proved to be the first step
in an ongoing preoccupation with Leibnizian themes and
variations.

Throughout my Princeton career I kept in touch with
Alonzo Church. Though an uninspired teacher, he was a
scholar of such substantial ability and vast erudition that it
was a stimulating experience simply to see him at work. He
now enlisted me as a reviewer of *The Journal of Symbolic
Logic* and made extensive use of my services in this regard.
During 1951-1953 I contributed to the journal some 40 reviews of papers on a wide variety of logical topics. This
experience of Church's mentorship provided a most useful
training in critical analysis and compact exposition.

During the second term of the 1950-51 academic year, a
visitor from Oxford, James O. Urmson of Corpus Christi
College, made a deep impression on all of us fledging philosophers at Princeton. A disciple of J. L. Austin, his seminar
on epistemology introduced us to the mysteries of "ordinary
language" analysis as cultivated by this master of the new
vogue of Oxford philosophy. We endlessly dissected how talk
about knowledge proceeds in the "ordinary language" of "the
plain man," contrasting this with the supposed distortions at
work in the convoluted knowledge-talk of philosophers like
Descartes—to the not insubstantial disadvantage of the latter.

In the early spring of 1951 I attended for the first time an
annual meeting of the American Philosophical Association
(or rather the Eastern Division thereof), held on the Swarthmore College campus. The Princeton philosophers contributed two car-loads or so, and I was included. I had never seen
so many philosophers in one place before—the 300 or so who
came struck me as an enormous throng. Nowadays we meet
in big convention hotels in the major cities, with nearly ten

times as many in attendance. The past quarter century has seen American academic philosophy change—be it for better of for worse—from a small fraternity of mutually familiar colleagues to a large, amorphous, and rather more impersonal profession.

Only towards the end of that academic year, in the spring of 1951, did I begin to give serious thought to the future. But whatever anxieties I may have had were soon dissipated by the offer of an Instructorship at Princeton for the academic year 1951-1952—at a salary of $3,500. This was less than many a graduate fellowship at this time or writing (1974), but was an amount which then seemed quite ample to me, and I took the naive view that my foreseeable future was now securely arranged.

With the conclusion of that academic year, my graduate studies came to an end as well. I now received my official commission as a Doctor of Philosophy—my membership in that truly international branch of scholars licensed to teach in institutions of higher learning throughout the world. And I now had a "handle" to my name as *Dr.* Rescher, an addendum which took a long time to sound natural to my ears. My doctoral work had progressed at surprising speed—yielding the Ph.D. in two years, when I was still only twenty-two years old.

The summer stood before me. It was necessary to put aside some money against the coming year's expenses. But it is one thing to have a degree, and something quite different to have a job—even a temporary one of the sort I had in view for the summer. I approached the office of Student Employment for ideas. A prospect developed there which I took up if not with glee at least with contentment. The Elizabethtown Consolidation Gas Company in Elizabeth, NJ (conveniently sited on the Pennsylvania Railroad's Princeton-New York run) had just converted from selling its own manufactured gas to natural gas imported on the Texas pipeline. In the confusion created by the change-over, its domestic customers had been systematically over-charged. The New Jersey Public Utilities Commission had ordered a repayment for all duly entitled customers. The company was consequently hiring a handful of young men (mainly college students home for the summer) to carry out the work of calculating these refunds. To this essential but infinitely dull task I dedicated my labors that summer at a recompense which, small though it was, enabled me to put aside several hundred dollars. For a happy conjunction of events made it possible for me to live very inexpensively.

The Assistant to the President—one Colonel Fox (U.S.A. retired)—was devoting himself to the hunt country of Virginia over the vacation and wanted some reliable person to take care of his house and female cat—the apple of his eye—in exchange for quarters in the place. I took on this assignment together with my friend and fellow student Jennings Mangum (a young North Carolinian who was soon to forsake philosophy for the greener pastures of banking), and it provided us with comfortable yet cost-free lodging for the summer period. One weekend when Jennings was away, and I in charge, the colonel's cat escaped from her huge complex of interconnectected cages—a vast multilevel structure that was veritably a cat-palace. Fortunately she reappeared after a day or two. When I met the colonel once more a week of so after his return, he complimented me on the care of the cat, stressing her plump and well-fed appearance. I worried about the implications of this circumstance, but happily the litter I saw with my mind's eye never materialized.

My closest Princetonian friends at this stage were James L. Cole—a fellow graduate student in philosophy—and his wife Barbara. The son of a psychology professor at Oberlin, Jim had strong interests in this field as well and ultimately transferred to it. Barbara was the daughter of a prosperous insurance broker from Penn Yan, NY. Jim had met her at Oberlin. She combined a fine sense of humor with an inveterate addiction to gossip. (She was also the greatest horse-enthusiast I ever encountered.) They were a couple blessed with infinite good will and good humor, and I became very fond of the Coles and grew close to them.

On two or three occasions I joined the Coles on vacation visits to the cottage of Barbara's parents on Lake Keuka near Penn Yan. Like many another happy young couple, they felt that all their bachelor friends should marry, and Barbara was in any case a natural matchmaker. She began bringing me together with various girls from the locality. None of them made much of an impression on me, save one, Barbara's old childhood friend Frances Short, to whom she introduced me in the spring of 1950.

Born in 1925, and thus a few years older than I, Frances was a slender, smallish girl, two inches or so over five feet in height, with a light complexion and blonde-brown hair. She had majored in Political Science at Lake Erie College, but she now lived with her mother and brothers out in the country near Rochester, N.Y., and worked in this city as a social service caseworker for the New York State Department of Public Welfare. Her father was the scion of an old WASP family whose mother, the first woman to earn an engineering degree at Ohio State University, had married Henry Howe Short, a pioneer in the electric-traction industry in the U.S. However the family had fallen on hard times during the Depression, and the father, its main provider, had died some years before I came on the scene.

Much impressed with Frances, I began to correspond with her in the fall of 1950. After courtship carried on by correspondence, and three brief visits in one another's vicinity, we were married in early September of 1951, at the outset of my Princeton instructorship.

Frances possessed many good qualities, being intelligent, thoroughly honest in head and heart, and straightforward in human dealings. But she also had some less positive traits of personality—traits which were ultimately to outweigh the good in the context of our relationship. She was tenacious about getting her own way with the things of everyday existence and intensely possessive of the people in her life. Character is fate, the Greeks said sagely. The personality of Frances already contained—as yet writ small—the makings of difficulty in fitting in with my own.

At first we occupied a small apartment consisting of the upper floor of a private house on Harrison Street (No. 185), rented out by the widowed and very talkative landlady who lived downstairs. But after two months or so we were fortunately able to move into unit No. 412B of the Graduate Student Housing Project on Butler Avenue—a cluster of pre-fab structures that had once accommodated Naval trainees in a World War II crash program. I embarked upon my teaching duties, and Frances secured a job in Princeton's Firestone Library. Since most of my compatriots in the graduate program remained on the scene, we led an active social life.

The teaching duties of my Princeton instructorship were not onerous. As best I recall, they consisted of one class (in the *Philosophy of Science*) and several preceptorials (in the *History of Modern Philosophy: Descartes and Kant*). The latter were an unadulterated pleasure, but the former posed problems.

At this stage, I generally geared my teaching closely to the assigned textbook. I did this partly from beginner's caution, but also because I have always believed that students should find reading and lecture material mutually supportive rather than wandering off in detached or discordant ways. (I think it unfair to ask the students to buy a book for a course and then not to teach them what's in it—however much one might also be *beyond* it.) Unhappily this basically reasonable policy proved counterproductive in the Philosophy of Science class because the predetermined text was rather a poor book. Perhaps, if I had been a more experienced teacher, the shortcomings of the text could have been overcome, but as it was, I found the going something of an uphill struggle.

The historical preceptorials went very well indeed, however, and I always came away from them with the feeling that I had really helped the students to gain a solid understanding of what these philosophers were about. (This impression was happily confirmed when some fifteen years later I met a young philosophy professor—his name now eludes me—who had been a student of mine on this occasion.) I became confirmed in the view that I had now found my profession: I felt that I could function effectively as a philosopher and teach successfully when dealing with material that was congenial to me.

I acquired my first car early in the Fall of 1951. Among my friends were Judson Lamour Ihrig and his wife Gwendolyn.

Jud was a very able young chemist than at work on the experimental research for his doctoral thesis. He was studying the effects of strong magnetic fields on certain chemical reactions, and reveled in the intricacy of his equipment—he was the most naturally gifted person at things mechanical I had ever encountered. Deeming it a disgrace that here was I, a young American male, quite unable to drive, Jud insisted that this should be put to rights. He would teach me himself and in my *own* car to boot. And so he took me to a junkyard where we bought an ancient blue Willis sedan for $30. We spent a couple of afternoons (and perhaps another $15.00 for materials) working on the car, with me sanding and repainting the exterior, while Jud put the nonfunctional electrical system to rights. Soon the car was running as nicely as can be, and for a month or so we would go out on occasional driving lessons, with Jud indoctrinating me into the mysteries of the manual gearshift. By Thanksgiving I was an accomplished driver, and greatly enjoyed my new-found mobility.

Late in 1951 I met Paul Oppenheim through the mediation of Carl Hempel, my old undergraduate mentor. Oppenheim had originally been a German financier, and had occupied a seat on the board of directors of I.G. Farben. A clever man, he had the sense to realize early on the rise to power of Hitler and the Nazis spelled a real danger to Jews. He liquidated all his holdings and took them—and himself—out of Germany in 1933, going first to Belgium, and subsequently to the USA. This prescience saved his considerable fortune. He invested this intelligently, and managed to live very comfortably on the proceeds in an elegant but compact modern house in Princeton.

Withdrawal from business enabled Paul to devote himself to his hobbyhorse, the promulgation of a particular philosophical viewpoint regarding scientific knowledge. He recognized that he could not, as an amateur, do this in a way that would exert any influence without securing the collaboration of able professionally qualified collaborators. Already in Belgium he had enlisted the help of Hempel, and they had collaborated in the middle 1930's on a book on the conception of *type* in the light of modern logic (*Der Typusbegriff im*

Lichte der neuen Logik). In after years, Hempel became Paul's academic talent-scout and during the early 1950's he recruited John Kemeny, Hilary Putnam, and myself (among others) to work on various projects with Paul. In the 1951-52 period I collaborated with him on an essay on the conception of a *Gestalt*, carrying out a line of investigation he had begun in Europe with Kurt Grelling some fifteen years before. This collaboration issued in a paper, "Logical Analysis of Gestalt Concepts," which eventually appeared in the *British Journal for the Philosophy of Science* (in vol. 6 for 1955). My own efforts had otherwise been absorbed largely in Leibniz and symbolic logic, and this work provided a useful occasion for further concern with issues in the philosophy of science.

Through the Oppenheims I came to meet some academic notables. The most eminent was Albert Einstein who was an intimate of Paul's—every Sunday morning they took a long walk together. Einstein lived up to expectation: Kindly and unassuming in person, and utterly eccentric in dress. (He went shirtless under an old sweater, and wore no socks, so that, when seated, his trousers rode up to expose his uncovered ankles.) He gave the impression of one who viewed life as made for thinking and best left undistracted by the trivia of the conventional properties. Bertrand Russell too was a friend of the Oppenheims and stayed at their house whenever he came to Princeton. (He was in town for a lecture at the time of his being awarded the Nobel Prize in Literature in 1951 and received notice of the award at the Oppenheims.) Russell seemed to exude an aristocratic condescension, regarding the ordinary mortals of this world in much the same way as operatic *prima donna* might look on the members of the audience—a necessary nuisance without whom one would be playing to an empty house. But Russell's evident self-esteem did not yield much to that of the almost equally eminent Hans Reichenbach, whom I also met several times at the Oppenheims.

No sooner was my new career launched on its way than a development occurred which at the time struck me as utterly catastrophic. As long as I had been a student I had had no draft problems at all, and as the end of my studies was approaching, my draft board had assured me in April of 1951 that these deferments would continue and that I could take up my post at Princeton without difficulty. But in November of that year the picture had changed. The draft levies for the Korean War had put increasing pressure on them, and they felt compelled to call me up. Notice now came that I would be inducted some twelve week hence.

When this bombshell burst upon me, I took immediate action. At the suggestion of a helpful mathematician, I arranged to call on John on Neumann at the Institute for Advanced Studies. At the appointed hour I was ushered into his office. It seemed vast to me and rather imposing. But the impressive little man came out from behind his large desk at the far end of the room, shook hands in a very cordial way, and was most friendly and helpful. I explained my problem to him, telling him about my training in logic and mathematics and expressing the hope that this could be utilized in some way in the course of my military service. (I passed in discreet silence over the fact that I had no stomach for routine infantry duty.) Von Neumann understood the issue at once, sympathized, and promised his aid. He had some ideas; would make some inquiries; and would be in touch with me again shortly. And he was as good as his word. Within a fortnight I had heard from him. His friend, an Army colonel whose name I have forgotten, was in charge of some sort of scientific activity at the Aberdeen Proving Ground in Maryland. His unit could use the services of bright young men with training in mathematics. Once the date for my reporting for induction was fixed, I should let the colonel know. Further arrangements would then be made and instructions given. I breathed much easier.

Nevertheless a serious blow had been dealt, and the period from mid-November 1951 to mid-February 1952 was very much of an interregnum in my life. The sharp break with normal plans for the future put my affairs into a condition of suspended animation. I carried on my regular activities in a routine, sleepwalking sort of way, always conscious of the great change that lay just ahead. But the time passed quickly, and early on the morning of February 17, 1952 I entrained to

New York to report for induction into military service. A turning point was clearly at hand and I looked with a mixture of apprehension and interest towards my projected new role as a junior scientist in Army service.

I had managed to travel a long developmental distance during this Princetonian period. Maturing as a person, I was now settling down in life as a married man. I had completed my higher education, written for publication, and placed my feet firmly on the initial rungs of the ladder of a professional career. That brisk midwinter day, the Pennsylvania Railroad carried from Princeton to New York someone substantially more educated and seasoned than the eager young scholar it had brought in the reverse direction only two and one half years before.

Seven

U.S.M.C.
Washington, DC: 1952-1954
(Age 23-25)

A rude surprise awaited me when I reported to the draft induction station at Church Street in lower Manhattan that chilly February morning in 1952. My papers—indeed every fifth set of papers—had a big black U.S.M.C. stamped on them. The explanation we simple: I was destined for the Marines. This proud volunteer organization was unable to secure enough enlistments to meet the demands of the military build-up for the Korean War, and had to resort to the draft. A random one-fifth of the inductees were being sent in this direction, and I was to be one of them. By one swift pinprick, fate burst the balloon of my carefully arranged plans for a research assignment at Aberdeen. My military career was to evolve in a wholly different direction, that of the United States Marine Corps, a sphere unhappily beyond the reach of John von Neumann's influence.

That night we were put up in an unprepossing Manhattan hotel, and the next morning we were gathered together, bussed to a local airfield, and embarked on a World War II vintage military biplane. The rude and unluxurious vehicle propelled sedately southwards towards the Carolinas. There was a refueling stop at Quantico, Virginia, and I recall my naive surprise at the substantially warmer temperatures encountered as we traveled south on this February day. The flight—my very first—was somewhat primitive, but not uncomfortable, and the time passed by rapidly, between conversing with my young Latin-American neighbor and reading in the first volume of Winston Churchill's *History of the Second World War*. (I wonder what strange inspiration led me to begin my new career with this rather martial bit of reading matter.)

Upon arrival at the airstrip in Beaufort, South Carolina, we were again herded into busses and transported through the subtropical coastal lowlands to our new home away from home, the sprawling Marine Corps Recruit Training Depot at Parris Island.

I shall be brief about the course of basic training itself. Its purpose was clear: to harden our bodies and to adjust our minds to the conditions of military service. The objective was to instill obedience and discipline in slack, soft, and wholly unmilitary young American lads. The measures taken towards these ends were certainly unenjoyable, but they were seldom cruel, and were unquestionably effective. The drill instructors' bark was worse than their bite, but sufficiently compelling to break us in to the disciplinary harness of military life. We entered Parris Island as ordinary civilians and nine weeks later emerged as fledgling marines able to operate rifles and pistols, convinced of the potential benefits of gasmasks, and exposed (at a safe distance) to the workings of flame throwers and hand grenades. I did not like the transforming process, but cannot gainsay its effectiveness—nor question its necessity given the aims of the enterprise. One illustrative episode still sticks in my mind. As we were being issued various item of clothing and other gear, someone told me to pick up "that jacket" and move along. I looked blank, for I had my jacket on. "That jacket," he said, pointing. "Oh," said I, "that's not a jacket, that's my coat." At that point a bystander corporal gave me a blow on the chest that knocked me down. "Don't you tell a Master Sergeant what's what!" he growled. I got the point—it's *their* system and, like it or not, you're going to have to do things their way.

As the end of basic training drew near, we were given classification questionnaires and interviews to determine how our efforts were going to be utilized by the service. The NCO in charge of this screening process was impressed with my competence at language—not so much the defunct (Latin and Greek) as the living (German and French). So he proposed assigning me a "military occupational specialty" category number of 0300, designating the Military Intelligence service, which employed linguistically equipped people for document translation, prisoner interrogation, and the like. I leapt at this idea with alacrity, being eager to serve where I could use my head instead of dedicating more rudimentary skills to being a rifle-carrier in the infantry. But once again, I learned how easily the best-laid plans can go wrong—especially in the military. For when it came to the actual assignment process, the only unit then actively seeking classification 0300 people was the Second Amphibious Reconnaissance Battalion at Camp Lejeune, North Carolina, and it was there that I was sent in due course to take up my first military assignment.

So many Parris trainees went on to Camp Lejeune that we were bussed there *en masse*. And so one fine Sunday afternoon in April of 1952 I arrived at this huge Marine base, whose bleak appearance and regimented arrangement I found overawing in a depressing sort of way. It was well after working hours by the time I found my way to the inauspicious prefabs that housed the unit for which I was destined. I was received by the current officer of the day, a friendly and enthusiastic young lieutenant who gave me a guided tour of the area and explained to me the nature of the unit's activities.

The military is always fighting the last war. In World War II as the Marines went island-hoping across the Pacific, frogmen were sent out from submarines in the darkness of night to reconnoiter the approaches, examine the beach area for obstacles, defensive installations, etc. It was to *this* sort of "intelligence" work to which I (a virtual nonswimmer—but with linguistic capabilities!) was now being assigned. I applied straightaway for the short leave to which new-trained recruits were entitled, determined to try to seek out some more appropriate line of activity.

I had heard that the Marines operated a correspondence school in Washington, D.C., and it occurred to me that this might well prove my best hope. Taking advantage of my leave, I made a bee-line for Washington to see what might be arranged. On arriving there I proceeded to search out the site of the Marine Corps Institute (MCI). This was not all that easy, because while I knew its site was at a certain address (as best I recall at 5th and G Streets), I failed to realize that there are *four* such addresses in the Washington grid system. But after a couple of false tries, I found the place in the Southwest quadrant. There I entered a large, old, red brick schoolhouse and proceeded to make inquiries of the Lieutenant Colonel in charge. Could they use someone with my training? To my pleasure and surprise, it turned out they could. The sergeant who was the instructor in higher mathematics was shortly to be discharged. Would I be able to grade calculus papers? I was willing, nay eager, for the assignment. Within the hour, a happy meeting of minds was reached by all concerned, and I left with the euphoric felling that I had managed—quite on my own initiative—to redirect the lines of my military career in a happier direction.

But all did not go so smoothly. On my return to Camp Lejeune I immediately applied for a transfer, only to have my papers "get lost" after being routinely disapproved by the commanding general, who was unwilling to see men pass from his command after less than a year's service. Not until two months later, and with intervention from Washington, did this finally get straightened out. (In the meantime I was, however, shifted from amphibious reconnaissance to less obnoxious activities in "Special Services," an operation which provided the troops with various forms of leisure-time support, from entertainments to correspondence courses.)

The transfer issue finally resolved, I waited eagerly for the day of transition. When it finally came, I hitched a lift on a Military Air Transport Service plane going up to Naval Air Station at Anacostia. (I also managed to collect the train fare for the trip—in the military one soon learns to have no scruples about cheating one's employer.) Thence I proceeded to my new home away from home, the Marine Barracks at 8th and I Streets, Southeast, the small but historic military station where the personnel assigned to the Marine Corps Institute were based.

"Eighth and Eye" was an unusual Marine installation. Then exactly one city block in size, it was shared by four mutually incongruous bed-fellows: the town-house living quarters of the senior Marine generals stationed at headquarters in Washington—including the Commandant of the Corps—as well as the U.S. Marine Band, the Drum and Bugle Corps, and the personnel of the Marine Corps Institute. One ironic fact which struck me only afterwards was most of those senior generals who lived in this complex, and under whose control my fate now lay—Marine Commandant Lemuel Shepherd, his Assistant Commandant Gerald Thomas, and the rest—were themselves young officers fighting in France at Soissons and Belleau Wood in 1917-18 when my father was an officer on the enemy side.

The Institute—a correspondence school pure and simple—was a rather strange sort of military operation and was staffed by an odd mixture of Marines. Many were young draftees—college men with a background in various academic subject. The others were professional Marines, World War II veterans who had decided to made a career of it, and who generally taught the more military subjects (map reading, weapon maintenance, etc.). Everyone got on pretty well. We were an informal, easy-going bunch and it required that constant vigilance of our officers to maintain the principle that we were Marines first and office workers afterwards. And day-to-day life around the barracks was not unpleasant. The people were generally congenial, and the food was quite good. (The baker—who produced goodies for us along with those for the bigwigs in the generals' quarters—was a true virtuoso.)

For the first few week in Washington I lived on base, going home to Princeton every second weekend on the port/starboard rotation scheme virtually universal for Marine installations. But immediately upon settling in at Marine Barracks,

I had applied for accommodations in a naval housing project. Informed that it would be half a year of so before this would become available, I turned to the rental market and set myself the (by no means easy) task of finding a reasonably pleasant but yet affordable apartment in the Washington area. After some weeks I finally located one, and made arrangements for the move from Princeton. But on the very morning that the movers started loading the van, I also learned that something had gone amiss and that the apartment would not be available after all. I set out immediately and had the good luck to find a suitable apartment at 3900 Fourth Street, deep in the Southeast suburbs. I concluded these arrangements just in time to notify the movers as they were ready to start from Princeton with our few worldly possessions.

An episode occurred during my service at M.C.I. that deeply affected my political orientation, and in fact turned me into a lifelong Republican. This happened during the 1952 presidential election campaign. We correspondence school people were all called together and given a lecture by our commanding officer, Capt. Charles Stevenson, to the following effect. He did not want to tell us how to vote, but just wanted to put some information at our disposal. It had been his observation over years that Democratic presidents generally favored the military services and Republicans administrations generally meant more stringent times. In particular, Eisenhower was no friend of the U.S.M.C. and had supported its absorption into the Army in the "unification crisis" of the late 1940's. While some of us might be indifferent to such considerations, those of us who were dedicated Marines should be careful in drawing our lessons from them.

These remarks proved profoundly counterproductive in my case. With attitudes shaped in reaction to my recent experiences I took the view that any opponent of the Marines was of friend of mine, and that any potentate who expected the military services to render value for money had entirely the right idea. And in due course, I was never to lose sight of the fact—which struck me as deeply symbolic in this light—that a Democratic administration took the country into the conflict which led to my rude extraction from civilian life, and that a Republican president had wound down the Korean war, and was striving to create condition under which my projected release from military service could be realized. In later years, the presidency of Lyndon Johnson, with its intensification of the Vietnam War after running a peace-platform campaign against the supposedly hawkish Barry Goldwater, was also to confirm my long-standing suspicion that, when it comes to war and war-like activity, Democratic presidents are given to talking in one direction and acting in another. Even at the height of the anti-Nixon hysteria in the wake of the Watergate scandals of the early 1970's, I was always mindful that this was the man who had successfully extricated us from the morass of Vietnam, and had done so under conditions more favorable than anyone had previously thought attainable. (As I saw it, the subsequent debacle in Indo-China was not Nixon's fault, but that of those who were intent on pulling him down, regardless of the cost to the nation's international standing and credibility.) In any case, it is curious how trivial developments of one's impressionable youth can often exert a totally disproportionate effect in determining the direction of future developments.

In the context of matters political, this period of life in the nation's capital proved one of the real advantages of my military service. Washington is—or then was—not only a very pleasant and livable city, but one made particularly interesting by the presence of the apparatus of government. Its newspapers, its people, and in fact its entire atmosphere of life is saturated with the ebb and flow of political affairs. And it affords a ring-side seat on the political arena that is in the highest degree broadening and interesting. (For example, I was able to attend one of the sessions of the Army-McCarthy Hearings in the spring of 1954.) Life in Washington was in many ways an educational experience, and while I was by no means happy about the circumstances which led me there, I nevertheless recognized that a silver lining came with the cloud.

A most grievous development for me during this time of military service was the death of my father in October of 1952, at the relatively young age of 62 years. His heart had been giving him trouble for somewhat over a year, but his condition seemed to have been stabilized by regimen and medication, so that his sudden death was quite unexpected. I took leave to help mother with the necessary arrangements and then returned to M.C.I. in very low spirits. I loved my father dearly and he meant a great deal to me in ways that are made no less real by the fact that they do not admit of precise articulation. When things go as they ought, the father plays a guiding role in the life of a son that differs not only in magnitude but in quality from that played by any other individual. With the departure of a parent something irreplaceable is lost for good.

Then and since I have frequently ruminated on the unhappy vicissitudes of my father's fate: the 1914-18 war, the economically difficult times of the 1920's, the destruction of his livelihood in the Hitler era, the transatlantic uprooting of the late 1930's, the collapse of his new-made livelihood in 1941, and the very straightened circumstances of the subsequent decade. Every phase of his adult life brought its own sort of hardship. Yet throughout, he maintained a cheerfulness, a good humor, and a dedication to intellectual interests that I do not for a moment believe I myself could have manifested in comparable circumstances. I greatly admire the even temper he preserved in adversity and the Stoicism with which he generally made the best of extremely difficult conditions.

Early in 1953 my name on the application-list for Naval housing was finally reached, and we were able to move into a small unit at the edge of the Anacostia Naval Housing project (right next to the Naval Research Laboratory—at No. 9, Compass Green). For the remainder of my military service this modest but comfortable wooden bungalow-style structure was to provide the home-base from which I set off in the mornings to do my stint at the Marine Corps Institute. Here we lived for the next year or so, struggling to inject an element of domestic normality into a life traumatized by the continual and diversified demands of the Marine Corps service.

In the spring of 1953 the Marine Corps Institute moved from the old schoolhouse in S.W. Washington to an upper floor in a large warehouse at the Naval Gun Factory not far from our base at Marine Barracks. After these changes, life settled once more into a relatively predictable routine. Reporting to the barracks for the morning check-in, we correspondence school marines rode in busses to our Gun Factory building and ascended by service elevator to our far-flung office loft. The mathematicians had a row of facing desks (partners-desk style) and we sat there hour upon hour, manning bottles of green ink and grading our papers. At lunch time the lads who lived on base were bussed back for their meal, while we "brown-baggers" who lived off base broke out our lunch-pails in the office and gathered around each other's desks in small congenial clusters. Weather permitting, one could go for walks about the interesting Gun Factory compound, or one might simply find a convenient packing crate to sit on and watch the Potomac flow by. In the late afternoon we bussed back to the barracks, gathering in the locker room for a quick change into civilian garb, and then departed for our respective domiciles. This, at any rate, was the usual routine, though there was ample variation, generally of an unwelcome sort—guard duty, drills, and inspections.

The position of the Marine Corps was—and I daresay still is—that one is a Marine infantryman first and a cook or recruiter or correspondence school instructor second. We were thus called upon for all those "duties" expected of a marine: guard-duty, clean-up duty, mess duty, etc. And once a week we got out our rifles to play soldier in Anacostia Park—until the city fathers complained of our tearing up their grass. We were then shifted to the National Guard Armory, a vastly preferable site because, being indoors, we were sheltered against the vicissitudes of the weather, and also because it was too far afield to march to, thus yielding the comforts of bus travel.

As marines stationed in the Washington area we were called on to participate in the staging of various ceremonials. In January, 1953 we marched in President Eisenhower's Inauguration Parade, and we later escorted the Declaration of Independence in its move from the Library of Congress to the

National Archives Building. We participated regularly in the Friday Sunset Parade, a display of military ceremonial then—and as far as I know still—put on during summertime for the edification of the public. Happily, I managed to escape virtually all the ceremonial details—because I wore glasses in those days, and the Corps disliked admitting in public that there were marines who lacked 20-20 vision.

There was, however, one very special service we were called upon to provide whenever Ike went (as he loved to do) to the presidential retreat in the Catoctin Mountains in Maryland—a rustic complex that F.D.R. had named "Shangri La," but Ike had renamed Camp David after his grandson. For some mysterious reason this was a Navy installation and we correspondence school marines furnished the perimeter security-guard while the Secret Service guarded the house with the President himself. I served on this special Presidential guard detail some four or five times. It worked roughly as follows. We would set out by bus on Friday afternoon for the drive of some two hours to the presidential retreat. By the time the President arrived in the late afternoon—by car from some nearby helicopter landing—our security operations was in place, consisting of a perimeter patrol by armed riflemen patrolling the inside of the wire fence enclosure. (Since our M-1 rifles held live ammunition, the inspecting Officer of the Day made sure one heard him coming on his rounds, in consequence of which some of the lads—I not among them!—made free to "sit down on the job.") We lived in basic but (in summer) perfectly adequate smallish cabins of the sort one might expect in a National Park. We ate in the mess-hall operated for us and for the Secret Service men by the Navy cooks from the Presidential yacht. (The food, as I recall, was of a very good standard.)

Had it not been for the nuisance of having one's weekend plans broken up, the Camp David detail could have been viewed as a not unpleasant diversion. One's guard-circuit involved a rather enjoyable if monotonous ramble through the scenic woodland paths. I shall always remember one particular morning in the spring of 1953 when I walked the 4-8 A.M. patrol through this very attractive tract of woodland,

with dawn gradually coming on and dozens of different species of birds awakening one by one, until the whole forest was
vibrant with song. I recall too one pleasantly balmy Saturday
that summer when I had nothing to do all afternoon but lie
on my bunk reading Benjamin Franklin's *Autobiography*
with great enjoyment, and with keen appreciation on the
shrewdness of the man. I had not read it before, but it has
been one of my favorites ever since.

The presidential week-end concluded, we would return to
Washington by bus on Monday mornings. On one occasion
we were given a guided tour of the main house after the
President's departure and got to see some of Ike's paintings
which I found surprisingly attractive. Though I saw Ike from
afar on several of these occasions, I never got to speak to him,
and don't think that any of us did, possibly excepting the
commander of the detail who may—I would hope—have
been accorded a personal word of thanks. One amusing facet
of the enterprise was the marked contrast between us "tough
marines," all in fact cerebral M.C.I. types, and the mere civilians of the Secret Service guard, a very rough lot answering
to one's picture of Miami Mafia enforcers, all ablaze in loud
sport shirts left over from the days of Harry Truman's Florida
vacations.

Of the many young men who figured among my acquaintances at M.C.I. three stand out as particular friends:

Herbert Curl was a young Ph.D. in biology—a limnologist
to be precise. Perhaps a year of two older than I, he also was
married and had a child. Possessed of a sedate disposition
and commonsensical outlook, he had a wry sense of humor
and was companionable in a somewhat self-contained way.
We were good friends at work, but had no contact off base.

C. Maury Jones had recently graduated for Princeton, which
gave us some points of contact. Maury was also married, and
his pleasant, outgoing wife gave birth to their first child
around this time. A graduate of one of the better prep
schools, he came from a wealthy background. (His father was
an affluent New York oddlot stockbroker who served in the
Esquadrille Lafayette in WWI and his mother a power in the

American Red Cross, and a *grande dame* of the best American type—maternal, yet clearly the bearer of considerable social and political weight.) Maury was bent on becoming a mogul in the advertising industry after completing his service. I have no idea how he subsequently fared in the pursuit of this ambition, but in any case he was bound to inherit a substantial fortune.

Walter Harman was a late comer who arrived at M.C.I. in early 1953. Perhaps a year younger than I, he was well enroute to a Ph.D. in zoology, and already held an appointment in the Zoology Department at Louisiana State University in Baton Rouge. His specialty was earthworms, and on his days off he scurried about the countryside collecting specimens. He was a pleasant, good natured, and rather easygoing young man. He frequently visited in our house, where his kindness and good humor made him always welcome. He was attracted to Gwen, an attractive and thoroughly pleasant girl who also came from Louisiana. He was then locked in a chronic struggle to make up his mind to marry her—which he ultimately resolved to what I am sure has proved to be their mutual benefit and satisfaction. I was very fond of Walter who always exuded the manner of a "gentleman of the old school."

Though at the time seemingly endless, my two year period of military service moved along day by day, and I daresay that on balance it went well enough. In June of 1953 I was promoted to corporal, thereby becoming a "non-commissioned officer," a status which entailed various small but useful privileges since NCO's are exempt from most types of dog-work. Later that year I even passed the various hurdles for promotion to sergeant and would have achieved this exalted rank—so I was informed—had my period of service been prolonged two months longer. My file contained several letters of commendation (relating to proposals of mine for improving the work of the office), and I think my superiors always found reason for satisfaction with my contributions. Though I disliked the service, I did not let this deflect me from my general tendency to try to do well at whatever task was put into my hands.

Perhaps this account has given a misleading "fun and games" tenor to my Marine Corps years. The thing I found most objectionable about military service was the combination of uncertainty and helplessness. One never knew what tomorrow might bring—a special guard detail, a stay with the president at Camp David, perhaps even transfer to "the front" in Korea. There was no way of telling what would come next, and whatever did come, there was no way of averting the decree from on high. This feeling that one's life lay wholly outside the grasp of one's own control was for me the most distasteful aspect of the whole business. My direst apprehension was a prolongation of the period of service by our being drawn into replacing France's collapsing efforts in Indo-China, and I shall be eternally grateful to Dwight Eisenhower for the fact that—despite considerable pressures—he did not permit this to happen during his administration.

What did military service mean to me? I would be less than honest to deny that I disliked every day of it and looked forward keenly to its termination. For I felt acutely the wastefulness of it all. I was an impatient young man eager to get on with the business of building my academic career, and I regarded the two years of my service as a massive loss of opportunity. I believe that the reason I became "indefatigable" in my professional work—as somebody once remarked in reviewing one of my books—was at least in part due to a sense of the need to make up for lost time.

One thing I learned about myself in the course of my service experience—somewhat to my surprise and regret—is that I am personally devoid of interest in military glory. I was more than happy to be stationed in peaceful Washington and considered myself fortunate not to have got anywhere close to Korea. The thought of participating in actual combat—let alone of actually distinguishing myself there—had no appeal to me. I do sincerely hope that if fate had placed me into this situation I would not have made a disgrace of myself. But I have always been genuinely glad of having had no chance to find out.

Only in eventual retrospect did it occur to me to wonder why I felt not so much as a twinge of guilt that here I was living in safely and (comparative) comfort in Washington rather than sharing discomfort and risking life and limb with my fellow marines in Korea. I think there were two reasons for this. One was that everyone else around me—marine and civilian alike—was in just the same boat. The other is that I saw this simply as a matter of the luck of the draw. Enough misfortunes had come my way—getting drafted into the marines included—that I saw no reason to feel anything but grateful for the silver lining that came with this cloud.

And I really cannot bring myself to regard this period of service as a total loss. There are many useful lessons that one can only learn under conditions of personal adversity, and I have had the not wholly welcome opportunity to learn some of them. I also learned some facts about human nature and about my own reactions to various problems and predicaments that were to prove of use in other situations. I experienced life with men under conditions of shared proximity, rubbing shoulders at close range with Americans of a type that would otherwise have been as remote from me as the natives of Patagonia. When one considers the relatively secure, comfortable, and mostly academic channels in which my own life has generally run, one might incline to think that here is a person who has no understanding of the lot of ordinary working people. Yet on various occasions, extending over an entire decade, I have been exposed to the totally routine and utterly mind-annihilating sort of work to which the daily efforts of all too many are perforced dedicated. During a formative period of my life I repeatedly saw the workings of "unskilled labor" from the inside: As an assembly-line candy-packer in the Lofts factory in 1943, as a counter-clerk in Bickford's diner in 1944, as a library-underling in the Jamaica Public Library in 1947, as a clerk in the Elizabethtown Consolidation Gas Company in 1951, and as a basic trainee in the U.S. Marine Corps in 1952. Edward Gibbon spoke of his teachers at Oxford as people "whose eyes are dazzled by the light of philosophy." He saw them as dessicated academics —otherworldly narcissists, given to contemplating their own intellectual navels. If nothing else, my period of military service prevented me from becoming a person of this sort.

Most of my younger colleagues have never done anything since the age of four or five except get up in the morning and go to school—first as a student, then as a teacher. This is a situation from which fate has preserved me. My service in the marines and even the subsequent period at RAND threw me together with people (and military people in particular) of a sort not to be encountered in academic settings. They gave me exposure to "the real world"—an experience by no means useless to a philosopher. Insofar as my reflections have dealt with issues of life rather than issues of thought alone, this is done in some measure to these years spent outside the precincts of the academy.

Then too, this experience taught me the fundamental aspects of military discipline—the basic pattern of life in cantonment that has not altered significantly since Roman times. These lessons were worthwhile not only for the human being but for the philosopher. From this aspect, my father's pet saying "*Das wird man Dir im Miltär schon zeigen*" ("They'll teach you about that in the service!") was to prove markedly true.

Still, throughout my Marine Corps service, I kept in touch with philosophy, finding some Sunday hours to devote to it even during the Parris Island months. During the spring of 1953 I taught Introduction to Philosophy in the evening program at American University—a strictly illegal proceeding for someone on active service, but one which brought me considerable enjoyment and a little money. At Alonzo Church's behest, I continued to write some reviews for *The Journal of Symbolic Logic*. And I managed to do a bit (a very little bit) of work at the Library of Congress to keep abreast of current work on Leibniz. The maintenance of my self-image as a philosopher was important to me.

As my discharge from the service began to draw ever closer with the passage of 1953, I had to give serious thought to the job problem. A letter from Professor Robert Scoon, then Chairman of the Philosophy Department at Princeton, offered a resumption of my instructorship there. But it was clear that this would be an interim measure, with little prospect for the long term given Princeton's otherwise sensible policy of not hiring their own graduates. After the upheavals of the past two years, I felt a strong disinclination to enter upon yet another temporary arrangement. And so I decided to look in other directions.

I wrote some fifty letters (unwisely on yellowish stationary) to the philosophy chairmen of various colleges and universities. The replies, though sometimes hopeful, were uniformly unproductive. The postwar student boom was just ending, and academic institutions throughout America were in a desperate state of retrenchment and decline. The academic job market was a shambles. Given my disinclination to accept the Princeton offer, the prospect of finding an appointment in philosophy looked very gloomy.

I thus began to think about other possibilities. For one thing, I was offered (at his instigation) the opportunity to succeed David Baumgardt as resident philosopher in the Library of Congress, but this somehow did not appeal to me. For another, it was now suggested that I explore the prospects of working for one of the various military think-tanks which were thriving in this era of the "Cold War" and the Korean conflict. The idea sounded potentially interesting, and I made the rounds of the Washington offices of various operations-research agencies ORO (Army), NRO (Navy), RAND (Air Force), and WSEG (Joint Chiefs). Both the latter two indicated interest in me; the others wanted only physicists at the time. But RAND's proposal was far and away the most tempting. They offered me a post in the Mathematics Division of their main office in Santa Monica, California, at the princely-seeming salary of $7,200 per annum. The job sounded interesting, and California had the appeal of novelty. The whole prospect seemed challenging—and anyway, no more attractive alternative lay to hand. I decided to accept.

By the end of May all preparations for the more to California were completed (down to the purchase of a new Chevrolet sedan—cheaper on the East Coast than the West and shipped cross-country at RAND's expense). One rainy day at the start of June, a Baltimore and Ohio train heading westwards to Chicago departed from the Union Station in Washington, leaving behind a city that had, for some two years provided the stage for my military service—such as it was. I left Washington happy to have this detour behind me, with a new and interesting-sounding job in a new part of the country lying ahead. The tune of "California, Here I Come" ran in my head, and I faced the prospect of new scenes and activities with a mixture of curiosity, hopefulness, and excitement.

Still only 25 years of age, I had now carried my education through to the doctorate and discharged my obligation of military duty. At last I could enter upon a regular job. And yet, though filled with the enthusiasm of youth, a certain apprehensiveness lurked at the back of my mind. Political developments had driven me from the land of my birth in 1938, international conflict had deflected me from a philosophical career into military service in 1952, and economic conditions had now blocked my prospects for a suitable academic post. Running beneath a surface layer of natural optimism was an undercurrent of awareness of the ever-present potential for unexpected and unwanted developments in human affairs. More than most people seem to do, I have always lacked an assured confidence that all will go according to plan and that we can count our lives secure against the untoward interference of "circumstances beyond our control."

Eight

THE RAND CORPORATION
SANTA MONICA: 1954-1956
(Age 25-28)

Chicago was the point of transfer to the Santa Fe Railroad, whose Superchief service then provided perhaps the most comfortable means of train travel to California. This railway journey in June of 1954 was a memorable one for me as my first transcontinental trip, featuring an array of vivid scenes: the "dark, satanic mills" of the steelworks at Gary, the active bustle of the Chicago railway stations, the seeming endlessness of the Great Plains, the barren panoramas of the California desert. Overall, the journey lasted two days and three nights—a limited time that yet seemed interminable to someone eager to get to its destination. But one sunny morning we finally pulled into the handsome Union Station in Los Angeles. After the luggage had been gathered up, a taxi provided transport to 1700 Main Street in Santa Monica, then as now home office of the RAND Corporation.

Housing accommodation was initially furnished in a nearby beachside hotel. But serious house-hunting began right away, since years of wandering from one residential make-shift to another had fostered an eagerness to settle and let down some roots. Upon seeking advice at RAND and inspecting various possibilities, it appeared that Pacific Palisades offered the most promising locality as an attractive and convenient residential area with affordable house-prices. While several days were spent looking, with some dozen houses actually visited, the final choice settled on the very first one inspected. This was an attractive single-level, California-style, three-bedroom house at 14907 Bestor Boulevard. With a handsome lawn in front and a sizable garden in back, the stuccoed house was prettily sited on a pleasant residential street, redolent with the perfume of Southern California flora. It cost a nowadays incredibly low-seeming sum of $22,000, but the realization of this then enormous amount called for every musterable penny of credit: not only a mortgage, but even a small loan from Florence Simpson, the helpful real estate saleslady who had assumed charge of these house hunting efforts. (Ever since I have always lived under my own roof save during periods of transition, and—comfort apart—this has proved a sound financial practice throughout a generally inflationary era.[1]) Occupancy of the house had to be postponed until the furniture van finally arrived, some days after Frances and I watched from the window of the empty livingroom the traditional 4th of July fireworks set off from a Navy ship anchored in Santa Monica bay. In due course we settled in and began to explore our new habitat, gradually growing accustomed to the shaplessness of Los Angeles and the unaccustomed semi-tropical beauties of Southern California.

When reporting to 1700 Main Street in May of 1954 I immediately came to realize that actually going to work was not going to be as easy as I had thought. One could not even get into RAND's principal premises without a protective escort, and new employees who as yet lacked security clearance were exiled to a separate outer region call "Quarantine." This was located in a side corridor just off the main entrance hall whose principal door led into the RAND building proper. The building itself was then only a fraction of its present size, and it housed only a fraction of the present work force—the over-all establishment amounting to some 300 people. There were few enough of us that the security guards learned to recognize everyone and to keep in practice, greeted them by name on arrival which gave rather a small town feeling to the place. The clearance period of some 4-5 weeks seemed interminable, and at the time I was impatient, though in retrospect came to view quarantine as rite of passage that amounted to "paying one's dues." My roommate in quarantine was Alexander Boldyreff, another incoming Mathematics Division researcher, who regaled me with tales of his wartime service in Alaska as an operations analyst for the Army Air Force. However, most of my time there was spent in reading material in the mathematical theory of games, which was then central to the interests of RAND mathematicians—thought as matters actually turned out I never made the slightest use of it in connection with any of my own work there.

As my pre-clearance period moved into its third of fourth week, a young man named Fred Thompson dropped by to ask if I might be interested in working with his group on some economic issues relating to air warfare that they were researching. This was the first time since my arrival that anyone at RAND had manifested much interest in my presence. So I agreed with alacrity, feeling that this would be a great improvement on the rather boring inactivity that was currently my lot. A week or so later my "Secret" clearance came through and I was finally released from quarantine. Strange to say, I viewed myself as liberated and felt like a free man within the confines of a tightly guarded classified facility that was actually more of a fortress than a public building.

My recruitment to project work at RAND was typical of its then-current mode of operation, at any rate in the Mathematics Division. By and large, work was done on a free-consent basis. The Air Force tried—often unsuccessfully—to persuade RAND to undertake a project. If the organization's directorship was interested, it tried to persuade one of its senior staff members that this might suit him. He in turn made the round of his otherwise uncommitted colleagues to try to recruit their collaboration. The voluntary contribution of effort was the rule, not just in theory but in actual practice as well.

The first project I participated in had as its aim the design of a large scale computerized input-output model of the workings of a national economy. The inquiry was bound up with the issue of how much damage the American economy could sustain in a war of aerial bombardment and yet continue to maintain a military effort. The leading spirit of the venture was Frederick B. Thompson, then in his mid-30's, who had earned his Ph.D. in mathematical logic under Alfred Tarski at Berkeley a few years before. Fred was a person of intense drive and energy, a super-salesman type. Intelligent and hard-working, he seemed to live for his work alone, driven by a strong yearning for recognition. I admired him for his good qualities and learned lessons from his bad ones, which included, above all, a tendency to set image above accomplishment. For Fred, to see his way roughly clear to solving a problem and then to convince other of his *capacity* to do so was quite enough; the need for completing a finished product available for general use was not recognized.

What particularly impressed me about Fred Thompson was the depth of his commitment to hammering away at the tasks in hand. When he arrived at work in the morning (never late and generally early) it was obvious that a good deal of thought had been given since the end of the preceding day to the nature of its residual problems, to the steps that lay ahead, and to the general organization of the work. And there was a kind of driving eagerness to "get on with it," an infectious and enthusiastic concern to push the effort forward to its next stage that exerted a near-inspirational impetus. Then and since I have regarded Fred as the very model of dedication to work and workmanship. Only as the end drew near did Fred's interest in the venture wilt. And so our computerized economic model—which I still consider as in some ways a pioneering achievement—was allowed to die by neglect on the very verge of completion. The futility of a powerful machine that ceased operations just short of producing an actually available result made a lasting impression on me, and made me determined that the fruits of my work would always be full-ripened and duly packaged for public consumption.

My second RAND activity was a joint effort with Fred and the economist Frederick B. Moore to make an assessment of the extent of the human and economic carnage that would be brought about by an all-out Russian nuclear assault against the U.S., given the best available estimates of their then-current capabilities according to USAF intelligence. The project was named VAMP for "Vulnerability of American Military Potential"—I myself dreamed up this acronym and was quite pleased with it. As best I recall, the project came to the conclusion that while the economy could readily restore the physical damage within a couple of years, we would have lost some 20% of the population in the attack—largely as victims to radioactive fallout—so that the destruction of life and its concomitant social disruption could be expected to put all considerations of an impact on economic productivity into the shade. It was the human not the material impact of atomic warfare that rendered it so horrendous.

After parting ways with Fred sometime in early 1955, I worked on a project on my own making: a speculative assessment of how, given current intelligence assessments of then-extant Russian military capabilities, a preemptive nuclear "counterforce" attack against U.S. retaliatory potential might be designed. Interestingly enough, considering the reputation for war-mongering hawkishness that RAND came to have in the academic community during the 1960's, all my own work there was primarily of defensive orientation, as indeed were most projects of which I had knowledge. RAND was responsive to the moods of the military, and, with Pearl Harbor still fresh in mind, the Air Force of the 1950's was more worried about being sinned against than sinning—Curtis B. LeMay perhaps excepted.

The head of Mathematics Division in those days was John D. Williams, author of a clever introduction to game theory entitled *The Compleat Strategist*. He was a person of rare quality. I did not get to know him well enough to gauge fully the creative power of his mind, but I could readily tell that it ranged far and deep. What struck me as the most original aspect of the man was his approach to research administration. His rule was to secure the services of people he deemed competent, and then to give them virtually unrestricted freedom, leaving them at liberty to work as interest and opportunity might list. This had mixed results. Some simply rambled off in pursuit of their own academic goals. Others dedicated themselves to the serious problems of the corporation, and their self-motivation produced a respectable average level of activity. It seemed to be Williams' idea that a high structure requires a base of seemingly wasteful proportions. Though I had my doubts at the time, I have since become increasingly alive to the possible merits of such a theory of administration.

Several among my Math Division colleagues made a particular impression on me. Among them was Norman Dalkey. Norm too had started out as a philosopher and had earned a doctorate in this field at UCLA. He was a person of great charm who combined a penchant for rather outlandish but interesting ideas with a certain disdain for the down-to earth labor needed to give them definite shape and substance. He came to do his best work later, when RAND's interests ultimately shifted from military to civilian concerns, and the atmosphere of the place became more congenial to socially oriented issues.

Lester Ford arrived in the Mathematics Division about a year after I did, and became peripherally involved in the VAMP group for a time. A gifted mathematician, he soon became interested in theoretical questions in queuing theory and network theory and drifted off into pure mathematics. But I got to know him and his large family very well (he had some seven daughters at this stage). Lester was a very easy-going young man with a good sense of humor and a relaxed, uncomplicated approach to the problems of life which struck me as admirable and sometimes amusing. I liked him greatly and we came to be good friends.

One of the most interesting people at RAND was Olaf Helmer, to whom I felt personally closer than to any other RAND colleague, thanks to the philosophical bent of his interests. Olaf was a German emigré with a mathematics Ph.D. from the University of Berlin and a second Ph.D. in philosophy earned under Susan Stebbing at the University of London in the late 1930's. He was a person of great charm, clever inventiveness, and a certain unrealism with respect to practical affairs. Futurology was his pet—a then unheard of sphere of inquiry. Because of our interest in some of the purely theoretical, RAND-disconnected aspects of the Delphi process, Olaf and I decided in early 1955 to meet once a week for an evening work session either at his house or mine. Frances and

I came to know the Helmers well. Olaf's wife, Maggie, was a charming and vivacious person, and I spent many pleasant evenings in their home in Mandeville Canyon Road talking epistemology with Olaf. He was a kindred spirit who helped to make my years at RAND more pleasant and the paper on Delphi that we published under the title "Epistemology of the Inexact Sciences" eventually had considerable influence both at RAND and at large.

It seems proper at this stage to say a bit more about RAND's concern with futurological studies—the so-called Delphi Method of expert prediction.[2]   Like many other intellectual innovations of 20th Century America, it was a child of the cold war. (Not until after the 1966 publication of Helmer's *Social Technology* did Delphi make much impact beyond the RAND Corporation orbit.[3]) And its start as a systematic enterprise was our aforementioned "Epistemology" paper, in which the theoretical foundations of the Delphi method were first elaborated.

The basic idea of the Delphi technique is to proceed by means of structured interaction among a group of predictors. This predictive process operates here without any face-to-face interaction among the group members. Instead, it uses a series of successive questionnaires to elicit responses from a panel of experts to arrive at an aggregate prediction about future developments. The experts are interrogated individually (usually by questionnaire) about their expectations for a series of hypothetical future events. A typical issue for a Delphi study might, for example, be the demographic question: In what year (if ever) do you expect the at-birth life expectancy of American females to reach 85 years? However, the experts do not meet to debate the question, but are kept apart from each other so that their judgment will not be influenced by social pressure or other distortions of small-group behavior. Instead, the Delphi process involves information elicitation punctuated by feedback stages in which earlier responses are conveyed to the group in a condensed, statistically summarized form. After the initial set of questionnaires is completed, the responses are assembled as statistical distributions, stated in terms of means and quartiles, supplemented by any pertinent comments by the experts. Then a second round is executed by the participants being provided with some aggregated information regarding the initial response. They might also be given the (anonymous) comments about and arguments for various positions. Respondents are then asked to submit revised estimates together with reasons for agreeing or disagreeing with the initial consensus. In the third (and later rounds) this procedure is repeated, with additional commentary and (depersonalized) exchange of information. Eventually, if the method works according to plan, the respondents will increasingly converge in their thinking, with a resulting narrowing of the range of estimates.

The Delphi method was received with eagerness in many circles and in the 1960's there was a vast proliferation Delphi exercises and studies. The empirical grounding of the methodology was subsequently explored in a series of ingenious experiments conceived by Norm Dalkey and carried through in collaboration with Olaf and Bernice Brown. However, I myself had no part in these later studies, having left RAND at the end of 1956 to return to teaching philosophy. I was a sort of midwife—assisting at the birth of Delphi, but leaving the child's raising up to others.[4]

Working at RAND afforded me an opportunity to meet many outstanding people—and to see some of them in action (for wargaming was then a vogue). Curtis LeMay, Charles Lindbergh, and John von Neumann were among the luminaries who came to visit. One extraneous chance encounter from those days also sticks in my mind. On one of my Washington flights on some RAND business it happened that Gen. Omar Bradley was a fellow passenger. Though a prime leader of our World War II efforts in Europe, a former Chief of Staff of the U.S. Army, and the Chairman of the Board of a major corporation, he did not travel in First Class, but shared humbler accommodations with ordinary mortals in the Tourist Class. He made himself available to his fellow passengers, strolling along the aisle talking with anyone who wished to chat, a step which—considering that he was not a candidate for public office—I found even more surprising. This episode was, for me, a useful lesson about leadership in a democracy, and I was impressed. Only in eventual retrospect did it strike me that Bradley's folksiness might have been every bit as much of an image-projecting pose as Douglas MacArthur's proverbial aloofness.

In this regard, one episode in particular opened my eyes. Late in 1955 or early 1956 I became involved in a collaborative inquiry—carried out at the behest of the Air Intelligence directorate—whose aim was to examine the prospects of a possible U.S.S.R. surprise attack against the U.S. in the oncoming missile age. One of the prime participants in this study, Jack Raymond, had a theory about a rapid build-up of Soviet missile forces which differed from the more conservative projection currently favored at RAND in the face of an evidentially counter indicated public concern about a "missile gap." Jack was in process of building his alarmist view into his contribution to the project. But when his more orthodox colleagues noted this, the result took the form not of reasoned counter-argumentation, but of a simple power-play that effectively ousted Raymond from the project. (Shortly after he left RAND for a much better job elsewhere—one of the several instances in my experience of a person ejected from one post putting forth under duress the initiatives that in fact lead to a major advance in his career, a curious phenomenon that often makes "failure" a highroad to "success.")

One distinctly unusual feature of the RAND Corporation of the early 1950's was its receptivity towards philosophers —due, I think, largely to the open-mindedness of John Williams. Not only were there Olaf Helmer, Norm Dalkey, Fred Thompson, and I who, though all in Mathematics Division, were philosophy Ph.D.'s, but there were others as well, including such consultants as Abraham Kaplan, John Kemeny, and Daniel Ellsberg. This philosophical presence, while amounting to no more than perhaps one or two percent of the staff, had a leavening impact on the prevailing ethos of the corporation. It engendered a greater receptivity to more speculative theorizing (such as the futurological interests of the Helmer-Dalkey-Rescher trio) and it strengthened the atmosphere of critical independence within which the group around Albert

Wohlstetter (father of the "balance of terror" doctrine) pushed for a radical revision of the Air Force's prevailing strategic policies in ways that eventually revolutionized the readiness posture of U.S. strategic forces. But in due course most of the RAND philosophers wandered off into other pursuits nearer and dearer to their hearts, for instance, Olaf Helmer into futurology research and I myself into philosophy professoring.

One lesson I had driven home to me during my years at RAND was the difference in cast of mind, intellectual approach, and—above all—operative effectiveness between the theoretician and the practical man of affairs. RAND had its quota of impractical, "mad scientist" types in those days—my friend Olaf Helmer being a good example of this species, and Herman Kahn a rather more opportunistic one. But it seemed to me that the views of such people never stood a chance of making any difference to the way in which things happened at RAND—the things that mattered. Between them and real influence in the corporation, either internal of external, there invariably stood a handful of practical men of "common sense," themselves not scientists either by training of intellectual inclination. The president of RAND, Frank Collbaum and his nearer advisors, a palace guard of influential consigliores—all solid and able men of limited vision and capability—were those in whose hands the fate of the corporation and its efforts actually rested. To say all this is not to say that theoreticians and speculators labor in vain. (The ideas of Marx, after all, have made a vast difference!) But it would seem that the work of the theorists begins to make an impact on the real world only when the men of action pick it up and turn it to their own ends.

I kept at philosophy in a desultory way during the RAND years. I read some of the professional journals and wrote a couple of (rather trivial) papers. On two or three occasions I attended philosophy meetings at UCLA. Looking back on it, I am sensitive to the difficulties of working "outside the context" without the stimulus of students and colleagues and formal commitments to teaching and lecturing. In this light, I came to feel a boundless admiration for C.S. Peirce, who produced first-rate work in philosophy for over 30 years in the splendid isolation of the wilds of the Pennsylvania countryside.

One interesting philosophical acquaintance I made at this stage was Rudolf Carnap, the eminent positivistic philosopher of Vienna Circle fame. Periodically Olaf Helmer, the statistician James Savage, and I met with Carnap at his house to discuss issues of induction and probability. Young whippersnapper that I was, I felt too much in awe of Carnap to enter freely into these discussions, although Carnap himself was actually an unassuming little man who made up for lack of sparkle with painstaking care and elaborate laboriousness. He was unpretentious, and at times almost diffident, but his evident dedication to the work in hand set an example from which a fledgling scholar could profit.

At this point it seems appropriate to say a few words about my religious development. I really cannot say that during my "suggestible childhood" religion played a more than marginal rile in the lives of my parents—or in my own. Nor did this situation change for some years after my leaving Germany for the United States at the age of nine in 1938. But I eventually experienced military service during the Korean War in my early twenties and while I never served at the front (and indeed never went overseas), nevertheless this experience —coming on top of my being a refugee from Nazi Germany —left me acutely aware of the contingency and uncertainties of human life. This sense of vulnerability and powerlessness served to make me more open-minded toward religion and more susceptible to its influences. Accordingly, religion did not become meaningful for me until I had to some extent matured and become settled in life—after the import of death had come home to me with the loss of my father, and the experiences of adulthood and its accompanying burdens of responsibility had matured me.

By the mid-1950s my mother had been drawn to Quakerism and had taken up work at the Friend's International Center at the University of California at Los Angeles, where I too was living at the time. After a period of attending the Quaker meeting in Santa Monica, I was ultimately motivated to join. Moreover, the entry into active membership in a Christian community was eased for me by the warm personal qualities of some of the people who then constituted the Santa Monica Friends Meeting. The Quaker emphasis on heeding that small, still voice within that continually calls us to higher and better things appealed sympathetically to my own natural tendencies of thought. It was in "centering down" in the productive silence of the Quaker "First Day" services that I gradually came to find within myself an increasing degree of Christian commitment.

Three aspects of Quakerism strongly attracted me: its utterly simple yet deeply meaningful mode of worship, its lack of any creedal commitments that might jar on a critical philosophical mind, and its dedication to peaceful conflict-resolution. (My experience of war, however distant, and of military service, however unwarlike, had convinced me that the way of peace is best, and that pacifism albeit somewhere between difficult and impossible in practice, is an ideal that merits all the support it can obtain. And this sentiment was reinforced, if anything, by my exposure to RAND's concerns.) In any case Frances and I now began to attend the local Friends Meeting in Santa Monica, and the fellowship that this provided was one of the pleasant highlights of these California years. I am sure that this development was one of the factors that led me to view with increasing favor the idea of eventually leaving RAND.

Only after getting settled in Pacific Palisades and adjusting to working at RAND and living in the Los Angeles area, a process pretty well accomplished by early 1955, did life become settled for Frances and me. Our marriage had heretofore witnessed a series of rapid changes, marked by repeated shifts in locale and career: its four years had seen us living in six different domiciles, with me following three very different careers—as a philosophy instructor, a Marine, and now as a RAND researcher. But at last stabilization seemed to be at hand.

This circumstance was, however, to prove shattering. The shifts and jolts of the recent years had masked the tensions and incompatibilities between us. The fact is that we were ill suited to one another in personality and, above all, in what we wanted from life. I loved travel and changes of scene, while Frances was glued to her home and hearth. I was a social creature, enjoying to be entertained and to entertain others, while she had no relish for the presence of others in her house. I viewed marriage as providing a domestic base for venturing forth into the activities of the environing world, while she regarded it as a safe harbor from whose security one would only reluctantly depart. To be sure, I never had been one to "go out with the boys." I did not hunt or golf or play poker or the like. But I have always relished work and its involvements—colleagueship, professional meetings, research-connected travel, etc. For Frances, any foray outside the domestic orbit on my part was virtual treason. She made marriage not a haven but a prison. The long and short of it is that we were incompatible—immersed in that not uncommon situation where a glib cliché like "the wrong chemistry" can render good service.

I long refused to look this fact in the face. I regarded myself as a "logical" person, and logical people hate to confess error. And various social and moral pressures were at work as well. But I now began to face up to the idea of a break with Frances and talked to her about it. However, she was dead set against divorce, which was apparently viewed as a heinous crime in her family because of some traumatic episode of the past. And I shrank from taking so decisive a step unilaterally. Things dragged along for some months in a thoroughly unsatisfactory condition, when external circumstances intervened. The inner strains of our relationship were once again dampened by outer challenges, and we agreed to hold our marriage together as we embarked on plans for a second cross-country move in a little over two years.

In March of 1956 I had gone to Washington for a few days to transact some RAND business with the Air Force intelligence people. Shortly after arriving, a telegram was forwarded to me telephonically to the Hay-Adams Hotel, where

I invariably stayed in the nation's capital because I found its solid old-world atmosphere congenial. The cable was from Howard Ziegler, chairman of the Philosophy Department at Lehigh University in Bethlehem, Pennsylvania, and requested me to get in touch with him. He and his colleagues were very interested in adding someone with my general qualifications as Assistant Professor in the department—a young Ph.D. trained in logic and philosophy of science, but with enough versatility to teach a wide range of subjects, and with some interest in the history of science. Ziegler was then chairman of the American Philosophical Association's placement committee, and had turned up my name in the inactive file, where it had rested since my job seeking days of 1953, when my discharge from service was drawing near.

This invitation came as a bolt from the blue. But since my Washington visit put me close at hand, it seemed worthwhile to pursue the matter. And so I journeyed to Bethlehem by train a day of two later. When I arrived I was met at the Pennsylvania Railroad station by the entire department—all three of them, Howard Ziegler, Adolf Grünbaum, and Thomas Haynes. What impressed me as we talked around the lunch table in the dinning room of the Hotel Bethlehem was the evident enthusiasm about me on the part of all concerned. There was no skeptical reserve, no element of "go ahead and convince us that we should really want you" about the discussion. They were all actually *eager* for me to join them I viewed this prospect, though wholly unanticipated and unprovided for, as altogether providential. While the proffered salary of $5,500 per annum was to be just half of my RAND pay, the chance to return to academic life exercised a powerful attraction. As I journeyed back to Washington by train late that afternoon, I turned the matter over in my mind backwards and forwards, and did not see how I could refuse, given my fundamental commitment to philosophy and to academic endeavors. To be sure, I did not see my way clear to beginning at Lehigh that very fall; there were too many loose ends to tie up in Santa Monica. But I did think that I could manage an orderly transition of my affairs in time to begin at Lehigh in early January of 1967.

And so I flew back to Los Angeles with my head full of the plans and prospects of impending change. Uprooted from academic work in February of 1952, I felt that here at last was a fortuitous opportunity to resume—just five years later—the pursuit of what I had for most of my adult life regarded as my natural *métier*. It seemed to me that destiny was calling, and I decided to bring my RAND career to an end.

In the course of the Vietnam War the RAND Corp. became one of the bogeymen of the Liberal Left in America—a symbol of all that was reprehensible about intellectuals in the service of a war-mongering establishment. (When I lectured in Oxford in the spring of 1974, one young participant told me of an American colleague who refused to attend because he heard that I had once worked for RAND!) Did I ever feel and qualms? I certainly did feel some occasional twinges—but perhaps not as many as one might think. For my own work at RAND was, as already described, largely concerned with matters of vulnerability and defense. Their upshot pointed towards the desirability of war-avoidance, and militated in a direction very much opposed to war-mongering. Moreover, I was too much of a realist to feel anguished. As long as nations maintain military capabilities— and in the present scheme of things it is not in the cards that they should soon cease to do so—they might as well conduct their affairs in this sphere intelligently, utilizing informed advice such as RAND was in a position to offer. The qualms that turned me away were not so much ideological but personal: a sense that "This was not for me." This sentiment was not yet (as of 1956) so strong as to impel me into an active pursuit of other possibilities, and indeed, might never have become strong enough to generate the requisite "escape energy" wholly by itself. But it proved to be quite enough that, when an unexpected opportunity spontaneously presented itself, I seized it eagerly.

As soon as I returned to California, planning got underway for the return "back East" (as Californians always say). The Bestor Boulevard house was put up for sale that summer, and we undertook and automobile excursion up the coast as far as Victoria, in British Columbia to make the most of the Pacific coast locale that was soon to be left behind. The house was sold in the course of this vacation and some temporary rental arrangement made thereafter. During that fall I wound up my affairs at RAND, and by the end of the year everything was ready for the transcontinental drive to Bethlehem.

I sometimes wonder whether, had fate not extricated me from RAND, I might possibly have become "trapped" there for good—quite outside of what I think of as my natural habitat in philosophy. I regretfully surmise that the answer is a definite *yes*. As I look back on it, I see that there was nothing inevitable about my reentry into philosophy. My cast of mind and personality is such that I would very possibly have settled inextricably into research and administration in RAND or some comparable less militarily oriented "think tank." With the passing years the prospect of return to Academia could have become ever dimmer. When I see people who have gone this route, the sobering thought comes to mind that "there but for the grace of God go I."

I thought (and still think) that I had managed to learn many useful things during the two and a half years at RAND—about human nature, about the workings of institutions, and about the ways of life in a domain outside the academic sphere. Although RAND itself was a rather unusual organization, I also learned something about practical affairs from some of the many very practical-minded people in its employ. Above all, I learned to work with other people and absorbed the significance and the technique of teamwork and collaboration. (The result has been that no contemporary in my field has published more collaborative studies than I, and that I have frequently been able to enlist my students as collaborators in my own work.) Then too there was the benefit of first-hand experience of the rather different life-style afforded by Southern California. With hindsight I have come to recognize that the RAND experience provided some very useful bits of intellectual nurture. For while RAND activities were clearly "beside the point," so to speak, from the narrower perspective of my philosophical career, my time there was not wasted even in this respect. I acquired a number of philosophically valuable lessons, in particular learning to appreciate the interest and utility of empirical investigations in the social sciences—especially economics and social theory—for working ethnic and social philosophy. My philosophizing in these fields has never moved at the level of arid abstraction that was almost universal in the 1950's and 60's, when any taking heed of the empirical realities was all too frequently seen as ill-suited to "doing philosophy" in the proper, *a priori* mode. Without this public-policy oriented concern for the concrete social realities, various books of mine in applied philosophy, such as *Distributive Justice*, *Welfare*, and *Unselfishness*, would never have been written.

How did I assess RAND itself? On balance I would say that I had great respect for the organization. It had some extremely able and far-sighted leaders—in particular John Williams of Mathematics Division and Charles Hitch of Economics. And it certainly had a wide and impressively competent array of talent in its employ in those times. As I saw it, RAND's main defect was its inability to bring these resources into a better focus. Some very fine work was being done by the organization (perhaps the best in its history), but I must say that its volume struck me as modest relative to the very impressive talents at the disposal of the enterprise. I suspect that to some extent the balmy climate, the beach-side site, and the "easy living" of Southern California tended to make lotus eaters of its staff.

Be that as it may, there were no regrets in my mind on that foggy California morning of January 4, 1957, when embarking on an eastward transcontinental drive in the same green 1954 Chevrolet that had crossed the country westward by train some two and a half years previously.

NOTES

1. [Note added in 1996.] The 1952 cost of this Pacific Palisades house was three times my then annual salary as an entry-level professional. Now in 1996 it would cost six times my annual salary as a very senior academic. The contrast speaks volumes about the inflation of house prices in the attractive areas of Los Angeles.

2. Of the numerous published accounts of the origins of the Delphi method, none gets the matter entirely straight. The story runs as follows: A precursor study that helped to set the stage was Abraham Kaplan, A. L. Skogstad, and M.A. Girshick, "The Prediction of Social and Technological Events," RAND Corporation paper

P-93 (Santa Monica CA, April 1949), subsequently published in the *Public Opinion Quarterly*, vol. 14 (1950), pp. 93-110. The use of the Delphi method itself in its initial, rudimentary form first occured in Norman C. Dalkey and Olaf Helmer, "The Use of Experts for the Estimation of Bombing Requirement: A Project Delphi Experiment," RAND Corporation Research Memorandum RM-727-PR (Santa Monica CA, November 1952). (Delphi was thus inaugurated in the context of think-tank strategy studies.) The theoretical basis of the Delphi methodology was first set out in a 1958 RAND publication (paper P-1513) later reprinted as: Olaf Helmer and Nicholas Rescher, "On the Epistemology of the Inexact Sciences," *Management Sciences*, vol. 6 (1959), pp. 25-52. A reasonably accurate outline of the history of *subsequent* developments is set out on pp. 85ff of Edward Cornish et al., *The Study of the Future* (Washington DC: World Future Society, 1977). See also Harold A. Linstone and Murray Turoff (eds.) *The Delphi Method: Techniques and Applications* (Reading, MA: Addison Wesley, 1975), which characterizes the multiply reprinted Helmer-Rescher paper of 1958 as a "classic paper" which "was very adequate for the typical technological forecasting applications for which Delphi has been popular" (p. 15).

3. The method in its developed form is described in Olaf Helmer's *Looking Forward: A Guide to Future's Research* (Beverly Hills: Sage Publications, 1983). For further references see p. 299 ff of Roger M. Cooke, *Experts in Uncertainty: (op. cit.)*, (Chapter 11, entitled "Combining Expert Opinion" is particularly relevant). Good discussions of Delphi are also found in Joseph P. Martino, *Technological Forecasting for Decisionmaking* (New York: American Elzevier, 1972), pp. 28-64, and in Harold A. Linstone and Murray Turoff (eds.) *The Delphi Method: Techniques and Applications* (Reading, MA: Addison Wesley, 1975). However, the very fact that the passage of years has not rendered these discussions obsolete betokens the forecasting community's disillusionment with this predictive technique.

4. For me personally, however, this collaboration with Olaf had an important long-term consequences. For these interactions set the stage for an ongoing interest on my part in issues relating to scientific prediction.

Nine

LEHIGH UNIVERSITY
Bethlehem, PA: 1957-1961
(Age 28-32)

On reaching Bethlehem, Pennsylvania in early January of 1957 at the end of my first and only coast-to-coast automobile trip, a few days were spent as houseguests in the Howard Ziegler's colonial-style residence near the center of town. Thereafter, a small but adequate apartment in a newish complex on the outskirts of town provided a new home.

It felt good to be "back East" again. Bethlehem was a thoroughly pleasant place, somewhat dreary in its industrial areas, but with attractive residential settings and an interesting historical localities dating from its Moravian heritage. With a population of some 60,000, the town was built on a rational, human scale—rather peaceful and old-worldish after occasionally garish exoticism of Southern California. I was thoroughly pleased to resume academic life is such an attractive and livable site. And the historic dimension was another attraction. I have a natural curiosity for background, and confronted with an old place or person or object I am always curious about the process that has led to the *status quo*.

Lehigh University was at this point a smallish institution. Founded in 1865 by the munificence of a steel magnate, the university by now had around 1,000 undergraduates in engineering, along with some 500 liberal arts students, and 500 in the business school. (There was also a small graduate program—mainly in the sciences.) Its diminutive Philosophy Department figured primarily in a "service" role, providing liberal-arts exposure to fledgling engineers and businessmen. The engineers in particular were able and hardworking students—if somewhat untutored on the humanistic side. It was a pleasure to teach them logic or philosophy of science, where the bent of their minds intersected with that of the subject.

At Lehigh I soon settled into the regular routine of a philosophy professor. As junior member of the department, I was called upon to teach a wide range of undergraduate philosophy offerings: logic, history of philosophy, theory knowledge, and various special subject (semantics, history or science). My duties during the initial years consisted in teaching four classes per term (each of them meeting three hours per week on a Monday/Wednesday/Friday or a Tuesday/Thursday/Saturday cycle). However, several of these classes were sections of the same course (usually two or three sections of logic), so that the number of distinct preparations was reduced. While this "teaching load" was a heavy one (at any rate, by the standard of later times), I had little difficulty in combining it with a wide spectrum of other activities. In comparison with RAND's eight-hour day, my schedule afforded a new-found freedom, and I managed to make some progress with my philosophical researches—and also with such outside efforts as the study of Arabic (of which more anon). All in all, I was happy and proud to be a member of the academic community once again. And I was delighted to be back at doing philosophy, relishing the opportunity to let my mind run in paths traced out by the great thinkers of the past.

The president of Lehigh at this stage was Martin Dewey Whittaker. He struck me as stuffy and unimaginative (an impression which, based as it was on rather casual contacts, may well do him injustice). His favorite anecdote—one heard it often from his lips—was the story of the man who had once given him the wise counsel: "Never explain your decisions! One generally reaches the right decision for the wrong reasons, and if you explain your reasons you will probably be

talked out of them and the decision as well."[1] Whittaker
apparently clung to this principle in and out of season, a fact
which hardly qualified him as an ideal of academic leadership.
As far as I could see, the brain of the University's administration belonged to Harvey Alexander Neville, its Vice President. A loyal old Princetonian and an able chemist, he
provided the institution with academic leadership and sense
of direction. I emerged from my various dealings with him
with an enhanced respect for his ability to combine dignity
with courtesy and helpfulness.

Howard Ziegler—the chairman of the philosophy department—was then just nearing the age of fifty. After undergraduate work at Franklin & Marshall College in his native
region of Pennsylvania (he hailed from Reading), he had been
trained as a Lutheran minister. But the ministry sat uncom-
fortably on his shoulders, and he gravitated towards academia, ultimately earning a Ph.D. at Columbia University with
a dissertation on a tertiary American thinker, one Frederick
Augustus Rauch. A person of many substantial capabilities,
Howard was an excellent administrator—painstaking, hard-
working, unselfishly mindful of the welfare of his subordi-
nates, and heartily devoted to the effectiveness of the
enterprise. Possessed of a friendly spirit and a good sense of
humor, he labored unstintingly to advance the interests of
Lehigh University and to enhance the quality of his department. Unusually effective in dealing with people at all levels—students, colleagues in other fields, and university
officials—he conveyed to everyone with whom he dealt a
concern for their well-being and care of their problems. He
was a true Christian gentleman, and his strengths of character
were matched by an attractive good humor and sweetness of
temperament. His principal shortcoming was a certain sensi-
tivity about his relatively modest abilities as a philosopher.
Yet he handled this admirably. Many department chairman
would in such circumstances have sought security in mediocre
colleagues. Not Howard! Dedicated to the good of the university, he went to great lengths to secure the services of really
able people. And, fortunately, they respected him as a very
superior person, greatly admired his flair for administration,

and deeply appreciated the care for their welfare that he constantly manifested.

When I first met with Lehigh Philosophy Department for a luncheon "interview" at the Hotel Bethlehem in April of 1956, Adolf Grünbaum had already been a member of the department for some years, having come there for his first post after earning his Ph.D. at Yale in 1950. His career at Lehigh had been meteoric, a mere six years seeing him rise from a fledgling assistant professor to an endowed professorial chair. From the very first, Adolf's attitude towards me was one of great cordiality and helpfulness, and ever since I always ranked him among my very best philosophical friends. It had been largely due to his activity—both in the classroom and in the cultivation of personal relationships among his colleagues—that the Philosophy Department of Lehigh and achieved a substantial reputation on campus, both among the faculty and the students. When I arrived in Bethlehem, Adolf's charming wife Thelma was pregnant with their (ultimately one and only) child—a little charmer called Barbara. We came to know the Grünbaums well and shared many Lehigh friends in common. Adolf was in those days laying the basis for work in the philosophy of space and time that was soon to earn him a world-wide reputation. Given the volatility of the academic profession in this era, I little thought when first meeting Adolf in 1956 that he would still be my colleague some twenty years later. [And now (1996) forty!] The collegial relationship between us has proved to be durable—and is invariably pleasant, owing largely to Adolf's congeniality, kindness, and fellow-feeling. I have always admired him greatly, and am impressed by the unusual degree to which Adolf combines toughness of mind with sweetness of disposition in his interactions with friends.

The only other member of the Department of Philosophy at this stage was Thomas Haynes. He was an interesting and engaging person. Intelligent and articulate, he had a pleasant, outgoing, and thoroughly sweet-tempered personality. Then in his mid-30's, he combined a curious mixture of ability and ineffectuality. He was certainly an intelligent person who read and thought a great deal. But all this intellectual effort bore no concrete fruit. For while Tom would talk of various creative plans, it soon became perfectly clear to anyone who got to know him even slightly that he would never discipline himself actually to bring to fruition any of the ideas and projects that enlivened his thought and conversation. His mode of intellectual outreach lay in the teaching of students: which he did most effectively, in the process evangelizing them with the 1920's era socialism he had imbibed in undergraduate days from some pupil of Elijah Jordan's, whose disciple he counted himself.

Outside the Philosophy Department, the Lehigh colleague with whom I had the closest ties was Carey B. Joynt, then (and for long afterwards) chairman of the Department of International Relations. Carey was a shrewd and clear-headed Canadian Scots Presbyterian: solid and upright to the core—combining sound judgment and good sense with a twinkle of wry humor. I saw a good deal of Carey, both socially and professionally. We shared interests in the philosophy of history, and in the place of ethics in international affairs, and wrote some articles in collaboration, as well as a never published study of the place of morality in international affairs. For me, Carey and his charming wife Anne were among the principal attractions of the Lehigh community.

Theodore and Marie Hailperin also stood high among the Lehigh people I came to know well. Ted was in the Mathematics Department at Lehigh and was a very able logician. Marie was a warm and charming person, and an excellent hostess. They had two attractive children, a boy and a girl, then just entering teenagehood. They lived in a functional little modernesque house off Pine Top Trail which they themselves had built. Even though Ted was somewhat hard to talk to, with the shyness and introversion not uncommon in abstract thinkers, the Hailperins were for me one of the real assets of the Lehigh academic community. (It was a loss felt keenly by everyone who knew her when Marie was struck down by cancer in the prime of life, not long after I had left Lehigh.)

We soon tired of apartment living, and in the fall of 1957 purchased an antiquated but attractive wood-framed Victorian town house in an old residential area near the center of town (at 215 Wall Street). The house had definite attractions—especially its location which afforded convenient access both to town and the university. But after a winter of struggling with the old coal-burning furnace we moved in the spring of 1958 to a convenient and modern Dutch-colonial style 3-bedroom house at 1815 Homestead Avenue. Located in one of the newer, somewhat more outlying residential areas on what were then the northwest outskirts of town, this house was to be "home" for the rest of the time in Bethlehem.

The winter of 1957-8 was not a good one for me. During most of it I suffered from some sort of (undiagnosed) viral infection that left me in an enfeebled, run-down condition for several months. By the spring of 1958 this had passed off and I was as good as new. However, this illness had had a curious side effect on me. For almost a year after, I found it just about impossible to sit still in a room full of people—I was too jittery. I could not bear to attend such functions as concerts or lectures. This phenomenon caused me a good deal of distress but mercifully faded away with the gradual restoration of physical vigor.

The academic life offers an exceptional range of opportunity. One is one's own master and disposes of one's own time to an extent truly unusual in modern life—particularly since the summer months are altogether free. My return to the "groves of academe" thus proved to be a liberating experience. At RAND I had been caught up in the 9-to-5 regimen of workday routine. Now the long hours of each day spread out before me—most of them uncommitted. On even the busiest day, my university duties took up no more than six hours, and so I enjoyed the luxury of having discretionary time on my hands. Moreover, I did not feel drained of intellectual energy the end of the day as I had at RAND and could now work for a several of hours in the evening, dispensing with a need for the soporific emptiness of television or light reading.

All in all, I was delighted to be back in academia. I taught a wide variety of courses during this period and was most pleased to reestablish contact with my old friends among the philosophers of bygone days. I found the contact with students most stimulating and gradually I made myself into an effective teacher. And I turned with relish to philosophical research and writing.

Various writing projects now preoccupied my attention. The first took me back to an old love on undergraduate days—the Presocratic philosophers. In the early months of 1957, I wrote an essay on "Cosmic Evolution in Anaximander"[2] which combined this interest with yet another, the history of science. It gave me pleasure to be able to show just how sophisticated the ideas of this "primitive" thinker actually were. Writing this paper gave me more pleasure than any other piece of work I had done since my Princeton dissertation, which had addressed the relation of Leibniz's philosophy to his work in science. My conjoint interest in the history of science and the philosophy of science was rather ahead of its time. The 1960's saw a wider trend towards the co-cultivation of these fields—to the extent that HPS ("history and philosophy of science") has become a well-established academic grouping. But in the 1950's this combination of interests was unusual.

I also much enjoyed writing a paper entitled "Choice Without Preference." It led me down various historical byways that gave me a vista of the charms of working in the "history of ideas." I read this paper at the Fullerton Club (at Bryn Mawr) in the fall of 1958 and at the American Philosophical Association meetings in New York that December. Its success on these occasions helped significantly to promote the profession's growing perception of me as a capable young man. Still, attending professional meetings is a humbling but salutary experience. When anywhere from 300 to 3,000 professional colleagues are present, one realizes how small a fish in the pond one really is. Most work on issues one has never even touched oneself. And even those who work on one's own topics are often uninformed about one's work—let alone taking account of it in theirs! (I have long ago schooled myself to regard such failures as grounds for amusement rather than regret.) The chastening thought comes to mind that is would make little if any difference to one's profession if one vanished from the scene and one's work were lost without trace. (The fact that others are in the same boat is of little consolation.) The most one can expect is the occasional encounter with someone who has profited from one's endeavors. And—alas, oh vanity of scholars!—how sweet it is to find on occassion that one has not labored entirely in vain.

I now also branched out in other directions. After my father's death in 1952 I had inherited his correspondence with his cousin Oskar in Istanbul, where he had emigrated many years before. My father eventually became his last remaining link with the rest of his family, and when father died I took up this correspondence with "Uncle Oskar." Though I never met him, I felt a deep bond of affectionate kinship with the crotchety old gentleman. Since this contact was to have substantial repercussion for me, it is necessary to say a few words about him.

Born in Stuttgart in 1883, Oskar Rescher pursued his university studies in Munich and Berlin, specializing in oriental languages. After taking his degree in Oriental Studies in Berlin around 1908, he habilitated as an academic at Breslau. He worked there as *Dozent* for some years, making annual forays to the manuscript collections of Istanbul, and around 1912 decided to take up residence there more or less permanently. Remaining a German citizen, he was called up for military service in World War I and served as censor for letters from Arabic-speaking prisoners of war. After the was he returned to Breslau as an Adjunct Professor (Ausserordentlicher Professor). Around 1925, he returned to Turkey, and became both a Muslim and a Turkish national during the 1930's. The years from 1920 to 1935 saw his happiest and certainly most productive period. His contributions to the studies of Arabic literary history gained him world-wide recognition as an expert in this area. But with increasing years he became increasingly eccentric. His scholarly influence was eventually curtailed by adoption of a particular and idiosyncratic policy as regards publication. Around 1925 he gave up publishing in scholarly journals, and thereafter, to the dismay of his scholarly colleagues, all of his works were published privately by him in editions of from 30 to 50 copies and distributed only to favored recipients.

As World War II neared, Oskar's financial circumstances tightened: he had some money in Germany, but could not extract it under Nazi regulations. This forced him to accept positions far below the level of his capabilities and attainments (e.g., after 1937 until the end of World War II he taught languages at the Military Academy of Ankara). He became an increasingly eccentric old man, given to writing German poetry with an Oriental flavor. He lived in a single room with some half-dozen cats to whose needs he catered more scrupulously than to his own. He was a scholar of profound learning and vast intellectual resources, who, but for his eccentricities, would have won an outstanding place for himself in Arabic studies. He died on 26 March 1972—some 60 years after first making Turkey his home—and lies buried in one of those vast necropolises that punctuate the outskirts of Istanbul.[3]

My correspondence with "Uncle Oscar" was to have a far-reaching result for me. For I now became interested in learning what was involved in being an Arabist. So I bought A. S. Tritton's *Teach Yourself Arabic* and began to work through it. Soon I was forgetting old material at the same rate as I was learning the new. I then transferred to the didactically superior text of Kapliwatzky. But after a while I came to realize that what I really needed was a teacher.

And so in early 1958 I began to commute twice a week during term-time to Philadelphia on a Reading Railroad passenger service that then still linked these two cities, stopping at a half-dozen hamlets in between. My destination was the elementary class in Arabic conducted by Professor S. D. Goitein at the University of Pennsylvania. He was a scholar of the old school, trained in pre-war Germany and knowledgeable in a wide range of philosophical and literary matters. Long service in Palestine—first under the British as a school inspector, and then as professor of Arabic at the Hebrew University—had reinforced his formidable competence as an Arabist. I enjoyed his classes, not only because they helped me with Arabic, but also because of the quality of the man himself. My classmates were mostly Jewish youngsters who had studied Hebrew since childhood and were now pursuing Arabic—a closely cognate language—as part of Semitic Studies. This gave them a considerable start at learning vocabulary and grammatical paradigms. Here was I, a mature adult of thirty and a professor at an institution of higher learning, and yet I was by no means the best student in a class of college undergraduates. The experience was humbling but also helpful. As a teacher one deals with material that has become second nature through familiarity, and it is easy to forget the difficulties of the novice. My struggles with Arabic kept this difficulty before my mind and made me more sympathetic with the difficulties experienced by my own students.

Initially drawn to Arabic by curiosity, my interest soon took a more scholarly turn. For I came to realize that while the Islamic philosophers of the middle ages had devoted much attention to my own pet interest, logic, and had done interesting work in this field, yet their discussions were largely *terra incognita*, virtually untouched by modern scholarship. So I now began to work in odd moments at bibliographic compilations on Arabic philosophers—first on al-Farabi, and then on the Arabic logicians in general. I entered upon this bibliographic work for two reasons. I thought that it would orient me in the field—to help me to gain a clear view of what had been done and what remained undone. And I felt that it would be a way of "paying my dues"—of making that contribution to the laborious routine of scholarship that could in due course earn a hearing from the specialist professionals for an outsider's work. While my proficiency in Arabic always remained sufficiently rudimentary to displease me, it was (in the early 1960's at any rate) sufficient to enable me to accomplish—over the next decade—a sizable amount of scholarship in various areas of Arabic logic that did not impose excessive philological demands.

One of the most rewarding results of my Arabic studies of this period was the restoration of a polemical tract by Alexander of Aphrodisias, an important Aristotle-commentator who flourished around 200 A.D. This text, long lost in the original Greek, could be recovered in an Arabic translation. For by outrageous good luck it was possible to unite two incomplete manuscripts, one from Turkey, the other from Spain, the former containing the first half of the treatise, the latter its second half, with enough overlap to put the unity of the text beyond doubt. After considerable delays in publication, the treatise was published in Pakistan and the Arabic text edited and translated in collaboration with Michael E. Marmura of the University of Toronto, an ideally patient and cooperative co-worker. (The opus has the distinction of bearing by far the longest title of any book I am connected with—*The Refutation by Alexander of Aphrodisias of Galen's Treatise on the Theory of Motion.* [Islamabad, 1965].)

During these Lehigh years, I also wrote a steady stream of scholarly papers on a wide range of strictly philosophical topics, perhaps a dozen each year. What I now regard as my most important philosophical paper of the Lehigh period was the *Philosophical Review* essay on "Belief-Contravening Suppositions."[4] This paper proved to be a very fruitful foray. It opened up the lines of thought leading towards my subsequent work on hypothetical reasoning and on the system-oriented epistemology of the coherence theory of truth.

My papers of this period manifested a diversified mixture of interests—in symbolic logic, in the history of philosophy (especially Aristotle, Leibniz, and Kant), in subjects like futurology and forecasting methodologies, and in some aspects of Arabic studies. Now around thirty years old, I was unwilling or unable to settle down to one particular specialty. (Even now, twenty years later, I keep more irons in the fire than most.) In fact, I believe this is why philosophy had such an appeal for me, for it accomodates and even to some extent demands a diversified spread of interests and competences. Nevertheless, I realize that many-sidedness exacts a price. For it is virtually impossible in the circumstances to polish one's skills in any one field to the fine edge of accomplished expertise. My colleagues who specialize in logic know the field better than I do, those who specialize in ancient philosophy know its texts better, and so on. It is only as a philosophical *generalist*—a combiner of many skills—that I could qualify as in any way outstanding. I am almost always satisfied with this, though there are also time when I feel pangs of discontent at being more of a fox than a hedgehog.[5]

As the 1950's came to a close, I undertook some writing projects of a larger scale. I turned my efforts at scholarship in Arabic philosophy towards the preparation of a general account of *The Development of Arabic Logic* (not completed until 1963 at Pittsburgh and published by the University of Pittsburgh Press in 1964). And at the invitation of St. Martin's Press I began work on an *Introduction to Logic* for beginning students (also completed in Pittsburgh and published in 1964). I also collaborated with Carey Joynt on a short monograph on ethical issues in international relations. (We submitted it unavailingly to two or three publishers—the time was not ripe for this theme, which came to flourish only in the post-Vietnam War era). These various forays provided my first experience at writing books for publication.

Throughout the Lehigh years I was professionally active not only in writing but also in other ways. I began to participate actively in the annual meetings of the Eastern Division of the American Philosophical Association. In December of 1957 I gave my first such paper at the Harvard University meetings, and in December of 1958 I presented the "Choice Without Preference" material at the Columbia University meetings, as mentioned above. In the spring of 1959 I served as external examiner for graduating philosophy students in the Honors Program at Swarthmore College. Growing recognition of one as a "promising young man" was attested by invitations to job interviews at various places, culminating in offers of assistant professorship at Cornell in 1958 and an associate professorship at Yale in 1959. In the meantime, I had been promoted to a tenured associate professorship at Lehigh in 1959, two years after arriving on the scene. My stature on campus—and in the philosophical profession—had grown rapidly during the first two years following my reentry into the academic world.

As I think back, I find it alarming that the move to Lehigh—so decisive for the whole course of my life—came about so fortuitously. The thought of that telegram from Howard Ziegler is always a forceful reminder for me that there is no rational orchestration to the flow of things in the affairs of life—it is just a matter of "one darn thing leads to another." Only with my appointment at Lehigh at the age of twenty-eight did my life's course get safely placed on its proper track. This process of getting well settled into one's career in almost invariably a time of trial and tribulation. When one reads a biography, it often seems that its subject was led by a series of sure steps to that destined line of endeavor which was to prove his ultimate life's work. But a closer look generally shows that this impression is very much mistaken—a person's younger years almost invariably include a period of false starts and indecisive trials, a time of an anxious contemplation of alternatives, a zig-zag motion in ultimately aborted directions with abrupt turning-points. At such times, things could have eventuated in any one of several ways. My early life included at least three such critical junctures: when completing high school—could my family afford to have me go to college?; when completing college—should I go on to do advanced study in mathematics or in philosophy?; in the period after my military service—would I turn up a suitable post in philosophy or would I settle permanently into some RAND-like career? Each of these episodes were crucial forks in the road, and each could conceivably have led to a totally different eventuation. Not until the Lehigh appointment did it become a settled matter that I would earn my livelihood as a philosophy professor—despite my having opted for this alternative when I chose graduate work in philosophy seven year previously.

Throughout the period of residence in Bethlehem we attended the local Quaker meeting (Lehigh Valley Monthly Meeting). At first it met in the assembly room of a private school in Allentown, but plan were just getting under way for the construction of a meeting house, and in due course a plot of farmland on the Bath Pike was purchased for this purpose. Here—some three miles north of the town center—was erected the new meeting house, which was inaugurated in early 1961, just before I left Bethlehem. Overall, I attended this meeting for some four years, and it came to mean a great deal to me, counting many fine individuals among its members. I served as one of the overseers after 1959, and thus had the chance to see at close range the inner workings of a

Quaker "parish." Perhaps this glance behind the curtain took away some of the magic. But I did continue to read widely in the literature of Quakerism and obtained a reasonable familiarity with its history and theology.

The condition of my marriage had undergone various changes in the course of these years in Bethlehem. The first months were a time of settling in—of making an remaking housing arrangements, of forging new social contacts, and of becoming active participants in the Quaker meeting. As was usual with our relationship, change and novelty in external circumstances produced an easing of inner pressures. But with the return of normalcy and stability, there came once more a heightening of those tensions between Frances and myself which made our life together difficult. Eventually there was little save the force of habit to hold our marriage together. However, a decisive change occurred in the spring of 1959 when it transpired that Frances was pregnant and tensions eased in the wake of yet another lapse from "normalcy."

The arrival of Elizabeth on February 20 of 1960—well after any hope of having a child of our own had been abandoned—worked a great change. A new and very precious person had entered upon the scene and a new situation had been created. In any case, our marriage, with all its various ups and down, had endured for almost a decade. Perhaps in the now-altered circumstances it would hold together for good?

During her stay in the hospital, Frances had contacted a staph infection, and so I mainly cared for Elizabeth during the first weeks of her life. Partly, perhaps, because of this we had a special bond and were always very close throughout her infancy. She was a bright child who learned quickly. (Her first word, "car-car," applied to a passing automobile, was uttered when she was only ten months old.) The pleasure of parenthood was perhaps all the keener for coming well after all hopes had been abandoned. Circumstances thus intervened once again to put the strains and stresses of a difficult marriage into the background.

Throughout this Lehigh period, I still maintained the umbilical cord of the RAND consultantship. Each summer I would spend some four or five weeks in Santa Monica, working at some short-term project—sometimes in the entourage of Olaf Helmer, sometimes on my own. Partly, I tended to view the RAND connection as "insurance" of a sort, in the event that my return to academic life were somehow to prove abortive. More importantly, I valued the opportunity to keep alive some personally rewarding and intellectually stimulating contacts.

The presidential election of 1960 was my first experience of politics as seen from a vantage point within a university faculty. True to my Republican allegiance, I backed Richard Nixon. In doing so I placed myself within the minuscule minority on our campus, which reflected the overwhelming tendency towards the Democratic party among American academics. My colleagues never ceased to pontificate with facile assurance about the superiority of their choice, but this only served to confirm my doubts. The favored fallacy of intellectuals everywhere is to overestimate the *external* bearing of their superior talents and training *within* their professional specialties. All sight is lost of a point I have always taken as self-evident, that common sense and a certain "rustic faith" in the traditional values and accustomed perspectives of ordinary people are better guides in conducting life's affairs than are the facile ideas of sheltered intellectuals.

At some point during the Lehigh years, I discovered the novels of Anthony Trollope. I cannot recall the specific occasion, but I do remember that I began with *Barchester Towers* and *The Warden*. Thereafter I wandered more of less randomly through the enormous corpus of this charming and uncannily insightful Victorian novelist. I am deeply grateful to this tireless writer for the many pleasant hours his labors have given me.

As the terms at Lehigh succeeded one another in the annual cycle that makes the academic a kinsman to the farmer, I settled more and more deeply into the grooves of campus life. The seasonal succession of academic rituals was a notable feature of life at a small university: the regular pattern of events from the social activities at the start of each academic year to the great end-of-year gathering of the whole faculty to honor the year's crop of retirees. Participation in the academic processions at the Fall and Spring commencement exercises was at that time compulsory for member of the Lehigh faculty. And so I must have sat through some ten commencement addresses. The medium does not lend itself to the production of significant results. Though these exhortations were usually delivered by eminent people, I do not retain the least recollection of the content of any of those addresses, and cannot recall the name of even a single individual who delivered them.

During 1959 Adolf Grünbaum had been negotiating with the University of Pittsburgh, at first with a view to his becoming Chairman of the Philosophy Department. After he declined this offer, it was succeeded in the spring of 1960 by his being offered the Andrew Mellon chair in philosophy. Adolf accepted this post, and moved to Pittsburgh that autumn. Immediately on arrival he impressed the administration with the desirability of securing my services. Negotiations began that fall which—after my also declining to serve as chairman—led to my appointment as Professor of Philosophy, to commence in the next academic year.

The timing of my return to academic life had been extremely propitious. With the late 1950's, a decade of rapid expansion came upon higher education in America. New institutions sprang up and old ones expanded greatly. The resulting shortage of qualified faculty created unprecedented opportunities for rapid advancement. I was a paradigm beneficiary of these circumstances: my career from fledgling assistant professor to a full professorship was compressed into a four year timespan. By dint of luck and serious effort, the "lost time" of the almost five years spent in the U.S.M.C. and at RAND had been made up. Interruptions and detours notwithstanding, I had been able to establish my claim to a full professorship at a major university at the still relatively young age of thirty-two.

The spring term of 1961 was thus to be my last at Lehigh University. In May of that year, the house on Homestead Avenue was sold and a move across the state to Pittsburgh undertaken. I looked forward eagerly to the challenges of this transplantation to a larger and more active academic environment, which offered, in particular, the chance to participate in the training of graduate students. Yet I did not leave Lehigh without mixed feelings. Bethlehem was a pleasant, comfortable place in those days—a small but eminently livable town. And I had been able to make many good friends in my brief time at Lehigh. All the same, I felt that there was no alternative to responding to the challenge of ampler opportunity.

NOTES

1. Actually, the original author of this advice was Lord Mansfield, who thus counseled an inexperienced judge. See J.S. Mill, *System of Logic*, vol. I, bk. II, chap. iii, sect 3.

2. Published in *Studium General*, vol. 12 (1959), pp. 718-731, and reprinted in my *Essays in Philosophical Analysis* (Pittsburgh, 1969).

3. His grave memorial was erected by Dr. Ayla König, the daughter of his old (1920's) landlady. She practiced dentistry in Istanbul and did much to care for Oskar in his later years. She supplied materials for the biographical notice of Oskar prepared by Dr. Leon Nemoy for the *Yale University Library Gazette* in 1972 on the occasion of Yale's acquiring a part of Oskar's collection of Arabic manuscripts.

4. *The Philosophical Review*, vol. 70 (1961), pp. 167-196; reprinted in H. Feigl et al. (eds.), *New Readings in Philosophical Analysis* (New York, 1972), pp. 530-45 and in E. Sosa (ed.) *Causality and Conditionals* (Oxford: Clarendon Press, 1975), pp. 156-64.

5. However, I wish that I knew far better than I actually do the languages (French, Latin, Greek, Arabic) which I have "learned" over the years.

Ten

PITTSBURGH:
THE FIRST YEARS
1961-1966 (Age 32-38)

Upon arriving in Pittsburgh in late May of 1961, our first residence was a rented dark-brick town-house on St. James' Terrace (No. 5313) in the Shadyside section, which had been found for us by Thelma Grünbaum. It was compact and convenient, and we were soon comfortably settled in. Although my post at the University did not formally commence until September, I began to acclimate myself there. I put in order my large, pleasant corner office on the 8th floor of Cathedral of Learning, and began to organize my teaching and writing in this new setting.

After some months of readjustment, house hunting began in earnest. It issued late in 1961 in the purchase of 200 Tennyson Avenue in the Schenley Farms area, no more than a three minute walk from my office at Pitt.

Pittsburgh itself took some getting used to after the quiescence of Bethlehem. While it has many pleasant residential streets, it has rarely managed to separate them sufficiently form vehicular traffic except in the suburbs. Almost nowhere in town is one secure against the sound of cars and buses. At the same time, the city has many attractive features. It is handsomely sited along the banks of great rivers. Its environs affords attractive and varied areas of countryside. Its downtown area—hemmed in by rivers—is a conveniently compact area for shopping and afford some very good stores. There is excellent music, the Pittsburgh Symphony in particular being a splendid resource. The museums, public libraries, and parks are very good and there is ample scope for the cultivation of cultural interests. And above all, from my point of view, the University of Pittsburgh is a great asset of the place.

It had not always been so. At this time in the early 1960's Pitt was undergoing the revolutionary transformation inseparably associated with the name of Edward H. Litchfield. Recruited in the 1950's from the deanship of the Graduate School of Business and Public Administration at Cornell, he was commissioned by Pitt's trustees—then the great men of the Pittsburgh power structure, especially Richard King Mellon and Alan Magee Scaife—to transform the University of Pittsburgh from a streetcar commuter college into a significant academic institution. A battery of Mellon Professorships and Mellon Fellowships were created, and over a period of seven years commencing in the mid 1950's some 70 million of Mellon dollars flowed into the treasury of the University. Great things were done and even greater things were projected. It was a heady and exciting era while it lasted, but it soon came crashing down in ruins, and the reasons for this lay in the personality of the man who stood at the center of it all, Chancellor Litchfield. He was too driving and Napleonic a personality to reach an easy accommodation with the magnates of Pittsburgh's moneyed establishment. A classic drama ensued in the clash between a volatile object and a stable mass, a clash in which Litchfield ultimately came to grief.

The Vice-Chancellor, Charles ("Charlie") Peake, whom Litchfield had recruited from a deanship at the University of Michigan, was an academic administrator of unusual quality because of his keen dedication to the furtherance of academic values. I knew him too late in his career to get a clear view of his merits as a professor of English, but as Vice Chancellor he devoted himself with buoyant enthusiasm to the support and advancement of scholarship at the University. He was active in the recruitment of good scholars and supportive of those already there. He was always accessible and ready to help an academically concerned department or individual in support of this cause. He was certainly a good friend to the Philosophy Department, whose ascent into a position of national stature was only possible because of his enthusiastic backing.

The acting chairman of the Philosophy Department at this point was Oliver Leslie Reiser. Born in 1898, Oliver was a pleasant and easy-going, somewhat other-worldly elderly gentleman. He had entered the service of the University in 1926, before my own birth, and was drawing near to retirement. Neither Adolf Grünbaum nor I were willing to take on the chairmanship, since our own work was making demands that could not be subordinated to administrative duties, and so Oliver continued in office for a time as acting chairman. This state of affairs was not without its problems. Oliver was a person of many attractive qualities, being an able teacher and a widely read philosopher, albeit one of distinctly eccentric interests in what most of us would view as occult phenomena. But he was totally ineffectual as an administrator. He was thus quite unfitted to the needs of the moment. In particular, he simply could not (or would not) take on the unhappy work of weeding out the lame ducks with which the department had become encumbered over the years so that the process of rebuilding could proceed. These people were his longtime associates and colleagues—he would do nothing to displease or displace them. However understandable this sentiment, it seriously depressed Oliver's stock in the eyes of the new-model administration of Litchfield and Peake. He was never offered the chairmanship, and while he seemed to accept this without rancor, his wife apparently resented it on his behalf, and put an end to his social relations with the rest of his colleagues as a result.

The recruitment of a new chairman was a priority task to which Adolf Grünbaum and I put our minds. Various efforts had already been made, but all had proved abortive and it was time to tackle the problem afresh. Adolf suggested an idea which I supported enthusiastically—that we should recruit Kurt Baier, who was then the philosophy chairman at the Australian National University in Canberra. Because of the distance involved, this had to be done without the usual for-malities of an interview, but with Charlie Peake's energetic support the effort was pushed through by correspondence to a successful conclusion. In the Fall of 1962 Kurt joined the Pitt department, a development which proved to be a stroke of good fortune for our common venture.

Kurt had been born in Vienna and had finished his legal training at the university there. In the wake of the *Anschluss* he had fled to England as a refugee, and with the outbreak of World War II was sent on to Australia as an emerging national. There he in due course did military service. After the war he returned to England for an Oxford D. Phil. and then took up an academic post in Australia. There his academic career had prospered, and he had acquired an attractive and gifted wife, Annette, a native New Zealander who was also a very able philosopher. A man of much charm and good humor, Kurt was an adept administrator who brought an urbane efficiency to the affairs of the department and with Annette's help did much to enliven the personal contact among its members.

It was a good time to have a capable hand at the helm. The people of limited ability—or less—who populated the depart-ment at this stage had to be encouraged to move on their way. And various opportunities were waiting to be seized. In par-ticular, great rumbling were shaking the Yale department and some very able people were sufficiently disgruntled to be willing to leave. Within a three year period, we recruited four Yale philosophers; first Nuel Belnap and Wilfrid Sellars (1963), then Jerome Schneewind (1964), and finally Alan Ross Ander-son (1965). This rapid accession of strength went a long way towards making the department into one of real distinction.

The most formidable of our Yale acquisitions was Wilfrid Sellars. Born in 1912 and then just past fifty years of age, he was now entering upon the period of his greatest philosophi-cal creativity. A stimulating teacher and pleasant colleague, he possessed a somewhat convoluted personality that made personal closeness difficult. But I have always admired Wil-frid as an immensely gifted philosopher and value him as a prime asset of our department. Periodically we lunch to-gether to commune about departmental affairs (always at the

Pittsburgh Athletic Association in Oakland, his invariable luncheon haunt). We generally see eye-to-eye on ends and usually on means as well.

The team of Anderson and Belnap afforded Pitt a potent resource in the area of logic. Alan Anderson was a logician of great creativity and insight—and a thoroughly delightful person to boot. His student, Nuel Belnap, was more complex, a creature of moods and crotchets who could also manifest great personal charm. He too was a logician of formidable capabilities. Alan and Nuel worked well together, making a smooth transition from the master-student relationship to collaborative idiosyncratic logical doctrines, they have maintained an open-minded accessibility to their colleagues of different persuasions.

The mid-1960's also saw the arrival of Richard Gale on an NSF postgraduate fellowship, together with his charming Japanese wife, Maya. A fellow of infinite jest, Richard soon found many friend in the department (as well as one or two no less enthusiastic detractors). We persuaded him to stay on—at first temporarily and then as part of the permanent establishment. Concealing a deep and vulnerable personality behind a veneer of surface conviviality, Richard has, over the years, been one of my good friends in the department. I regard him as a philosopher of deep dedication and very substantial ability.

It soon came to view once again that I had been fortunate in entering into academic work at a good time. The administrators of the old school, whose view of the world had been formed during the hardships of academic management in the 1930's, were moving towards retirement by the late 1950's and the cheese-paring attitudes of that difficult era were giving way to a new era of expansiveness. While Lehigh was still to some extent caught up in the trammels of this fading ethos, Pittsburgh under Litchfield had moved well beyond it. It had become an institution willing to back academic values in a forward-looking spirit, expending administrative time, effort, and resources on strengthening even so abstruse a subject as philosophy.

As to my own work, the first order to business after settling at Pitt was to clear the decks of unfinished projects left over from Lehigh days. And so I now completed *The Development of Arabic Logic* (a "Cook's tour" of medieval work in this field), and finished the *Introduction to Logic* which had been begun at Lehigh. I also wrote a small book on *Hypothetical Reasoning* to develop and extend the lines of thought begun with the "Belief-Contravening Suppositions" paper of 1959. Moreover, I now reached back to Princeton days and carried out my long-standing plan of writing an introduction to the philosophy of Leibniz, drawing on some of the materials developed in my doctoral dissertation. Almost overnight I changed from a writer of papers into an author of books.

During this period I came to occupy myself more extensively with symbolic logic and a steady stream of work in this field now began to flow from my pen. My attitude towards this subject was of a somewhat unorthodox slant. For I never looked on logic as an accomplished fact—a field fully formed and merely in need of systematization and exposition, but saw it as an unfinished and malleable discipline to be reworked and structured for the sake of its applications. I always gravitated towards those logical issues and areas that were of potential utility for the elucidation and treatment of philosophical issues, and viewed logic not just as a self-contained discipline, but as a body of machinery for the accomplishment of extralogical tasks.

In the spring of 1963 the philosophy department was ejected from the Cathedral of Learning. We had been sharing the eighth floor with the Computing Center, but now they were entering a phase of growth in personnel and equipment. It came to a choice between moving this center at a cost of thousands or of moving the philosophers and their handful of books. Needless to say, the finger was pointed at us. We were offered the seventh floor of the old Schenley Hotel across from the Cathedral, which had been used as a dormitory, but now, with the completion of the new tower residence halls, was being refurbished as the Student Union. And here I acquired as my office the very pleasant paneled Southeast corner room which I occupy to this day, and which had been an element of stability amidst many changes in the circumstances of my life.

Our main common effort during my first years at Pitt was devoted to building up a good graduate program in philosophy. And in this respect the move to Pittsburgh more than lived up to expectations, for the chance to teach graduate students was a highly profitable and enjoyable experience for me. Beginning in 1961 with a virtual *tabula rasa*, with little on hand by way of students, traditions, or instructional curriculum, we soon forged a strong program. We were enthusiastic and determined—and lucky in that some of the very best students we ever graduated came during those early years—Brian Skyrms, Ernest Sosa, and Bas van Fraassen to name only a few. The chance to associate with really able young workers in one's academic field is a uniquely rewarding and stimulating experience. (To speak of "teaching" them would be misleading, for the process of instruction is in such cases reciprocal.)

By the middle of the 1960's, as the department expanded, it developed a program of philosophical training that was as good as any on the country. Various studies of academic quality—in particular those of the American Council on Education—now began to indicate Pitt's philosophy department to be one of the top three or four in the U.S. Not only did we have an outstandingly able faculty, but we worked well together in an effective collaboration to this effort—in instruction, in program design, in recruitment efforts, in setting and maintaining a high professional standard. I myself contributed to this result in promoting the visibility of the department not only through my own work, but now also by founding the *American Philosophical Quarterly*.

Late in 1962 word was circulated at Pitt that the Chancellor was eager for the University Press to expand its list of scholarly journals, confined in those days to two or three somewhat frail entries. I had long realized that the number of philosophy journals was not keeping pace with the rapid expansion of personnel and activities. After some exploration, I thus proposed to the University the founding of a new scholarly journal in philosophy, and the result was the organization in 1963 of the *American Philosophical Quarterly* to be published by the University of Pittsburgh Press in a large double-column format (borrowed from the *Journal of the American Oriental Society*). Publication commenced in 1964 and the reception of the enterprise was favorable from the very outset. Everything went along swimmingly until the journal—The APQ as it soon became to be known throughout the profession—was suddenly plunged into a struggle for its very existence in early 1965. For the University now sank into the abyss of a financial crisis whose steady unfolding led to the departure of Chancellor Litchfield. Drastic economics were introduced into the operations of the University Press, and in consequence, Frederick Hetzel, then—as now—its Director, decided (sensibly in the circumstances) to withdraw the Press from journal publication and to concentrate its reduced resources wholly on books. Suddenly and unexpectedly the APQ was left high and dry without any publisher. The University severed its relationship to the journal, and I found myself saddled with the task of providing for its continued existence.

Rapid measures were called for, and after various consultations the problem was resolved in a most happy way when the Oxford publishing firm of Basil Blackwell—which already issued such reputable philosophical journals as *Mind* and *Analysis*—agreed to take the journal on. The negotiations with their managing director Henry Schollick, evolved smoothly, and the APQ went ahead most satisfactorily under these new auspices. By the time of its 10th anniversary in 1974, its subscribership had climbed above the 1,600 mark. All the indications are that in the initial decade of its existence this publication has managed to establish itself as one of the very best philosophy journals in the English speaking world.

For me personally, the APQ editorship has been a mixed blessing. On the one hand, success of my literary brainchild has been a source of satisfaction. On the other hand, I have also had to pay a price. The fact that I annually manage to displease some 300 colleagues with rejection slips has meant inevitable failure whenever my name has been put forward in candidacy for any genuinely elective office in professional associations. Colleagues to whom one has said "No" seemingly welcome the chance to reciprocate. Over the years I have occupied positions of considerable responsibility and trust in such organizations, but always by way of essentially appointive offices.

During this period I did a modest amount of miscellaneous reading wholly outside the domain of professional duty, averaging perhaps one book a month. To some extent this was sheer entertainment or escapism—a matter of relaxation and "breaking the circuits" of my official lines of thought. But half of it—the reading of autobiographies, biographies, and biographical novels (in particular Anthony Trollope's)—had a utilitarian aspect in providing grist for the philosophical contemplation of the structure of human life and the condition of man—an interest not unconnected with my eventual decision to write these pages.

The presidential election of 1964 was the first occasion on which I broke my by then usual allegiance to the Republican party—to vote *against* Barry Goldwater (rather than *for* Lyndon Johnson). I quite mistakenly gave credence to the propaganda—blared with mindless unanimity throughout the media—that pictured Lyndon Johnson as the personification of sweet reasonableness and peacemaking in contrast to Barry Goldwater's warmongering. As it was, the nation actually got Goldwater's policies behind the screen of Johnson's machiavellianism.

My position in national politics has always been straightforward. In my teens, I felt that FDR could do no wrong. He was the leader in power in a country that had opened its doors to my family at the time of our emigration from Germany, and stood in the role of our host-in-chief as it were. Thereafter, I came, during my twenties, to favor the Republicans, thanks to the counterproductive intervention of Capt. Stevenson of the U.S.M.C. in the 1952 presidential campaign. While my commitment to this party was by no means total, I judged that the Republican party leaders, on balance, possess a greater acumen in military and international affairs, and I have always felt that this was the area that really counted. A misstep in domestic policy or economic affairs might cause discomfort, but one in international affairs might get us all killed in this nuclear age.

A highlight of this period was the opportunity to pay a week's visit to Istanbul in September of 1964. This foray had a very particular purpose: to examine at first hand a certain Arabic manuscript on which I had been writing in connection with my study of the 4th figure of the syllogism.[1] I stayed at the Hilton Hotel and had a relatively pleasant time of it, apart from a stomach upset induced by venturing outside the orbit of European restaurants and sleep-deprivation due to a Turkish-style rock-concert extending far into each night at a nearby soccer stadium. Working in the Aya Sofya Library was a fascinating experience—and also a culturally broadening one, seeing that my omission to pay *baksheesh* to the library attendant led to my manuscripts becoming "lost" on the second day of my labors. (A kindly scholar in the library soon put me straight.) My great uncle Oskar's honorary niece, Dr. Ayla König, gave me guided tours of Istanbul and its environs (including the principal Bazaar, the offshore islands, the Sultan's palace, etc.). Oskar himself was away in Ankara—I suspect out of a purposeful reluctance to meet his remote relation and old correspondent face to face.

Around this time, I entered into a collaboration with the economist Herbert Simon of the neighboring Carnegie Mellon University. I had known Herb since RAND Corporation days, and should perhaps have described him as a polymath rather than an economist because of the impressive manysidedness of his talents and abilities. Together we wrote a paper on "Cause and Counterfactual," ultimately published in *Philosophy of Science* in 1966. The paper combined in fruitful symbiosis long-standing ideas of Herb's about causality with my own work on the epistemology of counterfactual hypotheses. I regard it as something of a model instance of interdisciplinary collaboration.

During this period my marriage went through a pattern of deterioration along by now familiar lines. At first, the business of resettling in a new environment, making new friends—and above all raising an infant daughter—had, as was usual with us, improved matters by providing external outlets for internal tensions and frictions. But gradually, as normalization proceeded and our lives settled into a stable pattern, all the old difficulties surfaced once again, and the 1963-65 period saw an ongoing intensification of these pressures. As a new academic setting released new energies and activities in me, Frances wrapped herself up ever more tightly in a cocoon of disapproval and resentment towards my work. By mid-1965 the situation had deteriorated to a point where I felt that even the hackneyed though telling argument that a married couple must remain together "for the sake of the child" no longer mattered. I have long puzzled over what impelled Frances into the ever-recurrent paroxysms of bitter discontent and recrimination. In retrospect, I can only conjecture that she was psychologically unable to share a husband with the requirements of a professionally demanding career.

This created an impasse. For twenty years, life's course had been shaping me step by step into a productive professor of philosophy. Even if I had wanted to reorient myself—which I did not—there is little I could have done about it. It became increasingly clear that no tolerable *modus vivendi* could be reached. By the summer of 1965 I had come to a settled resolve that there was no alternative to separation.

Shakespeare's *Hamlet* drives home the lesson that it is one thing to recognize a step as necessary, but something else to carry it out. Repeated trials showed the futility of trying through discussion to work out an agreed plan for "a parting of the ways." There was nothing for it but to take matters into my own hands by a unilateral step. One day in September of 1965 (virtually fourteen years to the day after our marriage in 1951) I simply did not return home after work, but moved into a room in the Webster Hall Hotel, having left behind a note to explain what was happening. This set up a flurry of activity—interviews with a teary Frances, the well-meant intervention of friends, and so on. But the situation was suddenly transfigured by Elizabeth's breaking her arm in a bicycle accident. We were reunited in the hospital, and I then returned to the Tennyson Avenue house, determined to pave the way for a more orderly separation. The next few months were difficult—the less said of them the better. But in March of 1966 I finally and decisively betook myself to a one-bedroom, furnished apartment in the Ruskin Apartments near the Cathedral of Learning in Oakland.

I had not anticipated the extent to which the depression and discouragement that goes with an upheaval of this sort create a destructive cycle. A man accustomed to life in domestic circumstances—a wife (however problematic), a child, and a dog, a house with garden and neighbors—cannot but feel painfully lonely in a small empty apartment. Above all, I missed Elizabeth intensely. Then just six years old and starting her school career in the first grade at Winchester Thurston School in Shadyside, she was a charming little girl at a really delightful stage of development. Though I never really doubted the rightness and necessity of my move, there is no doubt that the spring of 1966 was for me a time of distress and anguish of spirit. I simply lived on from day to day, clutching tight to my work as a sheet-anchor that provided a much-needed element of stability and balance in my life. Had there not been the absorption of my work to sustain me, I might well have broken down. During these difficult days, my old friend Adolf Grünbaum gave me moral support in a way that meant much to me and for which I shall always be grateful.

I lived in the Ruskin Apartments that summer, but in August 1966 moved to a pleasant two-bedroom apartment in a large stone house at 920 College Avenue in Shadyside section of town. I furnished the place with things bought very inexpensively in second-hand stores and "antique" shops. The process of homemaking helped to lift the fog of depression.

It is pointless to give more than a bare outline of the melancholy process of the ultimate dissolution of the marriage. In the fall of 1966 a separation agreement was arrived at with difficulty, and in the spring of 1967 a property settlement was worked out, which was followed by the formal divorce in July of that year. The settlement was financially ruinous for me: the Tennyson Avenue house and all its content and accouterments save for a few scraps of furniture became the property of my former wife, together with the whole of our savings, making a literal (if belated) truth of the marital promise "with all my worldly goods I thee endow." Also, a sum which at that stage exceeded half of my after-tax income from the University was to be paid for alimony and child support for the next fourteen years. On top of that, I had to pay a total of $4,000 to square the lawyers on both sides, a colossal sum as it then seemed to me, which I had to borrow since all existing assets had gone into the property settlement. Considering my resources at the time the burden was crushing. But I assumed it without hesitation and without dismay, seeing it as the only feasible way of putting an intolerable situation behind me.

A common quip has it that the only divorce worth having is an acrimonious one. (If there's any good feeling between the parties, what's the point of divorce?) But the lever of acrimony must find some *point d'appui*. Tragically, it was Elizabeth in the present case. I made no difficulties whatever about property of finances. Frances got whatever she and her lawyer saw fit to ask for. But the human element was more problematic. Frances was adamant on one point—there was to be no sharing of Elizabeth, no visitation rights, no access to her at all. I could not bring myself to accept this, and sought remedy in the courts. The wheels of justice ground slowly, and Frances fought every inch of the way. The hiring of lawyers and psychologists was the least of it. What I felt most keenly was the extent to which the child herself was pressed into service in this battle. For years I labored as best I could under the straightjacket of the occasional weekend visits I was able the extract through the legal process. I struggled to create some spark of intimacy and good feeling, but gradually I could sense the ebbing away of any shred of affection on my daughter's part. This erosion of my once-happy relationship with Elizabeth had been a source of much distress to me over the years.

This period of the ending of my marriage was certainly a time of pain, trial, and tribulation. Fortunately, the inexorable passage of time slowly led me back to a more cheerful outlook and restored normalcy to my attitudes and my social relationships.

One useful distraction during this difficult time was a collaborative research project on "Technology and Values"—a philosophical inquiry into the impact of technological change on human values sponsored by the Carnegie Corporation of New York and the International Business Machines Corporation who, in the ethos of the time, wanted to do something humanistic. (A decade later they would have sponsored a television program!) After trying in vain to interest philosophers at other institutions in an "applied" a venture, they came to Pittsburgh late in 1964, and persuaded the Department to take this on under the joint direction of Kurt Baier and myself. We organized the effort during the 1965-6 academic year, and eventually carried it through to a reasonable conclusion. The results of the inquiry were put into print in the book *Values and the Future* issued by the Free Press (in 1969—after much delay). An unqualified positive assessment of the project is doubtless unwarranted, but it was at any rate, a beginning—a pioneering foray into little-charted territory.

As Kurt Baier and I devoted part of our efforts to this project, we used the opportunity to bring some interesting visitors into the department as teaching replacements. On this basis we profited from the presence of some of the more venturesome spirits of European philosophy. I myself particularly enjoyed the visits that I. M. Bochenski of Freiburg and G. H. von Wright of Helsinki made in Pittsburgh in this connection.

For myself, the principal product of the "Values Project" (as we called it) was the writing of a little book on *Distributive Justice*—my first substantial venture into social philosophy—which I tried to unravel a knotty tangle of economic issues often obscured by political passion. It clear and dispassionate attention to matters of practical policy stood (so it seemed to me) in favorable contrast to the abstract generalities of most moral and social philosophy during the 1960's, when "applied philosophy" had not attained the vogue it was later to achieve.

Apart from work on the values project, the bulk of my professional attention during this 1961-1966 period focused on two not wholly unrelated, but still very disparate fields: the work of the Arabian logicians of the middle ages, and certain topics in symbolic logic. The half-dozen books I produced during these years are (if I myself may say so) not without merit, but nevertheless strike me in retrospect as afflicted with a certain shortcoming implicit in the very subject-matter to which they devote themselves. As late as the mid-1960's, something held me back from working creatively at the center of philosophy itself rather than merely nibbling around its edges. Only the calming atmosphere of a more settled existence ultimately encouraged me to undertake some really creative work on centrally philosophical issues.

The first phase of my life in Pittsburgh thus ended in dissonance. On the professional side I was now firmly settled in at a major university of large potential, and I had managed to accomplish work that secured me a place in the top stratum of academic philosophy. On the personal side, however, there was a state of unsettlement that could—conceivably—have blunted my potential as a creative scholar. Begun in hopefulness, this period closed in a condition of despondency and darkness of spirit, a condition that only passing time and changed circumstances would be able to erase.

NOTES

1. Ultimately published as *Galen and the Syllogism* (Pittsburgh: University of Pittsburgh Press, 1966).

Eleven

PITTSBURGH:
THE YEARS OF CHANGE
1966-1971 (AGE 38-42)

The 1966-67 academic year saw the beginning of a new phase in the unfolding of my professional career. For now, as I was approaching my fortieth year, a decade after resuming academic pursuits at Lehigh in 1957, my stature in the profession had prospered to a point where the University of Pittsburgh saw fit to accord me the distinction of designation as "Research Professor." This, of course, pleased me greatly. But the horizons were not unclouded. For the affairs of Pitt's philosophy department were reaching a crossroads.

After five years of service as departmental chairman, Kurt Baier was eager to resume writing and teaching. Since the most senior professors, who held "special title" appointments—Adolf Grünbaum, Wilfrid Sellars, and now myself —were exempted from this service, the Executive Committee of the department, after due deliberation, recommended to the dean that our colleague Alan Ross Anderson be invited to serve as chairman. This invitation—made with my own enthusiastic support—was in due course extended, and so it came to pass the Alan served as chairman from 1967 to 1970. But his tenure of this office was not without problems.

Able logician and fine person though he was, Alan was not cut out for administrative work. Early harbingers of the medical problems that brought him to a premature grave at the age of 48 in 1973 were already causing him difficulties. This left him with little patience for the minutiae of academic management. He tended to leave to others (often secretaries) the myriad small details whose proper handling makes for a well-run operation—without adequate supervision and with sometimes unfortunate results. Departmental affairs suffered visibly from the lack of a clear administrative focus. On the other hand, Alan was a fine scholar, a delightful colleague, and a man of truly superior quality—as was shown by his fortitude in the face of the cancer that ultimately laid him low. I had great liking and respect for him—and indeed had been a prime instrument in his recruitment to Pittsburgh.

The absence of a firm hand at the helm unfortunately brought many centrifugal forces into play. And this occurred at just the wrong time. For this was a period of stress and challenge—the era of Vietnam-connected student unrest across America's campuses.

The war in Indo-China had been on my mind ever since the days of my Marine Corps service. Towards its end, in 1953, an old-line sergeant harangued us as follows. We draftees who were about to be released ought not to think that we were saying good-bye to the Corps for good. The efforts of the French in Indo-China were failing, and the U.S.A. would have to go in to bail them out. We would soon be back in the Marines to assist in this enterprise. So prophisized the old sergeant, and I suppose one must give him credit for long-range vision. But, fortunately for me and my contemporaries, Ike did not see the matter in the same light, and entry of American soldiers into this conflict had to await the administration of his Democratic successor. But then as our involvement grew, something occurred for which my own generation, reared in the attitudes of the Second World War, was quite unprepared—the tide of political paranoia that swept over America's youth in the late 1960's. The graduate schools were filled in those days with young men who entered the academic arena to escape the draft and avoid "the real world" rather than because they felt any calling to the professional work in teaching and research. However, in taking refuge in academia, they did not leave behind their disenchantment with the existing order of things and their desire to "reform" it to their liking and convenience, but redirected their discontent at the established order of the academic world itself. Fortunately, we at Pitt experienced only relatively mild manifestations of these phenomena, but even that little was more then enough to be both dismaying and eye-opening. The malign developments of this period, and the fervor of its ongoing assault on traditional academic standards and values in the name of the politics of liberation, cannot be explained short of invoking the mechanisms of mob psychology. No observer of the academic scene in those days could ever again feel unmixed confidence that the era of "revolutionary excesses" was safely confined to the historic past.

In 1970, however, the Philosophy Department's affairs began to look up. In the fall of that year Gerald J. Massey succeeded to the chairmanship. Jerry was a highly conscientious and efficient administrator, and it was reassuring to sense a firm hand on the wheel once again. It took about two years to erase fully the disorientation and loss of morale that had come to infect the operation in Alan Anderson's administration. But in time the sense of common purpose and collaborative effort that had characterized the department in the earlier years of Kurt Baier's chairmanship was again restored—now in the more difficult circumstances of a much-enlarged department of twenty-four faculty members as compared with the dozen of the mid-1960's. We were most fortunate to find a person of Jerry Massey's superb administrative talents at exactly the moment when we needed this.

Among the offerings I taught this period, the most regular repeaters were courses on Leibniz, on Kant, on the theory of knowledge, and on the theory of induction and confirmation. All told, my teaching at Pitt has been pretty evenly divided between undergraduate courses and graduate courses, and I think they have been pretty evenly successful as well. During the hey-day of the era of the "student unrest" of the 1968-69 period, I had the repute of being a hard-liner, because I strongly supported the maintenance of examination requirements and was in general opposed to the then-rampant assault on all established academic standards in the name of *liberté, egalité, fraternité*, or whatever. For a time (roughly 1968-1971) this impeded my rapport with some of the graduate students, but, happily, the wind changed with the gradual restoration of an ethos more oriented towards learning than societal transformation.

The cloud of the academic turmoil of the late 60's had its silver lining when Wesley Wesley Posvar came to Pitt from the Air Force Academy to be our new chancellor. Less driven and less flamboyant than Edward Litchfield had been, he was also far more approachable and had his feet more firmly planted on the ground. Buoyant and positive in outlook, he had a real dedication to the academic venture, and was able to exercise a cheerful and calming influence upon the turbulent waters into which he had sailed. Coming at the end of a period of over-rapid growth, his administration has seen ongoing efforts to maximize opportunities in times difficult both economically and politically—particularly since a university must nowadays come to terms with pressures emanating from the wider community of which it is a part. An academic administrator has many constituencies, and is a servant to many masters. It is no small compliment to say that Wes Posvar has managed to walk this difficult and wobbly tightrope for years on end without ever falling off. (Unfortunately for Pitt—and for himself—he stayed in office until 1991, which prolonged his service beyond the time of its effectiveness.)

The 1967-68 academic year also proved to be a turning-point in my personal life. I had known Dorothy Henle since 1961, when Oliver Reiser and I interviewed and hired her as Administrative Secretary for the Philosophy Department, a year or so after she had initially come to the University of Pittsburgh to work in the Fund Raising Office. With the establishment of the *American Philosophical Quarterly* in 1963, she had become my Editorial Assistant for the journal. For years she had been part of the familiar, virtually unnoticed stage-setting of my workday world. But now, in the altered condition on my life that ensued upon the breakdown of my marriage, I gradually began to take notice. We sometimes played tennis at the Chatham College courts and attended an occasional symphony or movie together. As 1967 moved on, we saw more and more of one another. Dorothy was a charming, vivacious, and delightful young lady—endowed with an impressive degree of personal warmth and outgoing sociability. I was soon head of heels in love with her. In July of 1967 my divorce was finalized, and by the end of the year Dorothy and I were engaged. A new and much happier era of my personal life was now inaugurated.

At around this time I began to attend Sunday services in St. Paul's Cathedral in Oakland. Dorothy was a committed Catholic and it seemed sensible that we should join in worship. I cannot honestly say that I was drawn to Roman Catholicism on strictly theological or doctrinal grounds, although the theatrical aspect of the mass did evoke some response in my traditionalist nature. With each passing year since the iconoclastic time of adolescence, I have come to feel more strongly about the positive role of the traditional forms—that of worship included—in the shaping of a well-ordered and civilized life. To be sure, matters of doctrine or dogma never stirred me deeply. There are many ways to God, and I cannot believe that He is greatly concerned about the particular route one chooses. The Quaker deemphasis of matters of ritual (which I have always found congenial) itself seemed to prepare me to regard such matters of form as relatively unimportant, and so paved the way to acceptance of a highly ritualized religion.

On February 10, 1968 Dorothy and I were married in a small private ceremony at her brother's Penn Hills home. At first we continued to reside in the small but comfortable apartment at 920 College Avenue where I had been living since the summer of 1966. It was the middle of term-time at Pitt and we did not have a real "honeymoon." But late that April we set out to spend the summer in Europe. After a brief visit in Helsinki, we proceeded to Oxford for the Trinity Term (late April through late June), where I conducted a seminar on imperatives jointly with Richard M. Hare. We lived in Iffley in the just-completed Beechwood Flats apartments belonging to All-Souls College. In the course of our stay we came to like Oxford very much indeed. So much so, that we made the resolution—soon to be put into effect—of returning regularly to Oxford in the summers.

After the end of the Oxford term we took a week's holiday at Hastings—some of it at the television set watching the Wimbledon tennis-matches, but also making touristic excursions to Rye, Salisbury, Bath, and other spots of interest. In July we set out for the Continent in our ancient green Hillman car, crossing the channel on the Air Ferry. First we visited German relations in Hagen, and then set out on a circuit of lectures at various German universities, which enabled me to keep in touch with various German academic friends, including Albert Menne in Hamburg, Günther Patzig in Göttingen, Lothar Schäffer in Tübingen, and Wilhelm Totok in Hannover. Finally we spent a restful and very happy few days at Hinterzarten in the Black Forest. This was my first really extensive visit in Germany since leaving in 1938, and it took place under ideally pleasant circumstances.

Upon returning to England we stayed in London from late July to early August, combining tourism with my work at the British Museum on the Arabic manuscript by al-Shirwani that was eventually to be the core of my 1975 essay on temporal modalities in Arabic Logic.[1] In early August we returned to the Continent, making a trip up the Rhine by steamer from Mainz to Switzerland. There we stayed for a few days at Basle and then proceeded to the 13th World Congress of Philosophy in Vienna.

In early September we returned to the apartment on College Avenue in Pittsburgh. We now began househunting in earnest, for as the summer drew to a close Dorothy was just giving the early indications of pregnancy. We looked at almost a hundred houses all over the eastern section of Pittsburgh, but at last found an attractive, 1920's colonial-style brick house at 1200 Sheridan Avenue in the Highland Park section of Pittsburgh, which we bought in December of 1968. The house is compact yet roomy (with five bedrooms). Its three-storied layout is very conveniently arranged, and even before there were children we never felt that we rattled about the place. The location is in some ways less than perfect—Highland Park is rather far out from town, the University, etc.—but the house itself and its neighborhood have been thoroughly satisfactory. At any rate, it is here that we reside, live, and raise our family down to the present writing in 1974.

The neighbors—as it eventuated—were one of the real assets of the place. There were the Dickson Shaws across the way, who are the most pleasant and helpful neighbors imaginable; the Charles McGuires, whose daughter Vickie was for several years our babysitter and twice accompanied us on summer visits to England; the Samuel Passafiumes, whose mother Mimi lives a couple of blocks away and has for many years been our much-appreciated babysitter; and others as well. The human element is critical to the pleasantness of a residential site, and these neighbors have unquestionably made Sheridan Avenue a good place to be.

Having experienced very straightened circumstances in the impressionable first years after my family's emigration to the U.S.A., I have generally been prudent with money, doing without whatever I could not afford to buy outright, so as to avoid burdening the future with the debts of the present. But the years after the financially crushing divorce settlement of 1967 saw me becoming even more careful in money matters. I came to realize that drastic measures would be needed if I were ever again to stand on firm financial ground. A rigid frugality gradually remedied the situation and rebuilt my shattered finances. Much credit also belongs to Dorothy, who is a good manager and, while not a penny pincher, avoids anything approaching extravagance. I hope against hope that my children can learn to be sensible about money without acquiring this quality—as I myself did—in the hard school of financial stringency.

A succession of part-time visiting professorships—at Temple University during 1968-9, and the University of Western Ontario after 1970—were also helpful in rebuilding the family exchequer. (Our regular subsequent excursions to Oxford would almost certainly have been impossible without them.) Moreover, these academic visits were very useful to me in other ways. They enabled me to try out some lecture materials of a more experimental sort than might have been convenient on home ground, and various books of mine went through their trial-runs on such occasions.

With the passage of years I learned one valuable lesson: one must not sit back in life and await the development of favorable openings and opportunities—one must strive to *make* them happen, working to cultivate and develop them. (For example, I could well have waited until doomsday for the editorship of a major journal to come my way had I not simply set to and organized the *American Philosophical Quarterly* in the early 1960s.) To be sure, there must be opportunities, but these are usually so seminal as to be unrecognizable unless one is on the look-out. Good things are less likely to come to those who only sit and wait than to those who bestir themselves towards their realization. The wise man, said Plautus, shapes his own fortune (*sapiens ipse fingit fortunam sibi*), which may be a bit optimistic, but undoubtedly indicates what he should at any rate *try* to do.

Dorothy and I moved into the Sheridan Avenue house in January of 1969 just in time to prepare the nursery for occupancy. With the birth of Mark in April of that year and of Owen in November of the following year we were no longer a "couple" but a *family*, with two active and lively little boys. Aging is a centrifugal process. Youth is self-centered, but with the passage of years and the accumulation of experience there comes a gradual externalization of concern to embrace one's children and family connections. The arrival of Mark and Owen reoriented the pattern of our existence. There is no denying that the boys are sometimes a source of vexation and often a source of anxiety, but they are priceless enrichments of our lives.

I always sought a close interaction with my children, even when they were very little. I did my share—perhaps by the prevailing standards of the day more than my share—of feeding, diapering, and baby-minding. And of course as the boys grew up and could be played with and read to, we became very close indeed. A close relationship with one's children is surely among the most satisfying experiences of life.

Mark and Owen are active, bright and engaging little boys and a continuing source of pleasure and satisfaction to their parents. Few things in life give me greater joy than when one of the boys does something that makes me proud of him. I offer up a daily silent prayer for the success and for the happiness of my children, and to thank a kindly fate that has endowed them with the health, vitality, and charm they possess so abundantly. Their bodies require constant care and nurture and their minds amusement, stimulus, and information. It is difficult to know what to set down on paper about this sort of parental involvement—readers will either have a good idea through their own experience or will think the whole business rather bizarre.[2]

In the autumn of 1967, around the time when Dorothy and I became engaged, her sister Jacqueline married Peter F. Brown. The holder of a physics Ph. D. from Pitt, Peter is bluff, sociable, easygoing, and thoroughly good-humored. At that time he was employed at Bettis Laboratories, the nuclear research division of Westinghouse Electric Corporation. But he was not happy there, and in 1969 he took on a post as Assistant Professor in the Physics Department at Duquesne University. Dorothy was always close to her sister, who is in every way a delightful person. And so, as was only natural, the Peter Browns became a fixture in our lives, and our boys have made good friends of their daughter Alicia, who was born in 1970.

In August of 1969 the Browns accompanied us to Los Angeles for what was to be my final visit to RAND—now accompanied by baby Mark, born in April of that year. We spent some three very pleasant weeks, living in Brentwood admidst the old-time splendor of the "Villa Katzenstein"—a pre-war California-Spanish mansion that had once been the habitation of some movie mogul but now belonging to a family of this name. We did a good bit of tourism in Southern California (Disneyland, Marineland, Santa Barbara, etc.) At RAND interest had by this time shifted increasingly towards domestic affairs, and some of the themes I thought about on this occasion ultimately found their way into my book on *Welfare.*

In this connection, one public event of the late 1960's came home to me personally in an unlooked-for way. Ever since leaving RAND's employ in early 1957, I had been carried on their roster of consultants and had made occasional short visits to "keep in touch." Now, however came the time of the

Pentagon Papers scandal, when Daniel Ellsberg leaked to the *New York Times* a top secret Defense Department study of America's Vietnam War policies which he had illicitly copied whole on a consulting visit at RAND. This shook the RAND Corporation to its foundations. Harry Rowan, its new President, who in my day at RAND had been a minor planet to Albert Wohlstetter's sun, was now sacked, and everything was revamped—especially in the sphere of security. In rapid sequence the security clearances that gave consultants access to classified materials were first downgraded from *Top Secret* and then suspended altogether. It became clear that the relationship would be completely nominal, and I decided to terminate it. The RAND connection had, in any case, become of lessened interest to me over the years.

Colonial Williamsburg began to be a regular feature of our life at this stage. We first visited there in late 1969—again with baby Mark in tow. Almost every winter since we have set off on the eight hour drive to Colonial Williamsburg for a sort of mid-winter break in routine. We stay in the old-world comfort of the Williamsburg Inn, eat at the various colonial taverns, relax, rest, sightsee, and enjoy the off-season quiescence and old-world charm of this historical treasure-spot. The very uniformity of this experience: the helpful personnel of the Inn, the table-service of the "young gentlemen from the college of William and Mary" in the various public houses, the historic buildings, the Governor's Palace and its gardens, are all woven as ongoing threads into the fabric of our lives. (I pen these very words at one of the card tables of the Inn where I have often worked at my philosophical writings as well.) These visits contributed substantially to enlivening my interest in antiques, an interest that was to be pursued actively during our visits in England.

In 1968 I had the pleasure of editing a *Festschift* for my old teacher and friend Carl G. Hempel. It gave me much satisfaction to be able to acknowledge in this way my debt to someone I greatly admired and who had on various occasions been so helpful to me—who, indeed, from my earliest days as a philosopher had provided the role-model for a professor in the field.

In the early 1970's, work on issues of moral and social philosophy in the U.S.A. turned away from the abstract formalistic and linguistic concerns of the two prior decades, and addressed itself increasingly to the more substantive issues. Philosophy once more descended from its ivory tower to deal with those sorts of public policy concerns that preoccupy people in "the real world." The field of "applied ethics" sprung up and became fashionable. But while American academic philosophy arrived here in the early 70's, I myself was already on the scene in the 1960's, the book on *Distributive Justice* (1966) being a case in point here. The fate of my 1969 paper on the "Allocations of Exotic Medical Lifesaving Therapy" also exemplifies this circumstance. When medical ethics became popular among philosophers in the 1970's, this paper was one of the few things in print on the subject and thus, intrinsic merit aside, was reprinted and anthologized more often than anything else I ever wrote—I am aware of ten reprintings within some six years. (The enthusiastic reception of this paper rather discouraged than pleased me, because it drove home the not wholly welcome lesson that a philosopher gains easy access to people's attention only when he tells them what they are predisposed to listen to.) The book on *Welfare* which I wrote in 1970-71 was a later instance of this same tendency to philosophizing about issues of social concern. Its insistence that the best welfare program is a healthy economy is a lesson of the depression years that was seemingly forgotten in the America of the euphoric postwar years.

As the decade of the 60's drew to its close, I had attained a firm psychological base of operations. By now I had climbed the grassy pole of academic advancement to the pinnacle of a special professorship, and my family life was securely established through my marriage with Dorothy, the arrival of our first child, and our getting settled in our own home. These developments released new wellsprings of creative energy. Now forty years old, I had become a person of matured judgment and matured professional abilities as well. Sensing all this, I felt (no doubt subconsciously) that the time had come for me to undertake a work of larger scale than heretofore.

The timing for such a venturing forth was propitious. the period after the First World War had seen the diffusion of a more and more narrowly constricted view of the task of philosophy. The methodologically "hard" areas of philosophy, logic, the philosophy of mathematics, and the philosophy of science, were in; the methodologically "soft" and more speculative areas, metaphysics, substantive ethic, and social philosophy, were out. The spread of the logical positivist ideology so trenchantly articulated in A. J. Ayer's *Language, Truth, and Logic* typifies the culmination of this narrowing of views. Though I was myself largely reared in the ethos of this perspective, it gradually dawned on me that the mission of those of us who began to be active in philosophy after World War II was to reverse this impoverishment of our subject by the inter-war generation. Our task—as I saw it—was to work for a widened conception of the field, to effect broader synthesis, and to restore active concern for the historic problems of the traditional range of philosophical deliberation. We were to revive dedication to wholeness and system—not by abandoning the penchant for exactness and detail of the pre-war generation, but by fusing detail into meaningful structures, combining the older yearning for system with the new passion of exactness. It was thus to be our job to use the exact methods and rigorous standards of the inter-war generation as instruments for a renewed assault on the "big issues" of the field that had figured importantly in the historic span of philosophical theorizing.

More than any other creative intellectual discipline, philosophy has a special relationship to its past. Its task, to be sure, is not one of syncretism, of preserving and restructuring the tradition for its own sake. But is can always draw enormous profit from the work at hand by exploiting the ideas and arguments and visions of the traditions as a storehouse of tools for the accomplishment of these present labors. The basic issues of philosophy are perennial and crop up in a renewed, reacclimated guise in every era. And attention to the ways our predecessors have dealt with them is a resource of inestimable value in the accomplishment of our own work.

I was thus led to take a rather different view of the technical preoccupation of the minutiae of formal analysis which had come to the forefront in the philosophy during postwar years.

It seemed to me that the professions' passion for the detailed analysis of small-scale side-issues was getting out of hand. The situation was reminiscent of that of the simpleton who explained that he was looking for his purse on this side of the road because, while he dropped it on the other side, there was better light over here. All too often, philosophers were using their technical instruments on those issues of detail congenial to their application, rather than concentrating them on inherently important matters. Technical questions became preoccupations in their own right, rather than because of any significant bearing of the central problems of the field. Those who followed in the footsteps of Moore and Russell and Carnap often lost sight of the real problems—as these masters themselves never did. I viewed this tendency with increasing distaste, and felt that while detailed technical studies were indeed indispensable, their utility was purely instrumental, and lay wholly in their bearing on the large traditional issues of the field. Accordingly, when I now addressed myself to technical issues in logic and value-theory and philosophical history, I did so not simply for the sake of their intrinsic appeal, but because I saw a prospect of obtaining resources for addressing issues of wider philosophical significance.

This constructive orientation was important for me. In general, philosophers tend to fall into two classes: there are those who see themselves as *destroyers*—revolutionaries, demolition experts, removers of rubbish. The ancient skeptics exemplify this tendency, as do the Humean empiricists, and the logical positivists of the present century. On the other hand, there are the *builders* whose approach is conservative and who seek to secure and consolidate rather than to abolish received truth, with the key issues posed by questions such as: "What validates our standard logical procedures—or our moral judgments, or our cognitive claims, etc.?" Like Leibniz of Kant or Hegel, the builders too call ideas and conceptions into question, but with the very different positive aim of validating rather than destroying them. And while they too see the need for a fresh start (all serious philosophers do!), their orientation to the tradition is not one of abandonment but one of exploitation. It is certainly this latter, constructive and reconstructive school that commands my own allegiance.

Skepticism, negativism, and nihilism, may be a natural reaction to broken promises, but the risks of disappointment are surely preferable to the counsels of despair.

In any event, after 1968 the pattern of my philosophical work changed. For one thing, I stopped working on the history of Arabic philosophy (especially logic), thus putting an end to a venture commenced about a decade before. To be sure, I did no abandon my medieval Arabic concerns wholly without regret. But I had done pretty well everything I could readily do with the limited resources at my disposal. (I also sensed that while my philosophical colleagues were for the most part utterly indifferent to this work, some among them were actually hostile to it—unthinking partisans caught up in the anti-Arab ethos of Near Eastern strife.)

I now became increasingly preoccupied with mainstream philosophical issues of epistemology and metaphysics, and my philosophical work gradually came to assume a more continuous direction and more systematic aspect. The series of books that emerged so readily from my pen in the years after 1969—beginning with *The Coherence Theory of Truth*—were a systematic development of ideas launched during the just-preceding period and represented the culmination of lines of thought that originated at that stage. The fundamentals of methodological pragmatism were implicit in the last chapter of *Many-Valued Logic* (written in 1967; published in 1969). The imputational theory of lawfulness and the thesis of the mind-dependence of possibility go back to my essay in the *Festschrift* for C. G. Hempel (written 1968; published 1969), and this idealistic approach to natural philosophy was further developed in *Scientific Explanation* (written 1968-9; published 1970). These writings marked a turning point in my development as a philosopher.

I recall well how the key ideas of my idealistic theory of natural laws—of "lawfulness as imputation"—came to me in 1968 during work on this project while awaiting the delivery of Arabic manuscripts in the Oriental Reading Room of the British Museum. It struck me that what a law *states* is a mere generalization, but what marks this generalization as something special in our sight—and renders it something we see as a genuine *law* of nature—is the role that we assign to it is inference. Lawfulness is thus not a matter of what the law-statement *says*, but how it is *used* in the systematization of knowledge—the sort of role that we impute to it. These ideas provided an impetus to idealist lines of thought and marked the onset of my commitment to a philosophical idealism which teaches that the mind is itself involved in the conceptual constitution of objects of our knowledge.

My drift towards idealism was largely impelled by the realization, driven home through studies of the history of science, that scientific discovery is not a matter of "reading off what is writ large in the book of nature," but is the result of *interaction* between the mind and nature. This interaction process is such that the contribution of our strictly mental contrivances is every bit as significant to the overall result as that of "the real world" we are concerned to study. what we all science is an intellectual process in which we *construct* a frangible picture of nature using conceptual materials of our own devising, materials which inevitably bear the imprint of their mentalistic origins. The articulation and development of this idealistic perspective became the governing principle of my philosophical labors, providing a unifying focus for my long-standing fascination with the question of how the human mind comes to cognitive terms with the world it lives in.

There now evolved what has become my characteristic method of book writing. At any given time, I have three books under way—one that is essentially completed and is just being polished and refined, one that is actually in progress of being written, and one that is only in prospect and for which I am merely gathering ideas and materials in a jumbled file of jottings, notes, and references. This last-named item is of enormous utility. It means that when serious work on a project commences, I do not face a *tabula rasa*, but can virtually assemble a first draft from pre-existing materials. This tripartite method has served me well, and I can recommend it unreservedly to anyone who has a large writing project in hand.

This turning of my work into a systematic direction yielded over the six years beginning with 1968, a rapid succession of books which (I could sense) put my reputation as a creative philosopher on an entirely different footing. In any case, the year 1970 turned out to be the *annus mirabilis* of my professional career. In January of the year, Dorothy and I journeyed to an ice-cold Chicago, where I was awarded an honorary doctorate of humane letters by Loyola University at a small but impressive ceremony where Hans Küng and C. P. Snow were also among the awardees. This development seemed to me surprising and unmerited, and yet at another level perhaps intelligible as a gesture of pluralistic outreach from a thoroughly Catholic institution towards a younger philosopher (not yet to be classed as an extinct volcano) who combined analytic predilections with a sincere commitment to *philosophia perennis* and a pronounced sympathy towards traditional values and human concerns. The year also saw my designation as University Professor of Philosophy at Pitt, and my being awarded a Guggenheim Fellowship. The University Professorship in particular marked a change in my status. Instituted at Harvard in the administration of J. B. Conant, it was the aim of such professorships "to free a few particularly distinguished scholars from routine duties"[3] and just then stands the straightjacket framework of academia's departments structure, with the idea that no more than one percent of the faculty of the institution is to qualify for such recognition. At the relatively young age of forty-two I had completed the climb to the top rung of the professorial ladder.

A new sensibility came upon me in the wake of these developments. Having now attained a place of some prominence in the profession, I felt that I had to live up to it by producing the sort of work one would expect of somebody in such a position. I saw my professional advance lass as a reward than as a challenge.

The 1967-71 period was thus a time of innovation in my life: a new family, a new atmosphere in my department, a newly enhanced standing in my profession, and a new spirit in my work. I had entered into this period from a slough of despond; I left it with a sense of personal and professional security and a hopeful outlook towards new worlds to conquer. The old saw that "life begins at forty" is often mocked, but in my own case there was a grain of truth to it.

NOTES

1. See G. F. Hourani (ed.), *Essays on Islamic Philosophy and Science* (Albany: State University of New York Press, 1975), pp. 189-221.

2. I might just mention one of the little rhyme-cum-action jingles I concocted for the children's amusement during their infancy:

> In the middle of the night
> Slinks the purple hippadite
> Slowly creeping, slowly crawling
> Slowly 'round the corners grawling*
> On the hunt for little boys
> Whom it uses for its toys
> When those little boys it catches
> Then it pounces, grabs, and snatches*
> And with many fearsome grickels
> Then those little boys it tickles*
> (Accompany with suitable actions.)

3. Compare G. B. Kistisakowsky's obituary of Conant in *Nature*, vol. 173 (29 June 1978), p. 794.

Twelve

PITTSBURGH AND OXFORD:
1971-1974 (Age 42-46)

During Bethlehem days I once remarked jokingly at a cocktail party that nothing worthwhile was to be found in Pennsylvania west of Lancaster. A friend replied: "The people if Pittsburgh would certainly resent that!" And so, as fate's little ironies would have it, I was not only to move to Pittsburgh, but have now (1974) lived here for over a dozen years, have married a Pittsburgh girl, and am in the process of raising a family of little Pittsburghers. I am destined, to all appearances, to pass the rest of my life in this bridge-laden city. And I have grown sufficiently fond of the place to view this prospect, if not with unalloyed joy, at any rate quite without dismay. Pittsburgh has many assets as a community, and there is much about the town that is thoroughly likeable. In particular, Pittsburgh is a sensible place, where people tend to have a realistic, down-to-earth set of values, and where the traditional American work-ethic is still very much alive. It is a congenial environment in which to live and to do one's work—be it physical or mental.

The University, of course, ranks high on my list of Pittsburgh plusses—its Department of Philosophy above all. By the late 1960's our reputation had become secure as one of the very best departmentsin the country. And unlike most, we have since Alan Anderson's time once again become a harmonious group, interacting well with each other and transacting our business in a spirit of mutual friendship and helpfulness. To be sure, the period of rapid growth that typified the era of Kurt Baier's chairmanship of the department was now over. But this itself was fortunate, since we now had assembled a faculty of some two dozen, as large a size as is compatible with functioning as a coherent unit. There is no question in my mind that Pittsburgh is a good place for a philosopher.

All the same, one thing that has made living in Pittsburgh pleasanter for me is the chance to get away for some months in summertime—the unique advantage of an academic career. In this regard, a major change in the pattern of our lives occurred in early 1971 with the purchase of 100 Victoria Road, Oxford, a brick row-house typical of the urban England of the Edwardian era. The acquisition of the house laid the basis for a new pattern of life, with summers regularly spent in Oxford. At this writing in the autumn of 1974, we have completed our fourth visit there, and this arrangement has worked out most happily. It is greatly relaxing and restorative to have each year a period of relief from the Pittsburgh routine—and from the Pittsburgh summer heat. In June of 1973, however, our English domicile was transferred to 6 Cunliffe Close, a compact modern townhouse in a brand-new development located on the former site of the Greycotes School. Closely proximate to the Summertown shopping area, the house is also within convenient walking distance of the city center, being situated off Banbury Road at a distance of just over a mile from Carfax. Its garden (of whose designing I am rather proud) is sufficiently straightforward that it is not too strugglesome to keep it in good appearance.

As a residential setting, North Oxford is thoroughly pleasant but in one way disappointing. It is surely one of the most attractive and best preserved Victorian suburbs in existence, with its variety of large handsome brick and stucco homes in every style—from neo-Gothic to neo-Georgian—that was popular towards the close of the last century. But its potential is sadly unrealized, for the charm of the place is somewhat spoiled by an aura of scruffiness. Far too often the houses are ill maintained and the gardens are ill tended. Absentee landlordism is the root of the trouble. Many of those splendid Edwardian homes are owned by colleges. Some have become offices. Others are rabbit warrens of student accommodations. Some are rented to college fellows in a misguided paternalistic concern to spare academics the vexations (and benefits) of home ownership. North Oxford amply illustrates the principle that a property not in the hands of an owner-occupier is a property that is neglected.

A link to the University has come to be forged in the course of these Oxonian visits. The sub-faculty of Philosophy has invited me on each occasion to give a series of lectures on topics of my choosing. And so during each Trinity (Summer) Term of this period, I have presented, in preliminary form, the substance of a book on which I was currently working.[1] This chance to float my trial balloons before a capable and critical audience—generally containing several other visiting academics—has proved very helpful.

It is somewhat difficult to articulate the charm Oxford has for me. Part of it lies in those dreamy spires and castellated college structures that do credit not only to their long-gone builders but also to those who strive nowadays to preserve the physical appearance of this ancient university. Part of it lies in the manifest commitment to academic excellence that pervades every corner of the place. Part of it lies in a near-Quixotic dedication to old ways—to ceremonious pomp and the maintenance of tradition for tradition's sake. Everywhere one finds manifestations of a commitment to scholarly values expressed in ways sometimes charming, sometimes silly, but always impressive to those who themselves hold such matters dear. The Enceinia ceremony is an academic exercise that encapsulates all this to perfection—timeworn Chancellor, blasé honorees, Latin citations, academic humor, and all.

Regular features of routine in our Oxford summer create a pleasurable continuity: the "trooping of the colors" for the Queen's birthday celebration and Wimbledon tennis on the BBC; lunches at the Royal Sun (a charming old Inn on the road to Woodstock that produces a delicious *quiche Lorraine*) an occasional dinner at the expensive but excellent Restaurant Elizabeth opposite Christ Church or at the inexpensive but pleasant La Dolce Vita in Summertown. Such occasions make a repetitive design in the fabric of experience that always give one something to look back upon—and forward to.

Oxford and its surroundings have much charm and are especially well suited to the interests and needs of a philosopher. The setting is also congenial to our entire family. Over the years Dorothy had made many friends and the boys have may playmates. Here too we have more time to entertain guests and visitors—activities which, though we enjoy them, are not easily fitted into the busier Pittsburgh routine. Our theater-going seems principally to involve attendance at the New Theater or at the Oxford Playhouse for its London-bound trial-balloon productions. We also manage to take in some three of four films each summer many of them children's productions that we share as a family.[2]

Another favorite diversion is tourism, with a special focus upon houses of historical interest, for over the years I have acquired something of an amateur interest in architecture—especially domestic architecture. We have managed to inspect a fair proportion of the many "stately homes" on display within 30 miles of Oxford. This interest in historic houses forms part of a wider interest in history and in historical artifacts. Some time each summer is devoted to antiquing in the Oxford area. We regularly participate in auctions (especially those conducted by the estate agency firms of Buckell & Ballard at the Horse Fair in Banbury and Victor Side in St. Hugh's Church in Woodstock). And we search through a regular circuit of antique shops. (Some favorites are Phyllis White's small shop in Stanton Harcourt, and various establishments in Oxford, Burford, Moreton-on-the-March, Henley, etc.) Gradually we have managed to acquire an interesting assortment of miscellaneous items, and our Oxford house has a bit of the museum about it.

In Oxford I do not work at peak efficiency. The adrenaline does not pump quite so hard in the somewhat enervating atmosphere of the Thames valley. For this very reason my mind can range somewhat more freely there—it works well on issues of strategy while perhaps dealing less effectively with matters of tactics. I tend to work at sketching large projects whose detailed execution is more effectively handled in Pittsburgh. There is the leisure to do things that the more pressured pace of Pittsburgh does not admit of—to ruminate, to let the drift of thought wander loosely down the byways of personal affairs and professional concerns, and so to gain a fresh perspective on things.

Dorothy, too, has her own cluster of favored activities in Oxford. She takes tennis instruction at the Norham Gardens Tennis Club, participates in some of the activities of the University Newcomer's Club (nowadays not as a newcomer, but as an "old hand"), and she does brass-rubbing at miscellaneous churches in the area. Periodically she goes on a shopping trip to London. And then, of course, there are the various activities we do together: tourism, antiquing, entertaining, etc. Dorothy is a person of much enterprise and energy—active and outgoing—and life with her is a constant source of happiness.

The months we spend each year in England mean much to me. It is a refreshing change to live in the cultural framework of a cognate yet distinctively different society. I find our English cousins by and large quite congenial—particularly those of the older generation. There is, perhaps, less bonhommie than in America, and people tend to keep a bit more distant from others. (The lower noise-level of talk in restaurants, busses, and other public places in one rather striking token of this.) But it did not take me long to become persuaded that English people do not deserve their reputation for reserve and unapproachability. To be sure, they generally do not thrust themselves forward with a pretense of "hail fellow, well met!" joviality. But they seldom fail to answer friendliness with friendliness, and almost invariably go out of their way to be helpful to strangers. Except for the occasional eccentric academic—whom, after all, one can meet anyplace—I have seldom found that friendliness goes unreciprocated in England.

I am repeatedly surprised at the standard of living of academics in the United Kingdom. Like most British workers they are substantially less well paid than their counterparts in continental Europe and in the USA. And yet their lifestyle is generally comparable. No doubt this is in part because a very high proportion of them are married to professional spouses. Given their attachment to the good thing of life—annual holidays in the Mediterranean sun, children at private schools, imported wines, and the like, one cannot help being struck by the frequency with which English academics talk socialist cant from the comfortable vantage point of a bourgeois household. To an unabashed partisan of bourgeois values like myself, this seems downright hypocrisy. It a middle-class lifestyle is worth living and prizing for oneself, it is surely also worth defending in the sphere of ideology and political discourse.

Academics the world around are cut from much the same cloth and have many common interests and points of contact—their colleagues not least among them. If the old saw is true that servants talk about *people* and the gentry about *things*, then academics are servants. This is especially pronounced in England, because British academia is a relatively compact and tightly knit society—much like a small town. Everyone knows everybody and wants the latest word on their doings, and preferably their misdoings and mishaps. (This is particularly reinforced by the unwritten law of Oxford colleges that one does not talk shop on social occasions.) Oxford dons, to be sure, tend to have a somewhat insular outlook—as though everything worth happening happens in Oxford. To my surprise, academics in England are even more given to self-indulgence and self-advertising than here. (Only there is it standard operating procedure to line one's invitations up on one's mantelpiece for all the world to see that one is being asked to the Vice Chancellor's reception or the Provost's tea.)

Throughout these visits in Oxford the fellows of Corpus Christi College have taken me unto themselves as a visiting member of their Senior Common Room. An Oxford college is a most delightful sort of club. To be sure, as a dedicated family man with a ménage of his own in Oxford, I only eat in College once in a blue moon. But I often use the reading room, and often work in the Medieval setting of the picturesque old library. Having a foothold in college makes all the

difference in helping an academic visitor feel part of the
Oxford scene, and I am very grateful to Corpus for its cour-
teous hospitality, which has meant a great deal to me over the
years. Oxford affords an environment where a philosopher
can feel especially at home, because it is so clearly a place
where the things that matter to him are thought important.

All in all, then, the Oxford connection has greatly enriched
my life and widened my horizons. Such longish visits abroad
create a certain detachment from the surrounding bustle.
One is able to view things—both locally and "back home"—
with some detachment, and gains a fresh and broader perspective on human affairs, by no means useless experience for a
philosopher.

My oldest Oxford friend is R. M. Hare, the White's Professor of Moral Philosophy. I first met him around 1964 when
he came through Pittsburgh to give a lecture. When I planned
my sabbatical visit to Oxford in 1968, he arranged for us to do
a lecture-course on imperatives together, and it was he who
introduced me into his college (Corpus Christi), thus estab-
lishing a relationship of long-term duration. A fine scholar
and clever philosopher, he is a gentleman of the old school,
and I have come to be quite fond of him, and of his very
charming wife as well.

Jonathan Cohen of Queens College, who works in philosophical logic and language theory, and Rom Harré of Linacre
College, who cultivates the philosophy of science, have also
been among my closer Oxford contacts. Both are nonstan-
dard but yet by no means unusual Oxonian types, Jon as the
cultivated cosmopolitan metamorphosed into a bookish English country squire and active protector of rural England, and
Rom as the returned Colonial (from New Zealand) out to
show those stay-at-home fogies some new-world vitality.
Hettie, his vivacious wife, is something of a good-natured
one-member fan club for Rom, who in her eyes is a peerless
doer of fine and admirable deeds. They are a sweet couple.

Another person I see much of around Oxford is David
Taylor, who is in charge of journals in the publication department of Blackwells and has managed the *American Philosophical Quarterly* for this firm since it arrived there in 1965.
Dorothy and I have known him ever since our Oxford "hon-

eymoon" of 1968, and we like him much and enjoy his company. A graduate of Queen's College, Oxford, David is a chorister at Christ Church and an enthusiastic Latinist, which especially endears him to me. He is also an amateur playwright of considerable dedication and ability. (In 1975 I attended the opening night performance of his splendid comedy, *Ghengis Khan*, put on by the boys of Christ Church Cathedral School.) David is a person of unusual quality and versatility.

Yet another of our good friends in Oxford is Mr. William Sumpter, the gardener who first came in the summer of 1971 to take care of our Victoria Road garden. A World War I veteran then in his early 70's, he had retired as gardener at St. Edward's School some years ago, but was glad to take on a part-time job, and answered our advertisement in *The Oxford Times*. He lived nearby, in Hernes Road, and would come by on his bicycle once a week to cut the lawn and manicure the garden. A charming, dapper, little pink cherub of a man with a delightful sense of humor, he has endeared himself with the boys, whom he persisted in calling "Master Mark" and "Master Owen." Shortly before we sold the Victoria Road house in 1973, he was forced into retirement by circulatory difficulties in his legs. We continued to stay in touch with him and call on him and his very nice wife regularly during our Oxford visits. "Pop" Sumpter, as he came to be known around our house, is a point of contact with an older type of English workman, cheerfully class-conscious yet totally self-assured —a type now on the verge of extinction.

During the 1960's, I became increasingly active in international activities in philosophy. I came to hold various offices[3] and attended various meetings of international scholarly organizations, visiting Helsinki in 1962, Jerusalem in 1964, Vienna in 1968, Bucharest in 1971, Cambridge in 1972, and Berne in 1974 in this connection. My service as Secretary of the Logic, Methodology, and Philosophy of Science branch of the International Union of History and Philosophy of Science (an organ of UNESCO)—an office I held during 1969-1975—was particularly interesting. The post was no sinecure, for the Secretary stood at the hub of the enterprise, and all the business of this active international scholarly organizations passed through his hands. (I was most fortunate in this regard in serving with two immensely helpful and cooperative presidents: Stephan Körner of Bristol and Andrzej Mostowski of Warsaw.)

The Bucharest meeting of 1971 was my one and only foray behind the Iron Curtain in the years of the cold war. It came at a time of tension between Romania and the USSR, and the Bucharest airport was filled with tanks poised to stop a surprise attack. To assert their independence the Romanians had invited a Chinese military delegation to visit and also chose to assert their linkage to the West by putting on an official reception for the visiting philosophers in the great hall where high level governmental functions were mounted. At this reception I found myself, as an official of the International Union, being escorted off to be introduced to Nicole Ceancescu, happily the only occasion on which I have shaken hands with a dictator—or indeed with a head of state.

It requires considerable diplomacy to keep the organizational whip sailing smoothly along amidst diverse personal rivalries and international frictions. (Scholars can be every bit as primadonnaish as singers!) Handling potentially fractions interpersonal complications with reasonable adhesion to Sir Robert Walpole's principle of *quieta non movere* (roughly—"let sleeping dogs lie!"), my main accomplishment lay in furthering the division's proper work through a lively program of conferences and colloquia. During my tenure of office the organization grew substantially in numerical strength and in professional activity, so that I have at least the satisfaction of feeling that my period of service did more good than harm. But I found it fascinating to see how deeply the passions of academics could be aroused by stakes of negligible size and how engrossed people could become in jockeying for position in a situation in which there was in fact no real power to be jockeyed for.

I was active on other fronts also. In 1971, I organized *The Journal of Philosophical Logic*. I negotiated the inauguration of this journal with the firm of Reidel in the Netherlands and recruited my former student Bas van Fraassen as its initial editor. I take some justifiable pleasure in the success of this journal in the short course of its history. More importantly, however, the year 1973 saw the tenth anniversary of publication of the *American Philosophical Quarterly*. My literary offspring had not only survived it first decade, but has in its brief history managed to establish itself as a leading philosophy journal. I must confess that I am thoroughly pleased with its success.

During the 1968-1972 period I managed to regularize my relationships with publishers. My earlier books had appeared under a variety of imprints, but step by step I developed a closer and more continuous relationship with two publishing houses. For one thing, I became friends with Fred Hetzel, the able and enterprising director of the University of Pittsburgh Press, who had come to Pitt from Colonial Williamsburg a few years before. Initially the Pitt Press had published all my books on Arabic philosophy, but now, thanks to Fred's interest, it took on some of my regular philosophical work. The publication of three books over a six-year period confirmed this relationship: *Essays in Philosophical Analysis* (1969), *Welfare* (1972), and *Unselfishness* (1975).

In the course of our Oxford visits I also became friends with Jim Feather, the Managing Director of the publishing branch of Blackwells and a most knowledgeable and perceptive publisher. After completing his studies in Oxford, Jim was initially a newspaperman, but he soon made the transition into academic publishing and transformed Blackwells from a small-scale operation into a major publishing house. Blackwells had been publishing the *American Philosophical Quarterly* since 1966, but in 1971 we also reached an understanding as a result of which a steady stream of my own books has been issued by this house (*Conceptual Idealism*, 1973; *The Primacy of Practice*, 1973; *A Theory of Possibility*, 1975; *Methodological Pragmatism*, 1976). With both Fred and Jim, there has been a mixture of business and personal contacts, and it is striking here (as elsewhere) how greatly the element of personal relationship tends to smooth the conduct of business affairs. I consider myself fortunate to have two such conscientious and congenial publishers to deal with.

My philosophical horizons also continued to expand. I now launched a systematic study of two movements I had heretofore neglected: the Hegelian tradition and American pragmatism (and especially C. S. Peirce). Particularly in their stress on dynamic and evolutionary considerations in the validation of thought, both of these major figures of modern philosophy were to prove of substantial importance for the work of the "Pragmatic Idealism" trilogy (*Conceptual Idealism*, 1973; *The Primacy of Practice*, 1973; and *Methodological Pragmatism*, 1976) written during this period. This work led to my increasing commitment to an idealism based on the conviction that our conceptual tools reflect a predisposition to view the world in a way that takes human thought and action itself as its model and sees the unity-in-complexity of human beings themselves as the cognitive paradigm of a "natural system."

Teaching has always been near the center of my work-life, and during this 1971-74 period I taught a wide variety of courses. In time, my teaching interests came to focus on three areas: the history of philosophy, metaphysics, and the theory of knowledge—especially scientific knowledge. (My writing has run along just these same tracks.) As the years moved on I came to see myself, in relation to my students, as the diplomatic representative of a foreign civilization representing in their midst some of the great philosophers of the past, and especially some of the now-gone greats or near-greats whom I have known personally and whose work had, in one way or another, exerted some influence on my thinking—Rudolf Carnap, A. C. Ewing, W. T. Stace, and others.

While I have never taken the role of a remote Herr Professor towards my graduate students, yet I also never sought to be their "buddy," nor enter into a first-name relationship (as some younger faculty members began to do in the latter 1960's). Rather, I have tried to be their collaborator, their senior partner or colleague in an association of peers. I felt I had things to teach to my students not only about the substance of philosophy, but also about the spirit in which philosophical work is done and what it takes to be a philosopher—a serious concern for the issues, a deep desire to get things straight, a willingness to work, and a preparedness to put aside any affections or pomposities that can get in the way between the task to be done and the person who is to do it. Except for a time during the heyday of student activism in the 1968-69 era—when battle-line was drawn on an ideology largely based on age—I always maintained good personal relations with the great bulk of our graduate students. Whenever former students of mine do able work, I am as proud of it as of my own.

In the course of the 1970's, I began to be increasingly active on the philosophical "lecture circuit" as invited speaker at departmental colloquia, at conferences and congresses, etc., visiting campuses throughout the country—and making various visits abroad as well. During the four years of this chapter I presented two dozen major invited lectures in the U.S.A., and eight in Europe, an average of six *per annum* in the former category and two in the latter. Increasingly I gained confidence and developed a "style" for performances of this sort, and they were generally successful.

The year 1970 inaugurated another enlargement of the scene of my professional activities. My friend Robert Butts, an able philosopher whom I had known since my Lehigh days, when he was at Bucknell, had become chairman of the philosophy department at the University of Western Ontario in London, Ontario, Canada. On his initiative, I was invited to offer a course during the 1970-1971 academic year in the form of occasional visiting lectures. This invitation was renewed on a number of subsequent occasions. I would commute by air to Canada one Wednesday every other week during term to give a course for graduate students. These trips were somewhat demanding—I would set out from home before 7 A.M. and return to Pittsburgh late that day or early the next. But this ongoing link with an active department largely staffed with able young people was a source of stimulus and satisfaction. The philosophy students at "Western" were able people—and very pleasant too. Some of this lecturing I did in Canada during this period was by way of contribution to the routine teaching work of the department, but in the main I used these lectures as a sounding board for work in progress; for example, *The Coherence Theory of Truth, a Theory of*

Possibility and *Unselfishness*, were all presented in such lecture-courses. This link to "Western" faded away after Bob Butts put the chairmanship aside in 1973, but while it lasted it provided me with useful stimulus.

Along similar lines, I gave a series of lectures at the Catholic University of America during the spring of 1972. I was pleased to have the chance to learn something of the inside workings of this fine institution and to get to know Jude Dougherty, the enterprising head of its School of Philosophy. This visiting arrangement proved of value to me in affording an occasion for polishing yet further the materials of my Oxford lectures eventually issued in *Conceptual Idealism*.[4]

Some visits that did not happen also deserve mention. It has long been my desire to go "down under" to see something of New Zealand and Australia. Twice I had made all arrangements for an academic visit in New Zealand—in 1968 in Auckland and in 1975 in Dunedin. Both visits were canceled for the same reason: Dorothy became pregnant—with Mark on the earlier occasion and with Catherine on the later. Perhaps the fates intend this particular ambition of mine to go unsatisfied.

Throughout the 1970's I maintained a steady interest in the philosophy of Leibniz, writing, on average, one paper every two years on related topics. I participated regularly in national an international Leibniz congresses and conferences, and became an active member of that small international fraternity of members who interest themselves in the wide-ranging thought and multifarious doings of this great man. Over the years I have remained a dedicated Leibnizian, though, to be sure, I am not a Leibniz-scholar in that mode of total commitment which typifies the European philosophy-historians of the old school. Gradually I have gotten to know Leibniz well, not only as a thinker but as a person. I have learned, bit by bit, a good deal about his life and times and about the people amongst whom he labored. And repeated visits to Hanover have made me feel thoroughly at home among the few remnants of that much smaller town with which Leibniz was so thoroughly familiar.

A few words about Leibniz's influence on my own philosophical work are in order. I certainly do not view myself as
an adherent of his teaching or doctrine, but rather of his mode
of philosophizing. In this way he has been my model and my
inspiration. And I hope and believe that readers will sometimes find Leibniz astir in the pages of my own philosophical
works.

As Leibniz himself so clearly illustrates, the work of a
scholar or scientist has the unusual aspect that only a part of
him belongs to the institution that has him in employ. In the
main, his vocational identity and loyalty belongs to the professional guild of which he is a member by virtue of the
discipline he cultivates. On the whole, he knows his geo-
graphically remote fellow specialists—in philosophy or chemistry of whatever—better than his extradisciplinary colleagues
in the institution they serve in common.

Even today a disciplinary guild of academic colleagues
forms a truly international fraternity that largely transcends
political and cultural boundaries. The productive scholar or
scientist can walk into a laboratory or department in his field
at virtually any university or research institute in any corner
of the globe and take up almost instantaneous friendship[s
with others of extensive common interests and acquain-
tanceships. Here is a continuing heritage of that international
fraternity—then ecclesiastical—which created the university
system of the middle ages. Physicians, lawyers, and sundry
other professionals, all nowadays require for practice a certi-
fication governed by law, whose validity is consequently cir-
cumscribed by political boundaries (which operate down to
the state level in the U.S.A.). The university teacher—be he a
research scientist or a humanistic scholar—can take his Ph.D.
in hand and ply his trade in any corner of the world where a
university is desirous of his services. In theory even if not in
practice, the political divisions of national boundaries are
almost irrelevant in the practice of an academic profession.
The academic belongs to what is perhaps the only truly supra-
national professional confraternity that has survived the rise
of nationalism in the modern world.

Nevertheless, in my own case internationalism has its limits.
To be sure, I have lived a quarter of my life outside the USA

(the initial decade in Germany and the equivalent of a year and a half in England during this 1971-75 period). The most influential among my philosophical teachers (Hempel, Stace, Ushenko, Urmson) were European imports, and my general outlook in philosophy is thoroughly international. Of my leading philosophical heroes (Plato, Aristotle, Leibniz, Kant, Hegel, Peirce) only one is an American. Nevertheless, I unhesitatingly view myself as a specifically American philosopher—for three reasons: (1) the methodology I favor is a fusion of analytical techniques with historical concerns, an approach characteristic of the tradition of those modern American philosophers I admire most, from C. S. Pierce to C. I. Lewis and W. V. Quine; (2) my philosophical ambiance in terms of close personal and professional contacts runs heavily towards my American colleagues; and (3) the tenor of my philosophical thinking is oriented markedly towards pragmatism, which is generally—and, I think, rightly—regarded as the quintessentially American philosophy. Just as the language I speak best is an American English that no one would for a moment mistake for the British or Australian versions, so the philosophy I write is characteristically American.

This is perhaps the place to say a word about what becoming, nay, *being* an American has meant to me. It has, above all, meant belonging to a confident people—proud, capable, compassionate, and, above all, resourceful: a people of buoyant, can-do spirit that has always been glad to make room in its land for those willing to put their shoulders to the wheel of the world's work, encouraging them to make something of themselves, with a pat on the back for those who succeed and a helping hand for those who, through no fault of their own, cannot do so. Americans, I have always felt, are a people who can walk tall on the streets of other nations, confident that they represent a country that has not only the power but the moral quality that compels respect. At a banquet given late in his reign by William IV of Great Britain in honor of the American minister of the day, the king (with characteristic eccentricity) diplomatically declared that it had always been a matter of serious regret to him that he had not "been born a free, independent American, so much did he respect that nation, which had given birth to Washington, the greatest man that ever lived." I can see exactly what he meant, and feel thoroughly pleased that in my own case of kindly fate has seen fit to remedy the defect of the accident of birth. Wherever I detect traces of the American spirit of practicality and common sense and optimism and idealism in my personality or in my philosophical work, I welcome it with pleasure.

In youth and middle age one tends to think of oneself as immortal. Death, like other catastrophes, only befalls other people. The realization that one's days are numbered is neither pleasant not easy. (It shocks me to think that when Spinoza was my age—now 46—he had been dead for over a year.) In 1973 I experienced for the first time a bout of serious health problems. In the middle of August I had a text-book attack of appendicitis in Oxford. I diagnosed this myself, and drove myself, Dorothy accompanying, to the Old Radcliffe Infirmary, where this was swiftly conformed. It was an acute case, and within two hours they had me out of the operating theater where a capable lady surgeon had removed the troublesome organ. I spent several rather pleasant days recuperating in the private room which had fortunately fallen to my lot in the hospital, and then returned to Cunliffe Close to prepare for the return to Pittsburgh a week or so later. But I continued to have stomach pains. I attributed this to normal post-operative developments. However, a few days after our return to Pittsburgh, at Jerry Massey's start-of-the-year party for the newly incoming students, these pains became very severe. I returned home and began bouts of vomiting. That evening Dorothy drove me to University Presbyterian Hospital, where I came under the care of Charles Watson, an able professor of surgery at Pitt's medical school. It transpired that my gall-bladder had gone badly awry (so badly that gangrene had set in). Unfortunately, during the operation the anesthetist's breathing tube managed to traumatize on of my vocal cords which remained paralyzed some six weeks afterwards, leaving me in a condition where I could only whisper. (For a time, I wondered if I would ever again lecture normally.)

These medical troubles led me to realize that if some more serious medical disturbance had removed me from this scene, my children would know precious little about their father himself and nothing about his antecedents. And I felt keenly that in this even they would be losing a part of the awareness of their identity and thus a part of themselves. I resolved that they should not sustain this loss if it lay in my power to prevent it, and this was the origin of the biographical notes whose weaving together has resulted in the present book.

With each passing year I derive deeper satisfaction from my growing family. Children present an ever-changing panorama of challenges—and rewards. In Pittsburgh, Mark (b. 1969) and Owen (b. 1970) have both attended St. Edmund's Academy, a fine private boy's school located in the Squirrel Hill section of town. Mark began there in the nursery class for four year olds in 1973 and Owen in 1974. They continue there at this writing (1975), with Mark in the first grade and Owen in the kindergarten. They both enjoy the school and have profited a good deal from its caring and competent nurture. Their thriving baby sister Cathy (b. 1975) will no doubt attend the (coeducational) nursery school there one day.

A word should also be said about the boys' education experiences on the other side of the Atlantic. The Squirrel School in Oxford—where they began attendance at three years—is an unusual school, by American standards at any rate. It is run with a loose but kindly rein by Miss R. S. Bell, the spinster daughter of an erstwhile Oxford professor. Its home is a pair of old, large, rambling, late Victorian houses on Woodstock Road (off Rawlinson Road). The physical plant is plain and somewhat run down. But the staff is dedicated and the children are well taught in a caring and thoughtful atmosphere. Mark attended the Squirrel for part of every year during 1972-1975 and Owen was a year later in joining him there. They have enjoyed themselves there, and I feel that the school has done very well by the boys. In nine weeks or so at the Squirrel School in Oxford during the summer of 1974, Mark (then five) learned to read very well, and he does so now (early 1975) avidly and quite on his own.

Upon retiring from her job at Westtown School in 1971, my mother stayed there for a time, but in 1972 moved to a small flat overlooking the sea at Illetas in Mallorca. There we had a pleasant visit with her in the summer of 1973. She for her part much enjoyed her visits with us in Oxford, and in the fall of 1974 she moved into our house in Cunliffe Close. She seems to enjoy Oxford a great deal and had made many friends there. She is quite active—in the Ferry Center (the neighborhood activity center in North Oxford) and at Oxfam, where she does a good bit of volunteer work in the little shop on Oakthorpe Road in Summertown. Mother's presence in Oxford means that our English visits also offer a chance for the boys and their grandmother to spend time together, to the immense pleasure of all concerned.

On another front, however, familial affairs stand in a less rosy condition. Until the summer of 1971, Frances and Elizabeth continued to reside in Pittsburgh. I was thus enabled to preserve not, to be sure, a close and cordial, but at any rate a regular contact with Elizabeth. However that summer, after she had completed her Library Science degree at Pitt, Frances moved to Hanover, N.H. to take up a post in the library of Dartmouth College. She now refused me any visiting privileges at all, and so I had to pursue the matter in the New Hampshire courts, which entailed various visits to the handsome new red-brick courthouse at Grafton, N.H. This process dragged on until well into 1972, but in the end I was granted the meager satisfaction of one weekend visitation per month. Beginning in October of that year, I availed myself of this regularly, except during the summer months when we were away in England.

These visits went off pleasantly enough. Air New England's diminutive propeller-driven de Haviland biplanes provided a reliable though bumpy service from Boston to Lebanon, N.H. The Hannover Inn was a most pleasant place to stay and the town and its environs (especially Woodstock) afforded many interesting target for father-and-daughter tourism. But the contact between us was now too occasional for close cordiality to be maintained in the face of the psychological pressure upon Elizabeth of her mother's hostility towards me, which —contrary to otherwise plausible expectation—did not diminish with the passage of time.

In January of 1974 Frances and Elizabeth moved to Brighton, near Rochester, N.Y., where Frances took up a post in the library of the University of Rochester Medical School. This time there was no legal contest—my entitlement to monthly visitation was treated as a tacitly acknowledged fact. But as best I could tell, Brighton was not so pleasant locale for Elizabeth as Hanover had been, and she now seemed even tenser and less at ease than before. The passage of time brought nothing better than a continuance of the strained relationship between us which had been developing over the years—all of my wishes and efforts to the contrary notwithstanding. I know that I love Elizabeth with deep fatherly affection and would like to share her happiness and sorrows and be able to play some constructive role in her life. Perhaps someday when she is older it will become possible. "Where there's life, there's hope."

In the meantime, life goes on. In recent years I have done much traveling by air. I spent the bulk of this time on various writing projects, and so would estimate that a nontrivial fraction of what I wrote during these years was written aloft, the equivalent of a modest sized volume at any rate. The confined space of the cabin, the security against the telephone or other interruptions and the gentle hum of the jet engines all conduce to concentration. And the idea that a fixed but limited period is available for getting something done provides a useful impetus to "get in with it." (I write these very words at an altitude of some three miles on the Allegheny Airlines flight from Buffalo to Pittsburgh enroute home from a Canadian visit. My quota of work for this trip having been accomplished, I am devoting the residual time to these biographical notes.)

For the most part, however, we live a very home-oriented life, with house and children at the center of our horizon. Bit by bit, a good deal of work was done on the Sheridan Avenue property, both in the house and in the garden. The gradual introduction of various antiques and artworks has made this house a very pleasant dwelling. With the approaching completion of the sixth year of occupancy in January of 1975, I will have lived longer in this house than in any other during my adult life.

A word about diversions seems in order. One of my major pastimes is reading, primarily in English history and biography. (During the 1971-785 period I waded through the entire *Oxford History of England*.[5] Watching television is another favored leisure activity—even more prominent than pleasure reading in terms of time devoted to it. Drama is easily my favorite (especially the BBC serializations on the order of *The Forsythe Sage*, *The Early Churchills* of *The Pallisers*—some of which we saw as U.S. imports, some during our Oxfords visits), but I also enjoy the spy series (*Secret Agent, Man From Uncle*) and detective series (*Cannon, Ironside*). Then too we maintain an interest in the more traditional art forms as perennial season subscribers to the Pittsburgh Symphony and the Pittsburgh Opera Society.

A brief further word regarding my development as a philosopher. For a long time my work in this field followed the wind-drift of inspiration and interest. I would become intrigued by some issue, have an idea about it, and work it through to some reasonable conclusion. As a result my earlier productions—though manifestly competent—have the somewhat disconnected and scattered aspect of a series of *pièces d'occasion*. As I think of it from this perspective, it astounds me that I did not hit my stride as a systematic philosopher at work on connected topics of substantial scope until the age of nearly forty. Since I had found my way to philosophy well before I was twenty, and had earned the Ph.D. at the tender age of twenty-two, it has never occurred to me to think of myself as a late bloomer. And yet I have come to the reluctant recognition that only during my forties—when mathematicians and physicists are often already past their productive prime—did I begin to turn out the sort of substantial philosophical work that can, even remotely, lay claim to some scintilla of significance.

NOTES

1. Thus in 1971 I lectured on "Idealism," presenting the core of *Conceptual Idealism* (Oxford: Blackwell, 1973). In 1972, my lectures on "The Primacy of Practice" prefigured a book of that same name (Oxford: Blackwell, 1973), and my 1973 lectures on "A Theory of Possibility" outlined the book of that same title (Oxford: Blackwell, 1975). My 1974 lecture series on "Sympathy" ultimately saw the light of print as *Unselfishness* (Pittsburgh: University of Pittsburgh Press, 1975).

2. In quantitative terms, I would estimate that I nowadays (1973-1974) watch television for some twelve hours during the week, and average just under three hours per week of home-external forms of spectatorial entertainments like films and concerts (representing roughly two such outings every three weeks). The sizable difference speaks volumes for the impact of television!

3. Secretary General of the International Union of History and Philosophy of Science and Secretary of its Division of Logic, Methodology, and Philosophy of Science (1969-1975); chairman of the Finance Committee of the International Federation of Philosophical Societies (1973-78); Member of the Institut International de Philosophie (elected in 1971); Member, U.S. National Committee for History and Philosophy of Science (1969-1975); Member Bicentennial Program Commission of American Philosophical Association (1973-1976).

4. Published in 1973, but mainly written in 1970-1971. I have always been particularly fond of this book, seeing it as perhaps the first of my works as a fully matured philosopher.

5. In the course of 1974, which was a fairly typical year in this respect, I read:

> Robert Ensor, *England: 1870-1914* (*Oxford History of England*)
> Kathleen Norris, *The Treasure and Uneducating Mary* (an anthology of her short stories)
> Mrs. Humphry Ward, *Sir George Tressady*
> Samuel Pepys, *Diary* [for 1960]
> Maria Knoll, *Sophia: Electress of Hanover*
> Ruth Jordan, *Sophie Dorothea* [of Hannover]
> Elizabeth Longford, *Wellington: Pillar of State*
> Alan Palmer, *Metternich*
> Charles Petrie, *A Historian Looks at His World*
> Ralph Barton Perry, *The Thought and Character of William James*

Robert Adams, *Watership Down*
James D. Watson, *The Double Helix*

I wish that this list of "general," work-disconnected reading were much longer, but am very glad it is at least this long.

Thirteen

RETROSPECT:
1975 (Age 47)

The survey must end—even despite the continuation of life's steady flow of interesting new developments. Among these was the birth of Catherine Ann Rescher in April of this year (1975), enriching our progeny with a feminine dimension. New intellectual horizons have also opened up. *Methodological Pragmatism* (completed in 1974) awakened a concern for the evolutionary dimension of human knowledge. And *Scientific Progress* (begun in 1974) furthered my interest in the historical dynamics of the growth of science and technology—a development stimulated by reading *The Education of Henry Adams*. Yet, though a life story written in the midst of events does not end, it must be brought to a close, lest it metamorphose from an autobiography into a diary.

What then, of a synoptic overall assessment? Aristotle says that one cannot tell whether a life is genuinely satisfying until after this life has ended. And this is basically correct. As long as life continues, the prospect of an all-spoiling catastrophe is everpresent. Still, however vulnerable a judgment made in mid-journey may be to being upset by unforeseen developments, some attempt in this direction seems called for.

There is first of all, the fact that my life has unfolded during an era of war. My impressionable teens were lived in the shadow of World War II. My young manhood traversed the time of the Korean War, which occurred during my twenties and saw many of my contemporaries killed or wounded. The Vietnam War crept along its malign path during my 35-45 decade. All these conflicts touched my life in different ways, but most fortunately none prevented its running a relatively normal and undisturbed course. Living in an era of war, I have been able to grow up, marry, raise a family, and develop a professional career in a manner largely untouched by these cataclysms. I have managed to try to live a peaceful and productive life in an uncertain and destructive world—and think myself extraordinarily fortunate that this has been possible.

As I review the three decades of my adult life in writing these pages, the question inevitably arises: "Am I content with the course of things?" I feel there is no alternative but to take the complacent line of an affirmative answer. On the personal side, my wife, my children, and my friends are a source of much happiness for me. And I enjoy my professional life thoroughly and derive satisfaction from its varied activities: writing, teaching, lecturing. The chance to work at a subject of such inherent fascination as philosophy is of inestimable value to me. I do not say this with smug self-satisfaction, but with genuine amazement at my undeserved good fortune, seeing that someone who can find constant pleasure in living through his allotted role in life's drama is fortunate indeed.

I would not deny that on occasion I have done things that I regret—acts of thoughtlessness or unkindness, deeds done or things said in moments of impatience or irritation. But I have never idly and maliciously inflicted injury on another: my main faults have been those of thoughtlessness rather than of malevolence. (If the newspapers can be trusted, I have not sinned very much as the world goes nowadays.) Still, these errata—such as they are—are my sins, and it is only proper for me to feel ashamed of them, as I indeed am. I shall certainly not catalogue them, but it would be fatuous to omit an explicit avowal that I have my full share of human failings. I want to stress that, content though I am with my *fate*, I am far from being altogether satisfied with *myself*. For one thing,

I certainly would like to be more companionable and outgoing, instead of being rather shy and reserved and self-contained. But one does not select one's personality. One discovers gradually and partially what it is, and, for the most part, learns to live with it—though perhaps one may, here and there, manage to effect some (generally small) improvement.

Both as a person and as a philosopher I have generally gone my own way—without much regard to current trends and fashions. The editor of a scholarly journal soon learns that one simply cannot please everyone. But it is a hard lesson to learn that one can offend people—deeply and mortally—not necessarily by *doing* anything, but merely by what one is, as Spinoza clearly saw, something deep in each of us that wants and needs others to be like ourselves, and failure to answer to this need in others is readily taken by them as a personal affront. All the same, with regard to the petty conflicts and intrigues astir in any professional community, I have generally taken the olympian view that life is too short—and work too absorbing.

One characteristic aspect of my outlook on life is the substantial irrelevance for me of the *avant garde* thinking and the sophisticated cant of the day. A great part of the productions of "twentieth century culture" in the field of art, literature, and ideas strikes me as rubbish. My ruling interests, tastes, and values are largely those of an earlier era. Most of the books I value (historical studies aside) and most of the thinking I esteem, were available in the antediluvian days preceding the First World War.

In philosophy, too, "modern thinking" often leaves me cold. My allegiances and doctrinal sympathies lie with the great figures of the past—although the intellectual tools I use in argumentation and analysis are those of the present. It would be a caricature—with its typical mixture of truth and falsity due to the exaggeration—to say that much of my work in philosophy represents an attempt to deal with philosophical issues of my grandfather's day with the approaches and methods of my contemporaries. (The value of the history of philosophy is—as I see it—much heightened by the fact that so much contemporary work in the field is just plain dull.)

To be sure, a thinker may well pay a penalty for such lack of trendiness—by not being *of* the time, one may also fail to be *for* the time as well. But then it seems to me that a serious philosopher cannot ever truly be a "child of his time." He lives too much in the thought-world of other days, of Plato and Aristotle, Descartes and Leibniz, Kant and Hegel, Mill and Peirce. His co-workers are not his contemporaries at all, but the great thinkers of days past who have brought grist to his mill. Like most scholars in humanistic fields, a philosopher is fundamentally a member of his intellectual tradition and only superficially a member of his own biological generation.

The demands of the work are such that one cannot be a philosopher but a few hours each day—perhaps four of five at the very most. The rest of the time one is an ordinary person—husband, father, citizen, colleague, teacher, editor, administrator, or whatever—filling one's day with the ordinary activities of workday existence. And the issues of one's *happiness* in life rests ultimately on these, the ordinary-life concerns that affect all people. The teaching of Epicurus was not far off the mark: the surest path to contentment lies in schooling oneself to take pleasure in the commonplace and prosaic stuff that comprises the fabric of everyday life.

In conducting life's affairs I have by and large been a rather conventional person lacking a rather conventional existence. By nature I tend to be not so much a conservative as a conservationist. My concern for preserving the good is more intense than that for remedying the bad. I can suffer fools—readily, even if not gladly—but towards bohemians I feel an instinctive antipathy. I have nothing but contempt for those who expect the world to rearrange itself for their convenience and to reshape its whole system to facilitate their eccentricities. "If you want to 'step out of line', then be prepared to accept the penalty without whining about it" has always seemed to me to be perfectly proper and reasonable advice. But I tend to dislike those who want them changed simply for *their own* convenience, rather than on the basis of a disinterested and realistic view of the general good. I do not care for those who think and act as though the rules were made for other people, and have always detested the Bloomsbury

Syndrome—the penchant of intellectuals to think themselves a superior breed exempt from the rules and proprieties that hold for lower-cast mortals. The Bloomsbury people had no resistance to the virus of the dangerous delusion that the world revolved about themselves—with intolerable smugness they blindley mistook their own narrow and pampered world for the *real* world.[1] Among human failings, I find more tolerable those given to self-doubt than those given to arrogance. (As a person, I quite prefer Hamlet to Faust.)

Over the years I have managed to accomplish various things in philosophy in which I take satisfaction. In early 1975, the editors of the big German encyclopedia *Brockhaus* decided to include a short article on me, and invited me to indicate what I saw as my main professional contributions. I listed the following in reply: (1) The elaboration of a system of idealistic philosophy within the framework of the analytical tradition; (2) The development of a theory of inductive reasoning and scientific method based on the coherence theory of truth; (3) Contributions to the systematization of various philosophically oriented applications of symbolic logic (modal logic, many-valued logic, temporal logic, the logic of assertion, and others); (4) Contributions to the development and criticism of utilitarian ethics (especially in relation to distributive justice); (5) The rediscovery of the work of medieval Arabic logicians on the theory of temporal modality. It is a reputable record for someone still in his forties.

Lord knows, I have had my share of discouragements and disappointments. Consider one small example. I once entertained hopes of being invited to write the article on *mantiq* (=logic) for the new edition of the *Encyclopedia of Islam* that is now in progress, feeling that I have done more—and more interesting—work on Arabic logic than anybody else at this stage. Still, this invitation never materialized, perhaps because of the professional cliquishness of Islamists towards an outsider. Viewed with detachment such disappointments may seem small, but one does not feel them any less keenly for that—though to be sure, success in some areas is an anodyne for the pain of defeat in others. In any case, I have never allowed this sort of thing to affect my positive outlook and my determination "to get on with the work." Confident in my own mind that my philosophical efforts, whatever their short-comings, have a core of merit and creativity, I have become independent of a need for approval. (Though I readily confess that whatever words of praise have come my way have always been welcome.) One of the tremendous advantages of being a scholar is that, unless one makes oneself a hostage of others by seeking their approbation, one need labor to please no one but oneself.

At any rate, I have managed to accomplish a good deal by way of publication. The over-all picture here is presented in the accompanying Table 1. (I hope that this Trollopian touch will be pardoned in a Trollope admirer.)

None of my contemporary colleagues in philosophy have written so prolifically. To be sure, from a material standpoint the result is distinctly unimpressive. In one excepts the *Introduction to Logic* textbook, the yield of the remaining 22 volumes averaged some 2,000 copies sold and roughly $850 in royalties produced. A philosopher would certainly be ill advised to try to earn his bread with his pen. (As a supplement to an academic salary, the added income of roughly $2,500 per year was, however, not unwelcome.)

Table 1

THE RESULTS OF PUBLICATIONS THROUGH 1975

Title	Publisher	Pub Date	Copies Sold	Royalties Paid
1. Al-Farabi Bibliography	Pitt Press	1962	610	40
2. Al-Farabi's Short Commentary	Pitt Press	1963	960	180
3. Intro. to Logic	St. Martins	1964	17,710	13,470
4. Al-Kindi Bibliography	Pitt Press	1964	510	0
5. Studies in Arabic Logic	Pitt Press	1964	860	290
6. Development of Arabic Logic	Pitt Press	1964	1,020	250
7. Hypothetical Reasoning	North Holland	1965	1,503	410
8. Logic of Commands	Routledge & Kegan Paul	1966	3,320	290
9. Galen and the Syllogism	Pitt Press	1966	850	0
10. The Philos. of Leibniz	Prentice Hall	1967	5,960	1,490
11. Distributive Justice	Bobbs Merill	1967	5,390	1,730

continued

12. Temporal Modalities	Reidel	1967	1,038	300
13. Studies in Arabic Philos.	Pitt Press	1968	890	610
14. Topics in Philos. Logic	Reidel	1968	1,430	1,610
15. Topics in Philos. Analysis	Pitt Press	1969	1,150	1,360
16. Intro. to Value Theory	Prentice Hall	1969	6,470	1,780
17. Many-valued Logic	McGraw Hill	1969	1,540	1,500
18. Scientific Explanation	Free Press	1970	2,010	1,690
19. Temporal Logic	Springer	1971	1,260	1,040
20. Welfare	Free Press	1972	2,030	1,200
21. Coherence Theory of Truth	Clarendon Press	1973	1,730	1,650
22. Conceptual Idealism	Blackwells	1973	910	460
23. The Primacy of Practice	Blackwells	1973	940	470

Why then all of these books?—to return to the question posed at the outset. At first there was, no doubt, a mixture of motives—self-education, the wish to "make a contribution," and perhaps some yearning for recognition as well. These factors initially led me into authorship, but gradually there was a change—the hardening of habit, the settling into a certain pattern of life, the process of becoming someone who writes philosophical books. The best answer I can give to the question is simply that a slow evolution saw my emergence as a habitual—even *addictive*—writer. In the course of time the writing of philosophical books became my avocation as well as my work and *Nulla dies sine linea* ("No day without a line") my motto. When productivity is at issue there is no substitute for regularity.

Philosophical books are written for a wide variety of reasons: to dispel ignorance, to impress a faceless "them," to spread a gospel, to *épater les bourgeois*, and so on. Perhaps the most prominent reason is "to let off steam," to strike out at something that seems to us foolish or perverse. None of these were significantly operative in my case. With me, one idea unfolded into another in a natural sequence of events, and writing was a way of working out ideas—a mode of learning. As I myself see it, the prime factor behind my philosophical productivity has been not just curiosity (which could have been satisfied by reading instead of writing) but an explorer's urge to get insight into something first—before it comes to be a commonplace of the sort that everyone knows about.

The evolution of my work is thus in large measure a matter of tracing our the half-formed implications of my own writings, a process of an increasingly explicit development of what was implicit before. The recognition of the limitations and imperfections of my earlier performances has acted as a constant incentive to their extension and improvement. This endows my over-all work with an *exfoliating* character, akin to biological growth, with later stages giving a more elaborate—and in some ways altered—structure and content to the earlier ones. Ideas (like books) take on a life of their own, and frequently one that lies only very partially in control of their nominal "author."

The thematic pattern of my writing has had a cyclic structure, working in one area for a time, and then a second, and then a third, finally making my way round to the first again. In this way it has proved possible for me to keep up with a number of topics, managing (I hope) to strike a reasonable balance between superficiality and narrowness. A good philosopher, it seems to me, must be many-sided because the impetus to philosophizing is ultimately a search for systematic principles underlying the jumbled profusion of phenomena.

But what of that slippery issue of "success"? As I write these words, I am a man in middle 40's—his productive prime. My professional career has unfolded with remarkable smoothness: a Ph.D. at 22 years, a full professorship at 33, the editorship of a major journal at 35, soon followed by a University Professorship and the achievement of substantial roles in various professional societies. In strictly careerist terms, I have come far: the secretaryship of a major international professional organization (the International Union of History and Philosophy of Science), membership in the major international academy of the profession (the Institut International de Philosophie), repeated invitations to lecture at Oxford, an honorary doctorate, and the incumbency of a distinguished professional chair. Such tokens of "professional recognition" as can still come my way cannot add much to those I already enjoyed.

Yet all this is essentially irrelevant for what has become the fundamental issue of my professional life. Many productive years presumably still stand before me, and the real question is: Just how far can I go, not in such careerist terms, but as a

contributor to the work of philosophy itself? In each generation, only a modest proportion of philosophy professors manage to make some mark on the development of their
subject—to effect some difference in the way in which, eventually, at least some of its practitioners do some of their work.
The big question, as I see it, is whether—given health and
luck—I have what it takes to establish myself as a philosopher
belonging to this small but worthy band of significant contributors. Insofar as I am an ambitious person, it is in this
particular direction that my ambition lies. This may well be a
misguided, but it is surely not an ignoble aspiration. At any
rate, I feel I have the capability within me, and if the realization of this felt promise eludes me for reasons of my own fault
(rather than, say, because I am removed from this arena of
action by a falling meteorite) then—quite regardless of any
other "success"—I shall have failed by the one standard I
myself accept as valid.

Gradually, I have acquired the vision of a system of philosophy
geared to the idealistic tradition from Leibniz and Berkeley
through Kant to Hegel and Peirce, with the German idealists
on the left side, the English Hegelians on the right, and the
American pragmatists to the front. (Subconsciously, perhaps,
my being a German-American Anglophile is at work in mo-
tivating this fusion of traditions.) It has become my life's
task—my "mission," if you will—to proceed with the exposition and elaboration of this philosophical perspective of a
pragmatical idealism or idealistic pragmatism. The aim is to
become clear about the import and the credentials of various
sorts of human knowledge—above all in the sciences, in everyday life, and in philosophical reflection itself. The adequate
comprehension of the nature of these various realms of inquiry—and of their mutual interrelationships—is the formative purpose of the enterprise. The system as I see it in my
mind's eye is a substantial structure combining historical ele-
ments from the idealistic and pragmatic traditions with various original moves—a structure embodying traditional
materials, but built up with contemporary tools of logical and
conceptual analysis. Whether I shall have the requisite health,
staying power, and creative impetus to carry this project to a
reasonable state of completion, and how it will be received if

and when completed, remain the big open questions of my professional life. This story thus ends *in medias res*, in the middle act of a life-drama that remains to be played out amidst the pervasive contingency of human affairs.

Yet "no man knoweth the hour ..." What if my life were to end here and now? For one thing, I would not feel that I had lost out on a great deal. It has long struck me that there is a crucial difference between one's *chronological* life (in terms of mere years) and one's *cognitive* life (in terms of experience and learning), the latter being measured essentially in terms of the *logarithm* of the former. Experience, after all, is cumulative, and each new installment can only add its merely marginal increment of new lessons to the great body of what has gone before.[2] The resulting picture is set out in Table 2. On this reckoning, someone who dies at my present age has lived only some two-thirds of their expectable chronological life, but has lived almost 90% of their expectable cognitive life. Accordingly, I feel that I have already gained the great bulk of what life has to give in terms of its lessons and experiences, its joys and its usable sorrows. To die now would not be to lose out on all that much. (To be sure, I would, abstractly speaking, greatly welcome the chance to acquire the rest, however modest its scope.)

Table 2

COGNITIVE VS. CHRONOLOGICAL AGE

Chronological Age	log (Age)	log (Age) as % of 80 year Log 80	Cognitive Age on basis of 90 year lifespan
5	0.70	37	30
10	1.00	53	42
20	1.30	68	54
30	1.48	78	62
40	1.60	84	67
50	1.70	89	71
60	1.78	94	75
70	1.85	97	78

Were my life cut short, one principal regret would be the loss of work. I feel that there are still a score or so of good books left in me, I would be saddened by the thought that the philosophical edifice I leave behind would be so grossly incomplete in relation to what I sense it could, would, and should be. Above all, however, would be the loss of familial companionship of my marriage with Dorothy and the chance to see my children grow and develop. I reckon high the fortunes of those who—unlike my own father—live to see the children of their children.

I often brood about the fate of my children. Not that they have yet given me grounds for worry. But I want very much that they should make something of themselves in the world and yet be both good and happy into the bargain. The parents of children certainly give hostages to fate. Yet, even from a purely selfish standpoint, children are a great and good thing—with advantages greatly outweighing whatever sacrifices and anxieties their presence entails. They give one a stake in the future of the race. Without children, life is an empty and solitary affair—like playing chess with oneself. They add and element of interest and excitement that no substitute can adequately replace. Then, too, children provide a consideration which helps to make life meaningful—that there is someone to whom it matters over the long run what sort of person one is. And, of course, all of the egocentrism and "calculating" considerations are as nothing in the balance once the element of love and caring enters in.

Anyone who rightly reckons with the chilling insight that "You can't take it with you"—that we can carry exactly as little out of this world as we initially bring into it—is bound to recognize that it is right and proper to care for the quality of what one leaves behind it. It gives me satisfaction to feel that I would leave a worthwhile legacy to my children: a caring nurture, a fairly good, or, at any rate, a not really bad example in the conduct of life, a modicum of financial security. Yet that possession which, more than any other, I would like to bequeath to my children in one I cannot transmit to them, namely, good luck.

Kant repeatedly told his friends that no man in his senses would be prepared to live his life over again in exactly the same way. If the offer were made to me, I would not hesitate to accept it on these terms—though there are indeed many things that I would *prefer* to see altered. If the writing of these pages has done any one thing, it has helped me to realize just how fortunate a person I really am.

NOTES

1. John Maynard Keynes alone took steps to inform himself about it, and the rest of Bloomsbury found it hard to forgive this peccadillo.

2. Thus fresh experience superadds its additional increment dv to the preexisting total v in such a way that its effective import is measured by the proportion dv/v. And $\int dv/v = \log v$. On such an approach, an increment to one's lifetime has a *cognitive* value determined on strict analogy with Daniel Bernoulli's famous proposal to measure the *economic* value of incremental resources by means of a logarithmic yardstick. (To be sure, man does not live by cognition alone, and many other factors must doubtless enter into an *overall* assessment.) ADDENDUM (1985): When writing the initial version of this book in 1974, I deemed myself to have discovered the principle of the merely logarithmic growth of knowledge through experience. In fact, however, the sagacious Edward Gibbon anticipated it in his *Memoirs of My Life*: "The proportion of a part to the whole is the only standard by which we can measure the length of our existence. At the age of twenty, one year is a tenth perhaps of the time which has elapsed within our consciousness and memory: at the age of fifty it is no more than a fortieth, and this relative value continues to decrease till the last sands are shaken out by the hand of death."

Fourteen

SQUIRREL HILL:
1975-1980 (Age 47-52)

Here we are in 1985, and a decade has now passed by since the preceding pages were written. The time has come to continue the tale. Life's affairs do not stand still and the passage of years inevitably brings new events and changed circumstances to the fore. The reader who has persevered through the preceding pages has opened the door to the delivery of further detail.

* * *

In the late 1970's we moved our domicile from the rather suburban Highland Park district of Pittsburgh to the Squirrel Hill section, which to all intents and purposes is a small town unto itself. As our boys, Mark and Owen, settled in at St. Edmund's Academy, our life had became increasingly three-cornered—home in Highland Park, work in Oakland, school in Squirrel Hill. The starting and ending times for the pre-school and regular school sessions were out of phase, how-ever, greatly complicating the matter of transportation. Then too, after Catherine's arrival in 1975, the Sheridan Avenue house provided tight quarters. And so we now established contact with some realtors and began house hunting in a slow but steady manner. In the spring of 1977, one of the real estate agents with whom we were in touch drew our attention to the house at 5818 Aylesboro Avenue. Only two blocks away from St. Edmund's, we passed it frequently when taking the boys to school. We liked the house and arranged to buy it—delaying transfer of possession until our return from Oxford that September.

The Aylesboro Avenue house was a substantial brick residence, a typical urban house for a sizable American family of the pre-World-War I era. With ten principal rooms located on three floors, it had, ever since its construction in 1915, been in the possession of the Reismeyer family, from whom we purchased it. (The building-lot had been given to Mr. Reismeyer's mother by her father as a wedding present.) Built in the solid old Pittsburgh manner—with a good deal of interesting woodwork and stained glass, it combined considerable charm with substantial comfort—as well as convenience because of its close proximity to the crux of Squirrel Hill's shopping area at Forbes and Murray Avenues. It is a comfortable family house and we settled in easily and happily. The location is most convenient for school, shopping, and the varied offerings of Squirrel Hill Village. And the daily drive from home to the University through the seasonal changes of Schenley Park is every bit as much a pleasure as a necessity.

We have continued throughout the years our annual summer migrations to Oxford. It is remarkable that, at this writing in 1985, we have been proprietors of the Cunliffe Close house, bought in 1973, for longer than any other I have ever owned.) Our Oxonian visits have run a pretty uniform course—some lectures in the Sub-Faculty of Philosophy during Trinity Term (which runs until the end of June), a brief lecture visit to Germany or Austria during July of August, and some local tourism by way of day excursions. Then too there are such recurrent rituals as shopping in London, showing Pittsburgh visitors through Blenheim Palace, taking in a Shakespeare play at Stratford, and antiquing in the Cotswolds. A mixture of novelty and fixed routine, our Oxford visits have invariably been times of enjoyment and restoration.

Those Oxford summers offer something of a foretaste of retirement—I have no employment, no formal duties, no local obligations! As a "man of leisure" I can pursue my own activities at my own pace—which, for me, means a good deal of miscellaneous writing. Then too there is the chance to look at life as it goes on about me with certain distancing, seeing that we live in the community but yet are not of it. This sort of disengaged existence also makes it possible to take a more detached and reflective view of one's own life, a circumstance no altogether without value for a philosopher.

Since we arrive well before the end of the English school year, our children also have some Oxford schooling. All of them attended the Squirrel School at the intersection of Woodstock and Rawlinson roads under Mill Bell's tutelage. Mark thereafter attended the Dragon School for two summers, but subsequently changed over to Christ Church Cathedral School. Both boys then attended this institution year on year for the summer term—thanks to the cooperation of Hugh MacDonald, the benevolent headmaster—until their eventual graduation in the early 1980's. Catherine completed her Oxford schooling at age nine at St. Aloysius R. C. School on Woodstock Road. These schools not only taught the children various useful things but also provided them with friends to supplement their neighborhood playmates from "the close."

In early July of 1978, a month or so after we had settled into the Cunliffe Close house in Oxford, my mother left Oxford for a vacation in Freudenstadt in the Black Forest area of southern Germany where she had often visited with my father before the War. A few days after arriving there, she suffered a stroke that soon issued in unconsciousness. By the time I reach her it was already too late for any contact, and she quickly and quietly slid into death. I felt here loss deeply. Mother was my last surviving ancestor, and now on the eve of my 50th birthday I myself have entered—ready or not—into the ranks of "the old generation." It is never easy to lose a parent, and I still miss both of mine very much. After one attains the teen-age years, one no longer resorts to parents as confidants and consultants—one it too much concerned to assert one's independence from that sort of thing. But simply the knowledge that they are there, and available in time of need, is a great comfort. And this is particularly so when those parents are people of as much savvy and common sense as mine were. I can well understand why the elderly are inclined to "live in the past," seeing that it is peopled with those one loves. Throughout these years I continued to live in the past in another way as well, continuing my desultory but devoted reading of history and biography—perhaps some twelve or fifteen books a years. I made a point of reading material in German, French, and Latin as well as English to keep my linguistic equipment from getting too rusty. The Japanese attack on Pearl Harbor was a topic on which I read a good deal. (It has always fascinated me. Being thirteen at the time, I remember well the events of that bleak December of 1941 when the affairs of my new-found world were revolutionized by America's entry into that assemblage of cataclysmic events conveniently grouped together under the label of "World War Two.") During this period I made my way through all ten volumes of the California Press edition of Samuel Pepys' *Autobiography* and also read quantities of historical and bio-graphical material, particularly relating to the political and cultural history of England after the 18th Century.

During the latter 1970's our family situation assumed on a changed aspect. There were now three children each of whom makes a characteristic contribution to the fabric of the family: Mark as thoughtful of people and rather serious and intense, Owen as more easygoing and adaptive, Catherine, yet only five, as sociable and people-oriented. The children now began to be enjoyable not just as children but as people too. More-over my relationship with Elizabeth gradually assumed an increasingly cordial mein. She now began her college studies at the University of Rochester and lived on campus during term time. The maturation of years and the gain of psycho-logical perspective on her mother now happily made it possi-ble for her to achieve a markedly friendlier attitude towards me.

In the winter of 1978, I decided to join the Pittsburgh Ath-letic association—a club located across Fifth Avenue from Pitt's Cathedral of Learning, equipped with extensive facili-ties for exercise and athletics. The social side of the club had little interest for me, but its exercise facilities were something else. At mid-day I could cross the road, change into jogging cloths, run for a mile or so, shower, lunch, and be back at my desk—all within the confines of a single hour. For some years now (1985) I have done this routinely for three days a week whenever I am in town—to the benefit not only of my physical condition, but also of my spirits—and my intellect as well, since I generally manage to read a page or so of Cicero at the lunch-table. An increasing facility at Latin has been one of my real satisfactions during my 50's, and I try never to let a day pass without at least reading a Latin paragraph or two from some Latin author, ancient, medieval, or modern.

Such a period of retreat from the world in the midst of one's workday is a useful balm to one's spirit, particularly when one is involved in administrative duties. The Philosophy Department encountered a problem when the departure of its chairman created something of a management crisis. At the urging of the department's Executive Committee, I agreed to take over for one year, until some longer term arrangement became possible.[1] I did this reluctantly, however, hesitating partly because of the inevitable interference with my own work, and in part because it struck me as anomalous that a University Professor—who *ex officio* stands outside the departmental framework—should play an administrative departmental role. Still, the Department that had been my professional "home" for some twenty years was in a bind, and I swallowed my reluctance in the interests of the common good.

During the period of my chairmanship (1980-81) I concentrated my attention on matters of staffing and personnel. And I managed to achieve three substantial successes in this sphere: I initiated and conducted the negotiations with the affluent mother of our late colleague Alan Ross Anderson which eventually resulted in her endowing a professorship in his name; I carried through to completion the process, inaugurated in my predecessor's administration, of recruiting Wesley and Merrilee Salmon to the university; I arranged for four promotions in the Department (Robert Brandom and John Haugeland to associate professorships, Alexander Nehamas to a full professorship, and Kurt Baier's redesignation as Distinguished Service Professor.). Taking into account my initiative in Nuel Belnap's eventual redesignation as Anderson professor, I thus succeeded during my brief tenure of the chairmanship to arrange for the promotion of one-quarter of my departmental colleagues. Seeing that the recognition of talent is the foundation of a good and happy department, I feel that my brief time of office was a very constructive period. During the next few years, serious but largely unsuccessful efforts were made to lure each of "my promotees" away from Pitt. (We lost only Alexander Nehamas.) My labors towards making these valued colleagues feel appreciated by the university were, as I see it, an important positive contribution to the department's continuity.

I was glad, however, that the period of my departmental chairmanship was mercifully brief. I am not so constituted as to get great satisfaction out of playing an administrative role. Dealing with my colleagues in a way that made me responsible for accommodating their interests did not always manifest them in the most favorable light. But the helpfulness of Marj Boyle, the Departmental Secretary, and the supportive efficiency of Linda Butera, whom I brought along from the *American Philosophical Quarterly* to be my personal assistant, certainly helped to make the job a more pleasant one.

One curious later episode marred this period however. During my departmental chairmanship, one of my younger departmental colleagues (who shall remain nameless here) had vehemently opposed the appointment of the Salmons on grounds of Merrilee's involvement therein, whose abilities and merits he disdained—rather unjustly, as most of us saw it. When this appointment nevertheless materialized, he was furious with those of his colleagues he held responsible for this supposed outrage—virtually the whole rest of the department, but especially the "ringleaders," myself preeminent among them since I had conducted the negotiations of the Department's behalf. He withdrew from Philosophy, ultimately transferring to another department. But an opportunity for creating mischief soon presented itself—this time in connection with my directorship of the Philosophy of Science

Center. He had been a member of the Center for some time, but the term of his membership had expired, and the formalities of its renewal dragged out over some months, as administrative processes in academia often will. He chose to represent this delay as an aggression on my part, and launched complaints in various forums against my supposed assault on his rights and privileges. On three occasions over the next year I had to defend myself against his charges of administrative malfeasance—before a group of Center members, before a board of inquiry appointed by the Provost, and before a subcommittee of the Senate Committee on Academic Freedom and Tenure. My accuser obtained no satisfaction whatever in any forum, since on each occasion I had little difficulty in rebutting all charges of wrongdoing. His forays had no ultimate effect except to display the absurdity of his accusations before an ever-widening group of colleagues.

One other development of my chairmanship period was the university's decision to move the Department of Philosophy back into the Cathedral of Learning, whose 8th floor offices it had left in 1964. The move itself—now to the 10th floor—did not occur until a year or so later, but the die was cast. When this departure from the 7th floor of Schenley Hall in 1981 I left behind—not wholly without regret—an office of long-accustomed familiarity, whose occupation had witnessed some major transformations in my personal and professional life.

All in all, however, things were brightening up at the university. A great change came over the climate of academia by the late 70's in comparison with the situation that had prevailed a decade earlier. It was time of "normalization" of return to a more conservative and tradition-geared outlook. As the students' mode of dress became less exotic, so their behavior towards their seniors became less truculent. They even occasionally thanked one for services rendered rather than brusquely taking them for granted as no more than their due. Students—the graduate students especially—were now more serious in their studies and more friendly, alike towards their fellow and their elders. The neurotic distrust and baseless hostility to the older generation that had characterized the Viet-Nam protest era slipped unregretted into the past, and it became customary once more to proceed in a spirit of cordial collaboration—a development which redounded to the benefit of all concerned. This development pleased me particularly because I always liked teaching and enjoyed my personal interactions with students—particularly at the more advanced levels where a common interest in philosophical matters could serve as a bridge across the divide of years.

In any case, with the rightward turn of American political opinion in the Reagan era, my political persuasion took on a middle-of-the-road status once more. It is grounded in a deeply "bourgeois" attitude that regards the productive role of the middle class as the backbone of the country, and views the absorption into it of the economically disadvantaged as the goal of enlightened social policy.

In a very small way I too have been an entrepreneur. I had launched the *American Philosophical Quarterly*—the APQ as it soon came to be known in the profession—in the early 1960's as part of the ongoing expansion of academic activity in the U.S. after the end of the Korean War. Initially the University of Pittsburgh Press had been its publisher, but retrenchment in its activities in the wake of the University's financial crisis in 1965 led to its total withdrawal from journal publication. The journal then emigrated to Blackwell's in Oxford, where it flourished under the astute care of Jim Feather, the managing director of the firm. But after Jim moved to the U.S. in the late 70's, the relationship with Blackwell's deteriorated, and I resolved to repatriate the publication. It proved possible to work out a suitable arrangement with the Philosophy Documentation Center at Bowling Green State University in Ohio for their cooperation in the publication of the journal, beginning in 1981. The new arrangements with Bowling Green have been eminently satisfactory and the journal continues to thrive in a gratifying manner. I have always found the people at the "Doc Center" to be pleasant and cooperative in every way. Dick Lineback, its enterprising director and Jerry Slivka, its business manager were good colleagues from the start and eventually became friends as well.

The middle 70's saw the arrival at Pitt of Robert Brandom. Having just completed his doctorate at Princeton, he brought to Pitt a well trained mind of unusual penetration, as was already manifested in his job interview, which was one of the most impressive I can recall. After Bob's arrival, an exchange of papers brought to light some areas of common interest and after a time we collaborated on a book with the provocative title *The Logic of Inconsistency* (Oxford: Basil Blackwell, 1979).

My own philosophical research and writing continued to evolve in a constructive direction as well, with each successive year bringing along its quota of one or two books. I find it particularly helpful to set up at the end of each work-day the particular tasks that need to be accomplished on the next. Morning-worker that I am, this makes it possible to get off to a good start—without the impediment of having to stop and ponder at the very outset about what it is that one has to do next. These fell into several areas: the study of cognition in science (*Cognitive Systematization, Induction, Empirical Inquiry*) and in ordinary life (*Plausible Reasoning, Dialectics, Scepticism)*; and some theoretical issues about rational decision *(Risk)*. With the onset of the U.S. bicentennial I now interested myself more deeply in pragmatism, this quintessential American approach in philosophy, an interest that came to expression in *Peirce's Philosophy of Science* and in *Methodological Pragmatism*. The ideas of the latter had a particularly deep and lasting impact on my philosophical thought. Along with *The Coherence Theory of Truth* of 1973, this 1977 book was to constitute one of the principal formative landmarks of my philosophizing.

Arising sometime between six and six-thirty a.m., I managed to do around an hour's desk work at writing before anyone else in the family gets up. But throughout the day I write in snatches, seldom spending more than one hour at any one sitting, and often just thirty or forty minutes. (Perhaps with age my attention span has grown shorter?) These brief writing-sessions will be interspersed with various other activities. But by the time I retire for my sleep-preparatory reading at around ten-thirty or eleven, I have managed to put in several hours of creative effort. To be sure, most of my work-time goes not to writing but to the more routine tasks of academic work—correspondence, editing, preparing for or engaging in teaching, etc.

I am particularly proud of my 1978 book on *Scientific Progress*, which argues (in what I deemed to be an original and—I have always thought—rather insightful way) that the increasing technology-intensiveness, and thus the increasing costliness, of modern natural science is an inevitable feature of the problem-situation of scientific research. Such a use of philosophical perspectives to gain insight into a crucially important intellectual and practical area of human endeavor strikes me as particularly useful. I believe it was this book, perhaps via its subsequent German translation, that was primarily instrumental in my being awarded the Alexander von Humboldt humanities prize in 1983, and if this was indeed so, it represents one of those rather rare instances where what a creative scholar sees among his best work is also so deemed by others.

In any case, it seems fair to say that I have continued to grow and thrive intellectually because (and I really think *mainly* because) of my continued writing of books. These have given me constant occasion to learn new material, and extend my thinking into new directions. Setting oneself to meet new challenges is unquestionably something that makes life intellectually more interesting and rewarding. This is what my books have done for me and I am much indebted to them for it (to put it somewhat oddly).

And I am thankful too for the healthy development of my family during the period. It is gratifying to see the boys thriving in their transit towards more serious schooling—becoming increasingly active and independent in their reading, their bicycling, and their sporting activities. And little Cathy becomes a more charming and delightful little person with each passing day—and is growing remarkably chatty.

If I had to choose one key word to characterize the 1975-80 quinquennium, I would opt for *consolidation*. This period saw the continuation and accentuation of various well-entrenched aspects of my make-up. (At fifty, the leopard does not change his spots!) It was time when my activities as the paterfamilias, as a teacher and scholar, and as a peripatetic academic with a variety of intellectual interests all extended themselves further along some firmly preestablished directions.

NOTES

1. It was our Departmental custom to have senior faculty serve in the chairmanship for one or possibly two three-year terms. This arrangement has proved highly beneficial in assuring the department of an ongoing stream of new energy and ideas in its management, as well as providing for an informed group of "elder statesmen" in its personnel.

Fifteen

WANDERINGS:
1981-85 (Age 53-57)

The Philosophy of Science Center at the University of Pittsburgh dates from the 1960-61 academic year, which saw the arrival at Pitt of Adolf Grunbaum at is start and myself at its end, with Adolf serving as its Director and I as Associate Director during the early years. Eventually as my term as the Philosophy Department's chairman was nearing its end in the spring of 1981, it was proposed that I should assume the directorship of the Center. As with other administrative tasks, I was reluctant to take this on because of the primacy of my commitment to research (and small enthusiasm for administrative work), but once again there were no easy alternative, and so my colleagues managed to prevail on me to serve in the interest of the common cause.

The enterprise now stood on the threshold of a new phase of expanded activity made possible by a substantial grant from the R. K. Mellon Foundation. Heretofore, the Center had enjoyed the benefit of occasional postdoctoral visitors, but now it embarked on a systematic program to bring ten or more senior visitors to our campus each year, with at least five or six of these "Visiting Fellows" resident during every semester. This transformed the Center into a small-scale "Institute for Advanced Studies" in the general area of philosophy of science. Such an accession of philosophical talent, over and above the regular establishment of the departments of Philosophy and of History and Philosophy of Science, renders the University of Pittsburgh one of the most exciting places for philosophical study in the world, providing us with the stimulus of having an ever-renewed community of able researchers in this field.

The Center's program of Visiting Fellowships created a change in my personal life in bringing to Pittsburgh a steady stream of old and new friends. I had known some of these visitors casually for many years (Joseph Pitt and Rolf George, for example), but others (Aristides Baltas, Paul Humphreys, Klaus Mainzer, Lorenz Puntel, Oswald Schwemmer, and Roberto Toretti), who mostly came from abroad, I now met for the first time in this context. In addition, the visiting fellowship program gave me the chance to get to know more closely several colleagues whom I already knew well. Special mention is due to Timo Airaksinen of the University of Helsinki, who combines lively congeniality with personal warmth and philosophical dedication; Robert Almeder of Georgia State University, a philosopher of great human warmth and congenial friendliness; George Gale of the University of Missouri, a colleague of outgoing geniality and keen philosophical enthusiasm; and Jürgen Mittelstrass of the University of Konstanz, a scholar of energy, ability, and innate personal charm for whom I have great admiration and affection. This widened and deepened contact with colleagues from many countries has been a source of great pleasure to me, for almost invariably our Center visitors have been not only able scholars but very nice people as well.

The directorship of the Center was made much easier for me through the aid of Linda Butera, whom I brought over from the Philosophy Department as my assistant. Her cheerfulness and efficiency—and her talent at being "mother hen" to the visiting fellows by solving their practical problems—has made managing the Center far more pleasant than it would otherwise have been.

With the Center's move from Thackeray-Mervis Hall to the Cathedral of Learning in the spring of 1984, we finally acquired quarters where our visitors could be accommodated in convenient proximity to the cognate academic departments. For me this move was a homecoming of sorts, since I now once again had a station on the 8th floor of the Cathedral, where my office had initially been when I came to Pitt almost a quarter-century before. (To be sure, the Philosophy Department's move to the 10th floor of the Cathedral in 1982 had already returned my departmental office to this impressive structure.)

December of 1985 saw a major conference to celebrate the 25th Anniversary of the Center. On this occasion I enlarged the brief of Al Janis, who has been Associate Director for many years, and also brought my old friend Gerald Massey into the management of the operation as Associate Director for Academic Programs. Largely motivated by our enlarged activities, this enhancement of its administrative team positioned the Center for more extensive operations during its second quarter century.

Throughout these years, Oxford continued to play an important role in our lives. We would migrate there annually in early June and remain until early September. I would usually give some lectures during Trinity Term and would then settle down to a mixture of research and tourism. Over time, a modest degree of local academic respectability has come my way—as Oxford lecturer, adjunct member of Corpus Christi College, and occasional reviewer for the *Times Literary Supplement*.

One personally important eventuation of this period was my formal reception into the Roman Catholic church. Since marrying Dorothy in 1968, I attended mass regularly and gradually slid into the status of an unofficial member of the congregation of the Oratory at the University of Pittsburgh. Perhaps, ideally, the conversion of an intellectual to a form of religious commitment ought itself to be an intellectual product—a matter of secured conviction in theses and principles. But it certainly was no so in my case. Here it was primarily a matter of sentiment, loyalties and feelings of allegiance and kinship. Perhaps Pascal was right. If you would be a believer, he said, just go and do the things that believers do: Join a religious community in practice; associate with its people, attend its ceremonies, participate in its rites and rituals and socializings. Eventually you will then join the community in belief as well. So recommends Pascal, and so it was in my own case. After all, we do not come to our other allegiances—to family, to country or to culture—by reasoning but by association, custom and acculturation. Why should the matter of religion be all that different? As I see it, the impetus to religion (like the impetus to our other human allegiances) comes largely not from reason but from affects—from the emotional rather than intellectual side of our makeup.

In any case, after I had spent several years sitting on the fence as an "unofficial Catholic"—attending Mass regularly and participating in various church activities—the provost of the University Oratory, Father William Clancy, gave me a definite albeit oblique push. Taking Dorothy, aside one day, he asked her if I viewed him as somehow unsympathetic or unfriendly, seeing that in all those years I had never discussed my relationship to Catholicism with him. When I responded to this by arranging for a discussion, he put to me the question of what exactly was holding me back from joining the church. As I reflected on this, I came to realize that the answer had, in effect, to be *nothing*. And so I talked with Father Clancy in this sense, indicating that if he was prepared to receive me into the church, then, I, for my part, was prepared to go ahead. And so in March of 1981 I finally did so. Bill Clancy was not only a scholar and a gentleman, but he had a deep and sympathetic insight into the heart of academically minded people. He spoke little (at least to me), but his sympathetic concern encouraged me to think things through for myself.

There is no doubt that two intersecting factors were operative in inducing me to make a Christian commitment: a sense of intellectual and personal solidarity with those whom I could accept as role models among believers, and a sense of estrangement from those whom I deemed naively cocksure in their rejection of belief. For while I have lived almost my whole life as an academic among academics, I have always felt alienated from the easy certainties with which they generally view the world about them—confident that "they have all the answers." It has always seemed to me that the more we learn, the fewer answers we actually have, because the more questions open up. This aspect of things, which a religious outlook does or should encompass, seems to me to be something of deep and significant truth.

Of the many forms of human failings, the failure of imagination is one of the saddest. And one of the gravest failures of imagination is that of the person who cannot manage to project the concepts of a God worthy of ardent desire—a God whose nonbeing would be the occasion fro genuine grief. Compared with this, an inability to imagine a friend worth having or a spouse worth loving is a pale shadow—though all alike betoken a regrettable impoverishment of personality of the same general sort. Sensible people would clearly prefer to number among their friends someone who was willing to invest hope and trust in himself, his fellows and his world. To refrain, in the absence of preponderating reasons to the contrary, from letting hope influence belief—even merely to the extent of that sort of tentative belief at issue in a working assumption made for practical purposes—betokens a crabbed failure of confidence that has nothing admirable about it.

Religious belief alters our evaluative frame of reference, enabling us to view our own lives with a clearer and more enlightened sense of priorities. Its commitment to the larger, "spiritual" values helps us to realize the extent to which various issues that many people see as supremely important are actually trivia. This sort of view, at any rate, gradually became the substance of my religious outlook. As a philosopher, I had to decide upon my spiritual kindred in life. Did I want to align myself with the religion-disdaining Lucretiuses, Voltaires, Humes, Nietzsches and Bertrand Russells of the world, or with its theistically committed Platos and Plotinuses, its Anselms and Aquinases, its Leibnizes and Hegels? I was free to choose those who were to be my spiritual kinfolk, and I felt myself drawn toward those who saw humanity as subject to transcendent aspirations and obligations—and for whom forms of worship and religious styles of thought really mattered.

Some people are led to deepen their religious commitment by *thought*—by reflection on the rational fabric of theological deliberations. Others are impelled by *experience*—by a reception of some sort of sign or signal. In my own case, however, it came largely by way of *feeling*—through awe and wonder at the mystery of existence and, no less importantly, by a sentiment of solidarity with those whom I admired and respected as part of a community of faith transcending the boundaries of dogma and doctrine. There was no dramatic episode of conversion—no flash of light came calling me from on high. I simply and gradually found myself sliding along the unbroken slope from mere participation to committed membership.

In the final analysis, then, I have become and continued to remain a committed Catholic because this represents a position that, as I see it, is intellectually sensible, evaluatively appropriate, and personally congenial. Accordingly, the answer to the question of why I am a Catholic is perhaps simply this: because that is where I feel at home. It is a matter of community—of being in communion with people whose ideas, allegiances, and values are in substantial measure congenial to my own.

In any case, it was not dogmas and doctrines that drew me to Catholicism, but an inner need of a sort that is difficult to describe. It was not a need for relief from a sense of sin, nor yet a need for relief from the intimations of morality. Rather, it was a need for relief from a sense of isolation—the desire to feel oneself part of a wider community of spirits who are in some degree kindred, who share with oneself a sense of values and priorities geared to the spiritual dimension of our species and to a sense of human insignificance in the face of the awesome mysteries of our existence.

Has being a Christian made a difference to my philosophizing? An affirmative response is indicated by the fact that religious belief has affected my professional work in two ways. On the one hand, it has stimulated my interest in the philosophical aspect of some religious issues. (These interests are particularly reflected in such books as *Pascal's Wager, The Riddle of Existence,* and *Human Interests.*) On the other hand, it has also made me more sensitive to the evaluative and ethical dimension of human life. (These sensibilities are particularly reflected in *Ethical Idealism*, *Rationality,* and *Moral Absolutes*.) Being a religious person has amplified my philosophical interests, moving them beyond the "scientific" to embrace also the "humanistic" side of philosophical concerns. But on to other matters.

I now began to make regular academic summer forays from our house in Oxford to the Continent—especially to the German-speaking countries, where the academic year runs into mid-July. When in Germany I generally visit Hanover, that Mecca of Leibnizians. My friends, Albert Heinekamp and Wilhelm Totok at the Nether-Saxon State Library are always most hospitable and keep me informed of the activities of the Leibniz Society. During this time too, I made something of a study of the history of Hanover in the time of Leibniz, among other things making my way through all four big volumes of Georg Schnath's highly informative *Geschichte Niedersachens: 1670-1814*. I also repeatedly visited Austria by way of participating in the annual Wittgenstein symposia at Kirchberg. In this way I have gradually broadened my acquaintanceship among European colleagues.

And with the passage of years, my philosophical work has increasingly been making an impact outside the U.S.A. The translation of some of my books into other languages was part effect and part cause of the development. *The Primacy of Practice* was published in Spanish in 1980, and by the time that *The Limits of Science* appeared in German translation in 1985, I had six books in print in languages other than English—including one (*Dialectics*) in Japanese. Discussions of my work now appeared in philosophical publication outside the English-language orbit with increasing frequency. Over the years I have been elected to several international academies: *The Institut Internationale de Philosophie* based in Paris since 1975, and the *Academie Internationale des Sciences* based in Brussels since 1984. American philosophers who work in the "analytic" tradition are usually very provincial. I am fortunate in having been furnished with motive and opportunity to keep in touch with other intellectual traditions.

1983 brought a development that occasioned me great pleasure. The Alexander von Humboldt Foundation, which supports scholarship under the aegis of the German Federal Republic, awarded me its Humanities Research Prize. Some three of four of these are given internationally each year to humanistic scholars "in recognition of major research contributions in the humanities." This prize represents perhaps the closest approximation that we humanists have to the international Nobel prizes awarded to scientists (though is monetary dimension is incomparably smaller). It carries with it an obligation to spend a period of time lecturing in German universities, and during 1984 I made several trips on the German lecture circuit, visiting universities in various parts of the country.

Of the various university towns I visited in Germany, I found Konstanz especially pleasant. The circumstance that Konstanz is an historically interesting and most scenically situated town certainly helps. But it is the human element that counts. The philosophy department of the university consists of colleagues who are not only highly able but personally most pleasant. A degree of personal collegiality prevails among philosophers there that is unmatched at any other German university I have visited. I am especially close to Jürgen Mittelstrass, whom I have known for a long time—and whom we tried unsuccessfully to lure to Pittsburgh on one occasion. Klaus Mainzer and Gereon Wolters are also among my particularly good friends there.

In consequence of this renewal of contract with Germany, I have resumed a much closer relationship with the use of German language. My spoken German—which had been rusting way since my tenth of eleventh year—now received the benefit of enlarged practice, and I now also began to do more reading in German than I had been accustomed to in recent years. To some extent my psychological outlook shifted as well, for I am nowadays less inclined to see my German origins as belonging to the dead and buried past but rather as an enduring part of the fabric of my make-up. To be sure, I regard myself as a "100% American," but as one who—like so many others—is the bearer of a national and cultural heritage in which he takes both interest and pride. In this regard, my preoccupation with the philosophies of Leibniz and of Kant—steadily maintained both on the side of teaching and on that of research—have provided a connecting bridge to the heritage of my ancestral country.

As I now think back over the twenty-five years of my association with the Philosophy Department at the University of Pittsburgh, one thing that strikes me is the stability of this work environment. Six of my twenty fellow professors there, more than a quarter of them, have now (1985) been my colleagues and friends for twenty years or more: Adolf Grünbaum, Kurt Baier, Wilfrid Sellars, Nuel Belnap, Richard Gale, and Gerald Massey. This ongoing association represents a remarkable—and deeply appreciated—continuity and stability in a constantly changing world.

In surveys of quality in higher education, the Philosophy Department at Pitt nowadays scores in the top two of three. For the time being, at least, our reputation stands very high. Recognition of my own work has also continued to come my way. Honors bestowed on me include presidencies of the C.S. Peirce Society (1983-84), and the American Leibniz Society (1983-86). On various occasions my name has been put up in the contested elections of the larger philosophical societies (including Presidencies of our regional division of the American Philosophical Association, the Philosophy of Science Association, and the Metaphysical Society of America). But, for reasons already mentioned, I have never managed to succeed in such a contest and doubtless never shall.

The children repeatedly ask, with ever-renewed puzzlement, "But dad, just what does a philosopher do?" The answer is, basically, that he is a Cartesian *ego*—"a thing that thinks." His province is defined by the historic "big questions" of the nature of man, the character of our place in the universe, the ramifications of our interrelationships with one another, and the lessons of our experience in this "vale of tears." But of course while his fundamental concern is with these great matters, there is a vast proliferating host of increasingly localized and technical questions that must be addressed in order that one can properly deal with them. And it is largely with these more technical, subsidiary issues that philosophers nowadays deal (often, alas, forgetting in the excitement of this preoccupation to articulate those threads of linkage that bind their technical concerns to those great issues that constitute their reason for being.) The task of philosophy, then, is to orient and clarify our thinking about man's place in the world's scheme of things. Other branches of inquiry deal with matters of limited detail—the philosopher tries (or *should* try) to achieve broader perspectives—to provide, as best he can, a view of "the big picture." To do this adequately, is, alas, a well-nigh impossible task, but here, as elsewhere in life, one ought to do the best one can.

Living in "the land of opportunity," an American academic confronts the question: "If you're so smart, why ain't you rich?" As of the time that I held my very first regular job—the meager instructorship in Princeton at the age of twenty-three in 1951—I have never suffered from a lack of money for the needs of the moment. This is not because my resources were ample or my pay generous. Far from it! It was because Dorothy and I have managed to keep our wants modest and our expenditures small. At any rate, I have always *felt* affluent through making it my practice to "save for a rainy day"—to put by a bit from current university salary payments and —above all—to save the entire income from other resources—royalties, lecture honoraria, consulting fees, etc. By virtue of prudently conservative care, these savings have grown slowly but steadily. Only in recent years—with three children in private schools and family vacations becoming increasingly expensive—have we made some departure from this rigorous policy of savings. While I don't at all enjoy money management (philosophy is a lot more fun to think about), still I am not the sort of person who can walk away from responsibilities. The thing is to have enough money to free one from worries about having too little and yet not so much as to lead one to be greatly concerned about keeping it.

To be sure, prudence and modesty alike combine to suggest the inadvisability of exposing our financial situation to "the envy or pity of strangers" (as Gibbon puts it). After all, in this world wealth is something relative; it's all a matter of whom one chooses to compare oneself with—whether prince or pauper. My own appraisal of my situation it this: that fortuitous circumstances have rendered me affluent to an extent that exceeds my (relatively modest) requirements—and perhaps my deserts. Yet the contingency of fate—the fragility of human arrangement for the good—can never wholly leave the mind of one who had, like myself, spent a part of his formative years in Nazi Germany. Amidst the most secure circumstances there is a low voice that whispers at the back of one's mind "Don't count on it! I could all come crashing down." It is, I suppose, a bit like surviving a dreadful fire or earthquake—worsened by the realization that catastrophes are caused not just by natural disasters but also by man's malice and folly.

But let me turn from such gloomy musings to the warmth of the domestic hearth and the affairs of my family. Both Mark and Owen had been attending St. Edmund's Academy in the Squirrel Hill section of Pittsburgh since their kindergarten days, and as the years passed by, we all became involved with the school—especially Dorothy who was a volunteer worker in its library and active in various PTA committees. St. Edmund's is unusual in that, being administered by a corporation made up of the parents of its current pupils, it also involves those parents in many aspect of the life of the school—ranging from transporting children on school excursions to organizing money raisers of ingenious and diversified kinds. In the course of time, I too became more involved in the school. I was on the search committee that recruited Sterling Miller in 1979 to serve as the splendid headmaster he has proved to be. I was elected to the board of trustees in 1980, and served as its Vice President during my second term (1983-85).

The main contribution I made to the life of the school in this connection was to serve as chairman of the committee that mobilized the decision to transform St. Edmund's from a boys school into a co-education one and framed the policies and plans to put this change-over into effect. On close attention, it became clear to all concerned that no really constructive end was served by educating in a single-gender institution children of the impressionable years from three to thirteen who will have to go out to spend the rest of their lives in a two-gender world.

Having been a faculty member for almost all of my working life, it was interesting to see how the affairs of a school look "from the other side of the fence." Then too this was an occasion to get to know some interesting fellow Pittsburghers, such as my able board chairman David Smith, coming from walks of life removed from the academic—doctors, lawyers, bankers, and others of the "solid citizen" type who make a community hum.

But time marches on—and our children have all been continuing to grow and develop. In the spring of 1983 Mark graduated from St. Edmunds and is now (1985) an honors student at Central Catholic High School in Oakland, about to enter his junior year there, just sixteen years old and a bit taller than his father's six feet. He is currently passing through the "teen-ager" phase, which from a parent's point of view is surely the most trying stage of child-development. Owen (now fifteen) is also in the middle of this phase—though a bit less tryingly so, perhaps because, unlike Mark at his age, he has not yet "discovered girls." He is just starting his sophomore year at Shady Side Academy in distant Fox Chapel—described by one recent writer as "Pittsburgh's leading private day school."[1] He is performing well in his studies, and also promises (once teen-agehood is safely traversed) to become a very fine young man. Cathy now aged ten, is an absolute delight in every way—thriving, vivacious, and thoroughly good natured. She has attended Ellis School in Shadyside since the first grade and is by and large happy there. Educating three children in private-sector schools is not inexpensive (it presently absorbs roughly a quarter of my after-tax university paycheck). But it is worth every penny, since the atmosphere in these schools is more supportive than those in the public sector, so that academically minded parents have less of a struggle in counteracting unhelpful school influences.

As the children grew more mature, I found myself pushed increasingly into the parents' traditional dilemma—the tension between "maintaining control" and simply "letting go"—between paternalistic interference "for their own benefit" and willingness to let them stand on their own feet. I am quite sure that I do not have the balance right. Yet not to worry. They are fine people and I know in my heart of hearts that they will ultimately carve out a useful niche for themselves in the world. To be sure, it galls me when they don't "listen to reason" and accept parental direction in ways readily seen to be beneficial. But, alas, the principal lessons of life are ones that each person has to rediscover for himself—the extent to which we can transmit the instruction of hard-won experience to out progeny is very limited indeed. And so there are unquestionably times of annoyance and frustration during these years when the boys are passing through their teen-agehood with its skirmishes and uprisings. Fortunately, there are also those compensating times of love and fatherly communion.

In the earlier years of our marriage, we tended to take our week's midwinter vacation in Williamsburg in Virginia—a place I have really grown to love for its dedication to the excellences of a past era (a spirit that is bound to please someone dedicated to the history of thought). But in more recent years the children have yearned for "the beach," and so we have headed for Florida—Daytona or St. Petersburg. Everyone has a good time, except when they get too sunburned! A shady spot with book or writing pad does just fine for me.

My television viewing has fallen casualty to increased activity on other fronts, reduced to just a few hours per week. Partly this was because the newer programs appealed less to me as they became increasingly geared to the tastes of a juvenile audience. But the primary reason was the need to find some quiet time for my writing as the needs of the Center took up more of my office workday. Since I generally enjoy writing and actually find it relaxing, this exchange of television for work did not really exact a sacrifice.

One development of these years that has done much to brighten my life is the big change that has transpired in regard to Elizabeth. Virtually as of the day she moved away from home to live on-campus as an undergraduate at the University of Rochester in 1978, her relationship to me was revolutionized. She now became accessible, cordial, and downright friendly—towards me and towards our whole family. In the summer of 1983 she even visited with us in Oxford, and we are now all on the best of terms. After completing her under-graduate studies at Rochester as an English major with much success, she made a false start at graduate studies, and "dropped out" for a while to become a substitute school-teacher. She is now back in graduate school in the English Department at Duke University in North Carolina, concen-trating on the literature of the Victorian era. Her general development, and in particular the turn-around of her rela-tionship with me, has been among the really happy develop-ments of the past decade.

In effect, I nowadays have four jobs: as teaching professor, as prolific author, as administrative director of the Philosophy of Science Center, and as managing editor of several profes-sional journals. (All this in addition to the responsibility for a family of five persons with two houses in different conti-nents.) Someone less efficient and less organized than I could easily manage to make a full-time job out of each one of these tasks. Having already touched on the Center and on my writ-ings, I shall confine my present comments to those other two items.

Thirty-five years—more than the one-third of a century generally reckon as the span of human generation—have now elapsed since the time when I began my teaching career as Instructor in Philosophy at Princeton. Over that span of time one is bound to improve at a craft, and I am pretty sure that what I have lost in youthful ebullience has been compensated for by augmented competence. Certainly I enjoy teaching as much now as then—though I sometimes grumble about its getting in the way of my research. Though trite, it is never-theless true to say that college professors are lucky to earn their living at something that is so enjoyable.

In terms of personal satisfaction, the journal editorships have also been well worthwhile. I speak in the plural, because with the success of the *American Philosophical Quarterly* I was emboldened to launch a cognate publication focusing on the history of philosophy, the *History of Philosophy Quar-terly*, publishing its first issue in 1984, just on the 20th anniver-sary of the launching of the APQ. This journal too has got off to a good launch, attracting some 400 subscribers already in its second year. While the APQ has of course had to subsidize this new venture at the outset, there is little question that the new HPQ will in due course be able to stand on its own legs. It favorable reception among academic colleagues has certainly been gratifying. I would not have been able even to think of such an expansion of publication activity had I not had the benefit of secretarial and editorial support of the very highest quality for my journal operations. But during 1982-83 there was Donna Williams, and since 1983 Christina Masucci, to provide the necessary support at a level of exemplary competence. Still, a single person, however competent, could hardly have coped with the work had modern technology not come to our aid. The conversion of my editorial office to electronic word-processing in 1982 made possible a volume of correspondence and paperwork that would otherwise be unthinkable. (Even so, the amount of work we get done in our small office is totally unprecedented by university standards.)

Still, the bulk of my efforts have been dedicated to writing. Now writing philosophy is a lonely enterprise: the writer of philosophical books is on his own. Some people are easily bored with their own company. My own failing lies in the opposite direction. To read, to meditate, and—above all—to work my ideas out on paper is always a pleasure for me. What began as a diversion hardened into habit and ultimately perhaps even became a necessity. And for a scholar there is always also that matter of the companionship of minds long gone. Dealing with them via their books has been my constant task—and pleasure. For me it has been an active exchange since I respond to their writings via my own.

Anyhow, my philosophical work has gone on thrivingly. Each successive year has seen the appearance of a book or two with the agricultural regularity of spring lambs. After Jim Feather's departure from Blackwell's, my relationship with that firm eroded, and I have since had no regular publisher but have patronized a variety of houses, trying for a suitable publisher attuned to the character of each particular book—often a tedious venture. However something of a special relationship did develop with the university Press of America and with Jed Lyons, their enterprising Vice President and chief editor. He was instrumental in launching a "Nicholas Rescher Series" in 1983, which consists mainly of reprints of books of mine that had lapsed from print, but also includes several new titles. (It was Jed's interest in having this series include something of a biographical character that nerved me to the decision of including *Mid-Journey* in its scope.)

These lines make me sound rather the "loner" and perhaps in my work-life this in indeed so. But not in my family life. I am deeply fond of Dorothy and enjoy her company very much. Whenever I return home, she is the first person I seek out, and I never feel that I am really at home until I have exchanged news of the events of the day with her. I greatly enjoy the familial things we do together. My life without her would be empty indeed. And in a different way this is true of the children as well, for as they mature in years they change in status from one's "kids" to one's friends.

Edward Gibbon said that "an illiterate scribe may delineate a correct and elegant copy of penmanship, while the ... (pages) of the philosopher or poet are most awkwardly scrawled in such ill formed and irregular characters, that the authors themselves, after a short interval, will be incapable of deciphering them."[2] This observation is right on the mark in my case. It generally takes months for a new secretary to master my handwriting. Despite Miss Ferber's efforts in the 4th grade, I never successfully managed the transaction from the rugged German school-script to rounded Palmer penmanship, and the result has vexed successive generations of secretaries laboring over my writing which, without exception, have always been produced in long-hand. With age my handwriting has, if anything, gotten worse.

The salient feature of my later writings have been their concern for clarity not in handwriting but in ideas—above all for a clearer understanding of the nature of human knowledge—and scientific knowledge in particular. Just how are we to establish and consolidate such knowledge, and how far can we hope to press this project—these have been the main objects of my deliberations. I am particularly pleased with my book on *The Strife of Systems*, which the University of Pittsburgh Press published in 1985. It tries to develop a model for understanding the nature of *philosophical* inquiry along the sorts of line that philosophers of science have for decades been engaged in developing for *scientific* inquiry. It is a rather ambitious attempt to characterize philosophical inquiry in systematic terms. Taking its point of departure from the 19th Century German tradition of study of the "cultural science" as exemplified by Herbart and Dilthey, it gave a picture of "how philosophy works"—of what the actual process of philosophizing is like—in clearer and more explicit terms than any other treatment I know of. The epistemology of philosophy has been an underdeveloped discipline for a long time now, and what pleases me is the sense that I have made real progress in this complex and difficult field. Since philosophy is not only my profession but also my love, it is gratifying to feel that I have been able to contribute towards a clearer understanding of the process of philosophizing.

In the Germany of the academic old regime of the era before World War I, a senior professor (*Ordinarius*) of philosophy was expected to have a "system" of his own. Step by successive step, I seem to have moved gradually into this mold. To be sure, I fully expect my system to be every bit as obscure a century hence as is the case with almost all of those created by my predecessors of a century ago. I am certainly not so vain as to think that my work will be of lasting interest and am not such a fool that it is for "enduring fame" that I have labored to produce all those pages. My prime motive has been the pleasure inherent in the work itself and the satisfactions of enhanced understanding that these attempts at clarifying my ideas have brought in their wake. Learning is one of the most rewarding of human activities, and the experience of many years has taught me that the best way to learn is to write.

NOTES

1. David E. Koskoff, *The Mellons* (New York, 1978), p. 411.
2. Edward Gibbon, *Memoirs of My Life* (Harmondsworth, 1984; Penguin Library Edition), p. 63.

Sixteen

RETROSPECT:
1985 (Age 57)

In Roman times one became a *senex*, an old man, at sixty. But nowadays, when people generally live into their seventies and eighties, those who stand at the threshold of their seventh decade are still relatively young. All the same, when one comes to the far side of middle age, one encounters a tendency to look backwards increasingly to the past—a tendency that has begun to make itself felt in my case. For one thing, I have resumed closer contact with Germany, the land of my birth and my ancestry. For another, I have recently resumed acquaintance (only by mail, alas) with Philip Merwin, my old childhood friend of Beechurst days, of whom I hove fond memories and whose correspondence is clearly that of a really nice person. And I find myself giving increasingly serious thought to the possibility of organizing a 40th Anniversary reunion in 1990 for the draftees who staffed the Marine Corps Institute in the Korean war year of 1950-55. (Who knows if this plan will go ahead, but the very fact that I am thinking of it seriously says something.)

Over the long term there is, no doubt, a period of decline and dissolution ahead, such being man's lot on earth. But even so, there is the compensation of seeing the children grow and develop and begin to make their place in the world. Then too there are my brainchildren—my books. It is pleasant to see them making *their* way in the world as well, occasionally meeting with appreciative attention. "A mere bauble" perhaps; but one that cannot be entirely without value for a scholar.

"You can't teach an old dog new tricks." And yet I feel that I have changed and grown over the past decade. Not necessarily for the better. As a person I think I have become less naturally gregarious, and it takes increasing effort to keep in touch with people. I am not totally satisfied with this—I still want to maintain contact with others and to broaden my circle beyond those with whom "I go back a long way." But I have to work at this sort of thing more than I used to do. These are things one cannot control—or can at best control in part. One simply has to take them in stride as they come.

Still, with the contracting of my social outreach there is an expansion of intellectual impetus. Recently I have launched forth into fields quite new to me: the philosophy of religion (*Pascal's Wager*) for example, and metaphilosophy (*The Strife of Systems*). Perhaps I am to some extent compensating for diminishing flexibility as a person by enhanced flexibility as a thinker.

At the start of his *Memoirs*, Edward Gibbon wrote: "In the fifty-second year of my age, after the completion of a toilsome and successful work, I now propose to employ some moments of my leisure in reviewing the simple transactions of a private and literary life." Though older by several years than Gibbon was when he wrote these words, I cannot share his valedictory sentiments. My work has unquestionably not been as toilsome as Gibbon's—and certainly not as successful. Nevertheless, I feel that I yet have some good work left in me, bubbling away subterraneously in the hopes of finding its way out. My recent years have been a time of motion, both geographic and intellectual. During this period I have crossed the Atlantic four times a year, on average, and have carried on researched in a wide variety of philosophical topics. I certainly expect to cut back in the years ahead on physical journeys. But I hope and pray that the health and energy will be granted me to continue those interesting and rewarding mental journeys for many years, feeling, as I do, that I have some good books left in me yet, and that there is still much that I yearn to learn. May a kindly fate grant me this opportunity before the onset of that night where no man can work!

Meanwhile, the journey continues. *"Heureux qui, comme Ulysse, a fait un beaux voyage."* It has been a good journey so far. But, alas, no journey can be characterized as altogether happy before it is safely completed. And who knows what lies ahead? It is my nature to be apprehensive—the early experiences of my life have made it impossible for me to face the future with a feeling of assured confidence. Yet, though lacking confident expectation, I look forward with a combination of gratitude for the past and hopefulness of what is yet to come.

And so I conclude these pages with the dots traditionally employed in print to indicate the incompleteness of what is said . . .

—*Finis* though not yet the end—

Seventeen

TOWARDS THE 1990s:
1985-1989 (Age 57 - 61)

It is now 1995, and ten years have passed since the preceding chapter was written. Two reasons have impelled me to continue the story after this interval. One is the urging of some friends for updating of the account. (They probably spoke only out of politeness, but I have been naive—or vain?—enough to take them at face value.) The other, doubtless more cogent reason is that the old rationale still holds good, albeit in a lessened degree—the wish to maintain a record for the benefit of my progeny. Things do not quite stand still even in so quiet a life as ours has been, and there have been various developments that deserve to be added to the record. The chronological course of life involves an ever-changing redistribution of the balance between lived past and anticipated future. Given a "plausible lifespan" of eighty years the past-to-future ratio changes markedly over the years. The youth of twenty has three-quarters of his lifespan before him, the oldster of sixty is down to a mere quarter—an ominous reversal of proportions. And one's inclination to retrospect increase accordingly as one's horizons of anticipation shorten. But, even more, one comes to look increasingly beyond oneself to one's posterity.

And so it has gradually emerged—wholly unforeseen—that this is going to be an autobiography produced on the installment plan. Nothing was further from my mind when I first wrote *Midjourney* than the idea of its ongoing updating by decennial supplements. But there we are.

* * *

The transit of the 1980's saw our offspring moving towards adulthood with startling rapidity. With Mark graduating from high school in 1987, Owen in 1988, and Catherine entering high school in 1989, we now had no more small children in the family. Only Cathy—rapidly growing and at age fourteen already taller than her mother—has continued living regularly at home as the boys went off to college. Since "little ones" had been part of our domestic scene ever since Mark's birth in 1969, this transformation, in itself natural and healthy, produced a marked change in the patterns of home life as the demands of parenting decreased and the time of "carefree couplehood" drew nearer.

Our family situation also became altered in yet another regard. For Elizabeth has gradually become drawn into the family circle. Having interrupted her graduate studies she now, during this period of the late 1980's, has been teaching English in a middle school near Frederick, Maryland—only some four hour's drive from Pittsburgh, so that visits have become not only possible but regular. She has grown into a lovely young lady of good nature, sweet disposition, and delightful sense of humor. Her intermittent presence in our family circle is a happy occurrence that is enjoyed by all. When I think of the years of difficult effort to maintain a good relationship with her in the face of her mother's implacable antagonism, I thank my lucky stars that matters have managed to work themselves out so happily.

Still, one indicator of the thinning familial ties that come with the children's approach to adulthood has been their diminished participation in our summer visits in Oxford. In 1986 Mark remained in Pittsburgh to take some summer courses at Cornell, and in 1987 both boys stayed behind to work (Mark at Pitt and Owen on an archaeological dig). In 1988, the boys again stayed behind—Mark working at the "Riverside Review," a (now defunct) local newsletter published in Aspinwall, and Owen doing occasional caddying at the Fox Chapel Golf Club. So at this stage only Cathy remained a cross-Atlantic regular, and our link to Oxford became somewhat diminished. For one thing, the later timing of our visits make it impossible for me to lecture during Trinity Term, which decreased my contacts. For another, many of the families whose children were companions to ours during earlier years have now moved away from Cunliffe Close. Still, our summer visits to Oxford, shorter though they have become, continue, as always, to be enjoyable.

In the mid-1980's, we began to give a good deal of attention to finding colleges for our boys. In 1986 the family as a whole visited various campuses between the latitudes of Princeton, New Jersey and Williamsburg, Virginia (William and Mary). Mark and Owen also went off by themselves to Montreal to visit McGill. As a National Merit Scholar, Mark had a choice between various first-rate institutions, but it was McGill that became his choice and he started there in the fall of 1987. During the 1987-88 academic year I additionally took Owen to visit Notre Dame and Haverford, and he went on his own to visit the University of Chicago. In the event, he chose Haverford. I was—and am—rather perplexed by the strange, sort of "chemistry" that establishes a bond between youngsters and the particular college they find appealing. But having exposed the boys to a variety of excellent schools, we left the final choice to them in the hope that everything would be bound to turn out all right in the end. To be sure, one has one's own preferences in the matter, but as children begin to come into adulthood they should (and do) bear the corresponding responsibility for making their own choices—and the onus of living with them.

In the event, things did not work out for Mark at McGill. Drawn there by his interest in French, it turned out that he could not pursue it within the framework of their requirement structure because French did not count as a foreign language in Quebec. (He was never motivated towards the Spanish he had to substitute). And the institution proved to be much more crowded, routinized, and impersonal than one would have thought. Then too, the complexity of Canadian immigration arrangements was somewhat troublesome, with a good deal of paperwork needed to keep his entry privileges going. But the straw that broke the camel's back was a series of serious bouts of several strains of influenza that laid him low in early 1989. For several weeks, he struggled along with illness, aided only by McGill's Health Center's somewhat desultory attentions. We decided to bring him back to Pittsburgh, where ready access to first-rate medical services was at hand. And after a period of recuperation, he decided to continue his undergraduate work in home territory at Pitt, —not, however, living at home but at first in the Bruce Hall dormitory at Pitt and thereafter in a series of rented apartments. The idea of living at home under the watchful eye of mother and father no longer seemed practicable.

Owen, on the other hand, continued at Haverford more or less uneventfully, except for a very difficult Sophomore year, beset with discouragement in relationships with the opposite sex. The difficulty with the transit to adulthood is that one must make the shift to interacting with people on a totally different level and that this takes a lot of getting used to. In human life, adolescence is a deep dark forest where everyone must find their own way. Adults—especially parents!—can provide but little acceptable guidance.

Seeing one's offspring make their way into adulthood—changing imperceptibly from being children to being full-grown persons—can be one of the most satisfying experiences that human life affords. To be sure, this process is never without its travails. It is unlikely, for example, that one's children will generally do things as one would oneself prefer. After all, it is nature's way that children should develop into being their own person rather than someone else's. To count oneself fortunate it is sufficient that one's children develop not as one would have them but as one is content to see them be.

Throughout this period, Dorothy maintained an active schedule. Although she experienced from time to time a marked frustration at being un- and under-employed, yet, with Cathy still in school and living at home, she was reluctant to leave off homemaking. She has kept productively busy by serving on the parish counsel at church, playing tennis several times each week, helping to arrange varied parent's activities at Ellis, volunteering at the school library, and arranging various exhibits. As regards myself, I continued along what were for me by now well-established lines on the University domain, where teaching and writing generally occupied the forefront of my mind. And then too there were my editorial involvements.

When my friend John Kekes lamented in 1985 that there was no philosophy journal dealing with issues of politics and public policy apart from the left-liberal slanted *Philosophy and Public Affairs*—no vehicle of a centrist or neutral orientation—he planted a fertile seed in my mind. Once it became clear that the *History of Philosophy Quarterly* was going to succeed in terms of readership and contributors, I thought the time ripe to branch out to fill this gap, and in 1987 launched the *Public Affairs Quarterly*. It has been somewhat slower getting onto its feet than my other journals, but I continue to feel confident that it will in due course find a home for itself in the profession. I am convinced that there has to be a place where the emotion-evoking issues of this field—including such pressing questions of the day as abortion, environmental protection, or equal opportunity legislation—can be discussed in the cool dispassionate light of philosophically informed intelligence. Thoughtful and sensible people should be able to discuss public issues in a rational way.

As one grows older, one is increasingly less likely to extend their circle of friends in the absence of deliberate and concerted efforts. In this regard I have been fortunate here in Pittsburgh because of the Center for Philosophy of Science. Its annual crop of new visiting fellow brings on the scene a great many interesting people from all corners of the world, a circumstance that has made possible the development of a network of friends in many places. Naming names involves an invidious distinction, but without a few this line of reflection remains a bloodless abstraction and so I will mention John Forge in Australia, Michele Marsonet in Italy, Alfonso Pérez de Laborda and Wenceslao González in Spain, and Victor Rodríguez in Argentina all of whom now became close friends through the mediation of the Center. (There are many other and I apologize to all of them for singling out just a few on the basis of the volume of correspondence I have had with them recently.) I have always valued contact with scholars—at the personal level where possible and across the printed page where not. Insofar as I am able to maintain something of a youthful spirit it is through profiting by these challenges and opportunities of the world of ideas.

I have used the occasion of summers in Europe to visit various German universities, including Munich, Göttingen, Osnabrück, Bielefeld and—above all—Konstanz, where I have various friends, especially Jürgen Mittelstrass, Klaus Mainzer, Gereon Wolters, and Friedrich Kambartel. Konstanz is a most pleasant place in the summers, and the Insel Hotel, a converted old Benedictine Monastery, offers very pleasant, convenient, and comfortable accommodations. I enjoy not only the people, but also the scenery of the area, especially the boating excursions on the lake. It is fitting that a place which has so long been a cross-roads of European civilization at last has a university worthy its historic stature. On these German visits I also generally try to stop by in Hanover, to maintain my contacts with the Leibnizians at the Landesbibliothek. Dr. Wilhelm Totok, the Director and his right-hand man, Dr. Albert Heinekamp have always been especially cordial and friendly.

One feature of my circle of acquaintances—foreign and domestic alike—is that they seem to be quite different from the sorts of people one reads about in contemporary short stories, plays, and novels. I have been struck now and again by the sharp difference between the world of academic intellectuals and avant garde pundits, and the world of friends, neighbors, and fellow citizens at large as I observe them in daily life. They are for the most part ordinary, decent, upright individuals trying as best they can to live ordinary, decent, upright lives. The pervasive perversity and hypocrisy that punctuates the pages of contemporary literature and social commentary is very foreign to their spirit. Despite many and notorious exceptions, the bulk of one's fellows are mercifully of a far better sort than the people who populate the realm of present-day writers—a fact which raises interesting questions about the preference of our literary intelligencia for an emphasis on the less admirable side of human nature and conduct, a preference that their audience apparently does not share in comparable measure.

One development out of the usual course perhaps deserves mention. Like many another investor, I was badly mangled in the stock market crash in November 1987. As the earlier boom moved along relentlessly, I too was drawn in and made some fairly substantial stock investments. During the mid 80's they made good gains, but these were all wiped out (and then some) in that overnight market collapse. Its impact has led me to become an extremely conservative investor, one who would rather forgo a gain than risk a loss.

On my 60th birthday in July of 1988, Dorothy (with the help of the conspiring children) threw a surprise birthday party for me. It was an enjoyable and convivial occasion—with the usual comic contributions from a good many friends. But behind the cheerful surface lay a rather sombering thought as I now entered upon my seventh decade. Mercifully I have good health and a satisfactory (though doubtless somewhat diminished) reservoir of energy. Moreover, the flame of ambition for philosophical accomplishment still burns bright within me. Although I have completed a good deal of work over the years, I am not yet ready to sit back and rest on my laurels and various writing projects still vie for attention in my mind.

I now concluded that the time had come for me to put aside the directorship of the Center for Philosophy of Science. This office has had its rewards and satisfactions. But now that I was reaching sixty and had no right to count on more than another decade of work-time, I really wanted to be able to focus more intensively on my research and writing. So step by step I notified all concerned of my intentions and began to plan for an orderly transfer of administration to my old friend Gerald Massey, whose candidacy for the succession soon emerged as paramount. The process of transition itself was more demanding of time and attention than I had expected, but with light at the end of the tunnel—and a sabbatical year looming ahead—I managed to extricate myself with reasonable grace.

The Center had over the years become an institution of note, and its directorship is a position of some visibility and influence in the profession. It is often said that the abandonment of "power" in an institution involves a sense of loss and pain, but in the present case this phenomenon was notably absent. The diversion of my attention in other directions made it possible for me to view with a detachment close to indifference the Center's abandonment of some of my own arrangements. It is foolish to resist the inevitability that in an institutional setting every administration has to do things its own way and make its contributions where its own characteristic strengths permit. But on a personal level it did grieve me that the new Center administration was unable to value as highly as I myself had always done the services of Linda Butera, who had been my more than able assistant there.

Even as I was laying down the Center directorship, two new professional offices came my way—one of international connection, the other national in character. In the former case I was named to the Board of Directors of the International Federation of Philosophical Societies. This organization of organizations normally coordinates the work of the various national philosophical societies but in fact exists primarily to arrange for the big World Congress of Philosophy that transpire every five years. The other, more honorous office was that of President of the Eastern Division of the American Philosophical Association for 1989-90. The philosophers have no one national president but three regional ones (Eastern, Western, and Pacific). But since the Eastern Division is far and away the largest, and contains most of the historical and prestigious institutions of higher learning, its Presidency is the most prestigious elective office in American philosophy—the top of our profession's greasy pole, so to speak. For reasons explained above, I was quite surprised at my election—but nevertheless appropriately pleased. It is foolish—and eminently unphilosophical—to set much store by these things, but all the same such a token of recognition by one's colleagues is bound to welcome in a profession where the main form of collegial interaction lies in sharply criticizing one another's work. The Presidential Address I gave in Atlanta in December of 1989 was devoted to the topic of "Luck" and was designed as much to amuse as to instruct. It was very well received (and resulted in my publishing a book on the subject some years later).

One unhappy development on the professional front was Adolf Grünbaum's estrangement from the Department of Philosophy during the late 1980's, leading to his eventual withdrawal from the department's Executive Committee. Adolf believed himself—not entirely without cause—to have been mistreated by one of the department's members and the failure of various of his departmental colleagues to understand and support his position caused him great distress and chagrin. The result of this was a cooling between those department members who were seen by their colleagues as respectively, accepting or questioning the validity of Adolf's position. With the passage of time it became increasingly difficult to locate any middle ground between the two schools of thought, and the resulting tension unfortunately made the department a less comfortable place than it had always been heretofore.

This minor cataclysm in my immediate environment reminds me of the circumstance that I have (almost) passed over in total silence the really big developments of the day—the presidency of Ronald Reagan, the collapse of the USSR, and the reunification of Germany. This provides a vivid indication—if any is needed—of the fact that these autobiographical jottings are nothing like a discussion of the "life and times." They are concerned with the life alone and let the times look after themselves insofar as possible. And this is not an accident. In my earlier years the times were only too intrusive, what with emigration from Nazi Germany, resettlement amidst to the drama of World War II, military service during the Korean Conflict, and activity as a cold warrior (of sorts) at RAND. When these cataclysms faded into history and a "normal" life became possible for me, I decided quite deliberately to make the most of it. For better of for worse it has been my policy and practice ever since my return to academia in 1957 to focus my thoughts and efforts on my work, my family, and my personal endeavors (hobbies and social life included) and let the world of politics and public affairs go its own way. Let others mill around the hustings and man the barricades, I have my own more immediate personal tasks to attend to. That, roughly, has been my view of the matter, and for better or worse I have stuck to it.

Moreover, while as a concerned citizen these great developments enlisted my ongoing attention and concern, nevertheless as a philosopher they have left me (and, to all appearances, most of my colleagues) relatively untouched. For even philosophers are nowadays specialists whose particular preoccupation in philosophy of science of history of philosophy or personal ethics is largely disjoint from such issues of "current events." We all have our particular professional concerns. The lives of private individuals are—and in general ought to be—concerned with private matters. We are all obliged—and entitled—to get on with our personal agendas. To be sure, it cannot be helped that the world's great events can and do occasionally intrude into the lives of philosophers—but the fact is that when this happens it is almost always to the detriment of their work as such.

Not that I keep myself disconnected from the world's doings. Few people are more avid readers of newspapers than I, who can no more begin a day without reading the news than without eating breakfast, my mind being as hungry for information in the morning as my body is for food. It is just that I take a passive spectator's interest to developments, feeling no more called on to intervene in the political absurdities of the day then to send congratulatory notes to the parents involved in the "New Births" column.

During this period I have come to shorten drastically the time dedicated to the eminently wasteful occupation of television watching. Even as late as the latter 1970's, I still allotted some 18-20 hours per week to this pastime. But as of the early '80's I reduced this to some ten hours, enabling me to doubled my pleasure-reading time. With increasing years my interest in history and biography—in the doings of people—has steadily intensified. Not that I am particularly interested in matters of gossip and scandal. Rather, what interests me particularly is how people who have been *constructive*—who have made some positive contribution to the realms of human achievement—have managed to bring this off.

As a philosopher, I have always, of course, been interested in what historically influential people thought. But in recent years I have been increasingly interested in how they lived and in how they viewed the activities that were going on about them. And so biography acquired increasing fascination for me not only in its historical but especially in its philosophical aspect, with a special interest in the daily life of those philosophers (such as Leibniz, Kant, and Peirce) whose work is of particular concern to me. Getting to know more about them as persons, rather than just as thinkers, has been a matter of deep satisfaction to me. It is ironic but true that we get to know the people we *study* better than virtually all of the people we actually *know* personally.

One of my particular pleasures as my life entered its seventh decade has been the effort to learn something totally new for me, namely Spanish. In Oxford during the summer of 1987 I started looking into my mother's copy of J. P. Fitzgibbon and J. Roldán, *El español práctico* to "test the waters," as it were. Then in the January term of 1988 I began serious study by sitting in on a Spanish 1 class at Pitt. Over the ensuing terms, I also audited Spanish 2, 3, and 4. So bit by bit I worked up through the ranks until at last, by the spring of 1989 I became able to realize my goal of reading the novels of Benito Pérez Galdós in the original with some degree of ease and enjoyment. By the summer of 1990, I was working my way through *Don Quijote*, slowly but surely, with considerable pleasure in the process. Laboriously pushing beyond this point, I have also become capable of conducting a rudimentary conversation in Spanish — something I shall probably never be able to improve on substantially short of a longish stay in an Hispanic country. Language learning unquestionably exacts a price of tedium, but while progress is slow, it is also deeply satisfying. And for one in his 60's, there is also something reassuring about the discovery that one's mental process can still operate to productive effect in the acquisition of new material—despite such phenomena as an increasing tendency to forget people's names. Moreover, we all need an escape of some sort from the workaday routine of life's everyday course. Some find this in amusements, some in travel. But there is no more satisfying way to accomplish this goal than to make the transit into another thought-world.

The Roman author Quintus Ennius said that he had three souls because he knew three languages: Latin, Etruscan, and Greek. On this principle, I too feel entitled to claim several souls. But they all cry out for occasional nourishment, and so throughout these years I kept up a program of foreign-language reading to keep in touch with German, French, and Latin. I have had to read at least a couple of books in each of these tongues every year just to keep those mental circuits alive. While it is educationally stimulating (and narrowness preventing) to make forays into the thought-world of other cultures, I also find that the extra effort needed to read in a language that is not part of one's ordinary life is soporific. After several pages of such pre-bed-time reading, the brain is ready to settle down to sleep. Yet, nevertheless, even with a few pages per day one gets several books read in the course of the year. In reading as in writing, regularity is the key to getting things done. And I have found the process deeply satisfying and stimulating since each language ethos involves a different way of thinking about things.

In other regards too new themes of thought have come to the surface. Increasingly over the years it is the condition of man rather than that of nature that lies at the forefront of my thought. My interests have moved increasingly from the abstract ("knowledge," "science," "value") to the concrete—to man as an agent faced with real-life issues of decisions and action—in short to the inherent problems of the human condition. The reading of Miguel de Unamuno's *Tragic Sense of Life* (one of the earlier fruits of my Spanish studies) exerted a substantial influence on me in this regard. This somber Spaniard's profound and deeply cultivated insight into the place of the thinking human in the world's complex fabric of things offers productive stimulus to reflection.

Throughout this period my philosophical writing has continued unabated. Part of each afternoon and evening is spent at my old rolltop desk in my third-floor study at Aylesboro Avenue, perusing printed matter or pushing a ballpoint pen across a writing tablet. And year by year a book or two has emerged annually from the process. The settled habit of writing ideas out on paper has become a component of my make-up. Even if I were now (at the time of my 61st birthday) to stop productive writing and simply publish material already completed—which I have no actual intention of doing—I would be able to keep up my publication rate of over a book a year for the next five years, replicating P. G. Wodehouse's achievement of producing one book for each year of one's life.

The quinquennium at issue here (1985-90) has in fact been extraordinarily productive for me. I carried out a substantial series of investigations in several areas: philosophy of sciences (*Scientific Realism* - 1987) the theory of rationality (*Rationality* - 1988, *Cognitive Economy* -1989, *A Useful [Evolutionary] Inheritance* -1989), moral philosophy (*Moral Absolutes* -1989). I have observed in myself a distinct sort of evolution over the years. In my earlier years I was primarily interested in *abstractions*—in the "pure," strictly theoretical questions of logic and mathematics. Then, in my middle years, my interests graduated to the sciences of nature (particularly cosmology and biology) and society (particularly economics). As I grew older, however, they became increasingly humanistic and oriented themselves more heavily towards the creative activity of *homo sapiens* in the realms of literature, politics, and intellectual culture. Issues of "philosophical authropology" concerned with various aspects of the human condition have thus recently came into increasing prominence in my work. The books on *Ethical Idealism* (1987) and *Human Interests* (1990) reflect this phenomenon.

When making plans to lay down the directorship of the Center for Philosophy of Science, it struck me that there was one particular writing project I wanted particularly to pursue with the added time now at my disposal. Over the years, I have developed my philosophical ideas through a great number of publications dealing with a great variety of topics. But in talking with colleagues, it soon became apparent to me that the systemic interconnections that bind these varied discussions into a unified and coherent whole were apparent virtually to myself alone. And so I was struck with the idea of writing a connected exposition to give a unified overview of my philosophical ideas to their systemic interconnections into closer view—to write a book, or group of books, presenting my "system" of philosophy. Increasingly I felt a need "to put it all together" by producing a work of substantial synthesis, a systematic and synoptic exposition of the lines of philosophical thought that I have developed over the years in the course of so many books and articles. This is a project that has engaged much of my attention during the period from 1988 to date (1990). It will ultimately issue in a trilogy which is moving well along towards completion and has been accepted for publication by the Princeton University Press. In intention, I want to make these books into my very best, but whether I shall bring this off remains to be seen. The idea that this culmination of my philosophical labors will be published by the University at which they commenced just forty years ago pleases me very much.

The closing months of 1989 saw one further change in the pattern of our lives. We had promised Cathy a dog for some years, originally intending to acquire one to ease the house's emptiness when her brothers went off to college. With one thing and another, the step was postponed, but now we finally went through with this. Repeated family visits to the dog pound ultimately resulted in the selection of "Pepper"—a mixture of beagle and black Labrador retriever, with the latter predominant. We had at first thought of a puppy, but Pepper, a mature and handsome dog of three years, appealed to us—and especially to Cathy—by his friendly ways and intelligent responses. It did not take him long to convert the whole family—the boys included—to a firm belief in the benefits of dog-ownership. The species certainly has a natural talent for working their way into the affections of humans!

Somewhere deep inside me there is also an architect trying to get out—or rather, perhaps, a real estate developer. In the autumn of 1987 I bought at auction an apartment in "The Brittany" in Sewickley, with the idea that we might use it if Cathy transferred to Sewickley Academy. I had the idea that one could buy bargain properties, improve them, and then sell at a profit. This first experiment of a Sewickley condominium soon convinced me otherwise. While that rather drab apartment was soon turned it into a thing of beauty, it ultimately it was sold it at a profit so small that it turned into a loss after discounting the transitional costs of maintenance and marketing. The lesson I drew is that real estate ownership is only worthwhile if one gets some sort of use or benefit from the property. This idea was soon put to work. The spring of 1990 saw the purchase of inexpensive little house alongside the Allegheny River in Verona (address 153 Fairview Avenue) with the idea of having it available for guests and for visiting Center fellows. Maintaining an extra house is a bit of a bother, but it does render a real service. Only time will tell whether this is a good idea from a financial point of view, but in the meantime I rather enjoyed transforming a house that was dark and drab into one that is light and cheerful. I am a great believer in trying new ventures and projects from time to time, keeping up with those that prove a success (with Cunliffe Close in Oxford as a pre-eminent example), and "cutting one's losses" with those that prove otherwise.

Throughout this period, Dorothy and I also continued to house-hunt on our own account in a rather desultory fashion. We hoped to find a neighborhood that offered easier access to friends. But every time we came near to finding a suitable house, one difficulty or another stood in the way. The problem is not just inertia, but the fact is that 5818 Aylesboro Avenue is such a comfortable house in such a convenient location that anything short of an *ideal* solution soon comes to be viewed as not quite good enough—and, of course, absolutely ideal solutions are very hard to come by in this life!

In this regard one other idea came to the fore. Over the years, I have come to find long sunless winters increasingly oppressive, and welcome the idea of midwinter breaks in a warmer climate. The thought of a *pied à terre* in Florida or some other warm climate for regular occasional use over the winter months has of late become a more attractive prospect.

To be sure, I am not a beach person, but thoughts of early morning walks among palm trees and an evening cup of tea watching sun set over a body of water have come to have an appeal. Still, the whole idea may well die of malnutrition.

Be this as it may, the onset of the 1990's saw some shifting in the allocation of my efforts—in professional life from administration to more concentrated writing, and in personal life from offspring-focussed involvement to other concerns. Whether for good or bad, such changes do at least have the productive effect of preventing life from settling into too much of fixed rut. As I have said repeatedly, it is a good thing for even an old dog to learn new tricks.

Eighteen

CHANGING PRIORITIES:
1990-1995 (Age 62-67)

The new decade opened auspiciously for me with the award in the spring of 1990 of the University of Pittsburgh's "Presidents' Distinguished Research Award." The monetary bonus of some five thousand dollars, helpful though it was, had less significance for me than the token of recognition by my university colleagues of my philosophical labors during three decades at Pitt, where with the passage of years I had become the senior serving University Professor. I was particularly gratified by the award because I realize that all too often people whose work is esteemed elsewhere are not particularly appreciated at home base.

In this connection, the celebration in the fall semester of 1991 of my 30th anniversary at Pitt also afforded me much satisfaction. Under the joint sponsorship of the Philosophy Department and the Center for Philosophy of Science, a weekend conference was held in November of that year in which many old friends and former students played a part—culminating in a celebratory dinner attended by over two hundred people. Though one cannot but have mixed feelings in passing this sort of milestone, it is likewise impossible not to be pleased by the support of so many friends and colleagues. In the context of the occasion Dorothy was asked to arrange a small exhibition at Hillman library, and she did a splendid job of it.

With the passage of years, a new sense of priorities sets in. I now began to withdraw systematically from editing the philosophy journals I had founded in earlier years, arranging for the editorship of the *Public Affairs Quarterly* to be turned over to Nicholas Capaldi of the University of Tulsa in 1991, that of the *History of Philosophy Quarterly* to Andrew Reck of Tulane University in 1992, and that of the *American Philosophical Quarterly* to Gary Gutting of the University of Notre Dame in 1993. With the journal editorships well provided for, I now limited any activities on this front to the less demanding duties of elder statesmanship. Moreover, I now proceeded to curtail my administrative involvements at the University. The object of these measures was to "clear the decks" to facilitate a more single-minded dedication to research.

An interviewer once asked what part of philosophical work has given me particular pride and satisfaction. In response I made two points. The first is that, plausibly enough, among my many books I should look on some with more favor then others, and that some are my particular pets—*The Coherence Theory of Truth* and *Methodological Pragmatism*, for example—because they gave particular impetus to the inauguration of ideas that were seminal for the development my thinking at large. But the second—and more crucial—point is that it is the body of my work as a whole on which I place paramount weight in this regard. For what has been characteristic of my philosophical labors—and is rather unusual in the present scheme of things—is their comprising a system, a complex yet nevertheless (as I see it) unified and cohesive body of thought that weaves a great many key issues together into one coherent fabric. Systematizing was popular in the nineteenth century, but fell almost wholly out of favor in the twentieth. But I myself am something of a throw-back to the past in this regard, since, as I see it, any really adequate philosophical position must be systematic and to forego this larger aspiration is to abandon one of the salient missions of the entire enterprise.

Over the years I have produced a vast amount of philosophical writing. To my mind, much of this forms part of one single project—one unified vision of a systematic philosophical position. But because I wrote in such a way that each book stood on its own feet as an independent unit, this systematic aspect of my philosophical work has been apparent to only a minute group of my philosophical colleagues. In the profession at large, people who knew one bit of my work remained blissfully oblivious to its relationship with others. Often I would encounter reviews to the effect "This is an instructive discussion of the issue, but its treatment of aspect X of the issue is somewhat cursory and in need of development" with the writer oblivious to the fact (footnote references to the contrary sometimes notwithstanding) that topic X has been the focus of yet another book of mine. It ultimately struck me as useful to me to make the systematic unity of my work apprehensible by producing a systematic treatise that would weave the various themes and theses together in a readily discernible way. And so I projected a trilogy on *A System of Pragmatic Idealism* to present my substance of my philosophical ideas in three volumes, the first devoted to epistemology and philosophy of science, the second to value theory and moral philosophy, and the third to metaphilosophical issues. These three books were produced with comparative ease and efficiency. The completion of their publication in 1994 (soon after I had reached the traditional retirement age of 65—a practice now happily obsolete) was something of a high point in my professional career.

I was pleased to get these various books into print because I felt it important to give a clear and effective expression to the philosophical position I had developed over the years. The central, formative theme of my philosophy is set by the idea of the limits and limitations inherent in the human condition. This means, in particular, that our human knowledge of the world—our natural science—is imperfect and imperfectable. But at just this point my caution turns in a more positive direction. For I emphatically reject the negativistic tendencies of the age—skepticism, indifferentist relativism, and the like. Nihilism of all sorts, and of the epistemic variety in particular, are all anathema to me. For, so I believe, while we cannot achieve perfection in the cognitive venture, we can achieve adequacy. As the pragmatism that I favor sees it, we seek information for the sake of action, and this issue of implementational adequacy provides an objective—thought- and wish-independent quality control for our beliefs. When it comes to implementing efforts in a matter of reality's harsh and unindulgent taskmastership. Our thought-life is indeed a matter of ideal constructs devised by intellectual artifice, but the efficacy of our implementation in action of these con- structs is a matter of reality's uncompromising operations. Accordingly, the pragmatic standard of efficacy in applica- tions is capable of effecting a clear division between mere flights of fancy on the one hand and rationally sound construc- tions on the other. And so, while I am in many respects a philosophical idealist, I temper this idealism by an important concession to realism—a recognition of the quality-control exerted through the primacy of effective praxis.

The bicentennial of the French Revolution in 1989 occa- sioned my reading and thinking about the nature of social order. The defect of much of the 20th century political theo- rizing among philosophers is its penchant for utopian ideali- zations. The idea that humans are imperfect creatures whose management calls not only for intelligence but for restraints seems to be uncongenial to an age gone to emphasizing rights at the expense of duties. This political concern led me to project a book—entitled *Pluralism* (1993)—whose emphasis on social diversity was largely directed against theories of Jürgen Habermas for whom, as for so many contemporary Europeans, social consensus is the prime requisite of political health.

Also, continuing my long-term involvement with Leibniz I published (in 1991) an edition of his classic *Monadology* suited to the use of students. And thereafter I wrote an essay called "Leibniz Finds a Niche" detailing the developments surrounding his coming to Hanover in 1676. This foray into pure history provided me with an activity of interest and entertainment for some months. For, as indicated above, it can be both enlightening and illuminating to see a philosopher not just as a mind preoccupied with ideas but as a person dealing with the sorts of issues that confront us all in life.

With my *System* trilogy completed, I resisted any tempta- tion to put my pen away and close up my writing desk. Even before the project was finished, new stirrings were already at work as several other projects also pushed their way into my thoughts and onto my working agenda. Reflections regarding philosophical methodology and metaphilosophy in connection with that third system volume led me to embark on a new book, entitled *Philosophical Standardism* (1994) to set out more fully the lineaments of a philosophical methodology which, recognizing our limits, foregoes the universalistic aspirations of traditional philosophizing, in conceiving the aims of the philosophical enterprise more modestly, this approach makes its pursuit at once more practicable and productive.

In Europe (and especially Britain) it is common for academics—of whatever specialty—to bestir themselves in some branch or other of belles lettres. Some impetus in this direction arose in my spirit from time to time, but it was only in my mid-60's that I took any actual steps. First I produced a couple of short stories that distinctly left me unsatisfied. Then I shifted into a somewhat more poetic mode—not in the way of serious poetry but in that of animal fables in the manner of Aesop, complete with morals.[1] These productions evoked a somewhat fonder response in my spirit, and I saw them finally reach the light of print in 1994 in a small volume entitled *Animal Conversations* with illustrations by an artist whom I had met at the Sunday outdoor exhibitions at the University Parks in Oxford. I got much pleasure from writing these fables and hope that here and there a reader will get pleasure from them too. One likes to think that the vast mass of humanity that surrounds us contains here and there an unknown friend—a kindred spirit of sorts. It is in this belief and this hope that my little forays into literature—these very pages included—were undertaken.

While much of my effort during this period was dedicated to the production of two major epistemological projects—namely two (yet unpublished) books on *Objectivity* and on *Prediction*—I also turned backwards to publish a series of retrospective collections of earlier essays and papers in different areas of philosophy, including metaphilosophy (*Satisfying Reason*-1995), social philosophy (*Public Concerns*-1995), epistemic economics (*Priceless Knowledge?*-

1996), and the history of philosophy (*Essays in the History of Philosophy*-1995). Much of this material, mutually published in journals, needed easier access. I also brought to expression (in *Process Metaphysics*-1996) my long-standing interest in process philosophy which—together with my commitment to pragmatism—represents the decidedly American tendency of my philosophical influences. In terms of publication, these were banner years. The underlying motive of all of this revival of my past philosophizing was to supplement my now completed "System of Pragmatic Idealism" trilogy by making available in conveniently accessible form to a new generation of philosophical colleagues some of the laboriously excogitated philosophical positions and tendencies represented in my own work.

As I laid down the journals new arrangements had to be made at the university for my continuing secretarial support. As a result, Estelle Burris came into my office in 1994 and soon made herself indispensable through her diligence and versatility. I must say that I would not be able to be half as productive as I have been without having someone of her capabilities at my disposal.

It is relatively uncommon for philosophy to bear closely on practical affairs. But it does sometimes happen. From a London *Times* report of 19 July 1993 I learned that the Commission of the European Economics Community has for some years adopted as its formal definition of poverty having an income below half the average. This is exactly the standard for which I argued in my 1972 book on *Welfare* (see pp. 101-2). While I cannot claim the credit to *origination*—apparently I was, unbeknownst to me, anticipated by V. R. Fuchs—I can at least lay claim to that of *vindication*.

Early in 1993 I was contacted by a literary agent, Jim Hornfischer of Literary Group International, who had somewhere come across an article of mine and thought I should be writing for an audience wider than that of fellow professionals alone. After some exchanges back and forth, it was agreed that that 1990 presidential address on "luck" would make the basis of an interesting book. On this basis I proceeded to write a book of this title which analyzed the role of this prominent element of the human condition. It was published by Farrar-Straus-Giroux in late 1995. They printed some 10,000 copies where only 2,000 actually sufficed for my philosophical books, and paid what I saw as a handsome advance. With this venture into "trade" publication I experimented in outreach to what was for me a new and different audience—the wider popular readership outside the domain of professional colleagues. How the book fares in this regard remains to be seen, but it is certainly off to a better start than any of my more technical efforts. And in any case, I feel that the topic of the book is one that lies near to home for me, seeing that the role of chance and luck in my own life has certainly been prominent. On the negative side, the outcome of that fateful lottery which led to my being drafted into the Marines instead of the Army affords an example. On the positive side lie those chance developments which led the Lehigh philosophers to seek me out at RAND and restore me to the academic world that I regard as my natural habitat. And on a lesser scale there was the incident that the *Luck* book itself chanced to be read by an editor who induced me to contribute an article on the topic to US Air's monthly magazine—surely the first time that the substance of a presidential address to the philosophers has resurfaced in so popular a medium.

Speaking of RAND, in May of 1991 I attended a small political philosophy conference in Santa Monica. During the free intervals I took walks down memory lane along various parts of town—and I also made an excursion to Pacific Palisades as well to look at my old house there. What a strange Rip-van-Winkle-like feeling. Many things were familiar: streets, buildings, and scenes. And yet—no people. Of dozens of friends and acquaintances whose names stuck in my mind after this interval of almost forty years, the telephone directory yielded but a single name (that of Norman Dalkey). And I could find only two vestiges of my presence in this place during 1954-56: a book from the public library which I had taken out when it occupied a different site) and a fir tree I had planted at the Bestor Boulevard house and which had now grown to truly impressive proportions. (By my next visit in 1996 it was gone.) It is a humbling feeling to get a sense of how the winds of change blow away all our footprints in the sand. In view of this, I must consider it fortunate that my job, at least, has been an island of comparative stability in the sea of change, with more than half a dozen of my departmental associates at Pitt having now (1995) been colleagues of mine for over 25 years.

Our history is a manifestation of our hold on life itself. As someone with many German friends and relations, I never succumbed to the negative stereotyping occasionally encountered among the 1930's refugees of identifying the German and the Nazis. In fact, as the years went by I gradually came to the conclusion that it would be fit and proper to reclaim my German heritage and to reassert—at least nominally—my linkage to the land of my fathers. And so in the early 1990's I availed myself of the prospect of dual citizenship and applied for a German passport. Like so many of my fellow countrymen, I see myself in ethnic terms, as a German-American—who, America being what it is, is no less of an American for the presence of that hyphenation. And the fact that being a German natural now carries Euro-citizenship in its wake is also convenient given my many dealings with people there.

Throughout these years, we have also been continuing our annual summer visits to Oxford, which are always enjoyable and make for a very welcome break in the ordinary routine of Pittsburgh life. On the other hand, the very fact of their repetition is, now—after more than 25 years—rendering them somewhat routine and stylized. In part this is welcome because we get to see many of the old Cunliffe Close friends again—Robin and Jane Burch, Sue and Charles Steiner, and Sally Mason. We use our summer's leisure for relaxation and, in my case for some leisurely work. (Many is the book at which I've made good progress over the summer period.) And we cultivate various interests old and new (as with Dorothy's growing collection of scenic watercolors by Ken Messer—some the product of special commission). But as we ourselves grow older and less flexible, and as the children mature and are increasingly unwilling to be uprooted from their accustomed routines, it becomes clearer year by year that the days of these summers migrations are numbered.

And in one way this English summer break is nowadays less of a chance "to get away from it all." The telephone, the fax machine, and the convenience of express delivery service have brought our Cunliffe Close house much closer to my office in the Cathedral of Learning, greatly increasing the speed —and, alas, also the volume—of communicative exchanges.

The early 90's were fateful years of transition in the development of our family. In December of 1991 Mark graduated from Pitt with a major in English, going on in the fall of 1992 to do graduate study in this field at the Clemson University in South Carolina. Owen graduated from Haverford in May of 1992 with a major in Philosophy, thereafter pursuing graduate work at the University of Guelph in Canada. He took the M.A. there in 1994 and thereupon entered the doctoral program in philosophy at the University of Rochester. With Elizabeth working on her doctorate in English at the University of Toronto, and Mark having studied for some time at McGill, it seems that by some quirk of fate most of the children are destined to pursue some of their studies in the land of our neighbors to the north.

Cathy is nowadays an undergraduate at Drew University in Madison, NJ—although at the moment (Fall of 1995) she is away on an Junior Year Abroad program in Florence, Italy. Her interests are shaping up in the direction of anthropology and art history. Her years at the Ellis school had seen Cathy develop a well honed set of social skills which later stood her in good stead. Both at college and during the summers abroad in England, she has gathered in a diversified and sizable group of friends of both sexes. Dealing with brothers had given Cathy a talent for making friends of boys rather than "boyfriends"—a circumstance not always easily comprehensible to the girls who eventually become girl-friends to the boys. She gets on splendidly with people of all ages varying from the young children with whom she works in her English summer camps to adults—even oldsters—of all sorts. I am very proud of Cathy as someone who has developed an impressive array of social skills and has made of herself a "people person" of unusual effectiveness.

A particularly notable familial development during this period has been Elizabeth's marriage to Robert Morrison of Toronto in June of 1995. This occurred at a period when she is in process of completing her Ph.D. in English literature at the University of Toronto (and I greatly hope that she will now persevere to bring this project to its conclusion). Robert too is a Ph.D. candidate in English—a highly intelligent and serious minded young man, who returned to academia after a period in the business world. They seem well suited to each other and their union evokes paternal good wishes and hopefulness. Elizabeth is one of the brightest, nicest, most delightful people I know, and deserves nothing but the best of life (irrelevant though that may be for the issue of actual fate and fortune).

In the present condition of things it is not easy for young people in any of the economic classes from the poorest to the richest to know where to set one's feet on the paths of life. Choices lie before all of them and it is not easy to figure out in which direction to resolve them. I hope and pray that in the fullness of time the children will each find a line of endeavor from which they can draw not only economic benefit but personal satisfaction. As things stand, I am somewhat surprised to find that my little family is becoming such a brood of young academics—and am also somewhat worried by this because I think that the profession is falling on harder days.

Still, while present times are in various ways difficult for young people, there are also compensations. My formative years unfolded in conditions where war seemed the normal thing. I narrowly missed World War II, reaching eighteen in 1946 just after its end. Then, during the Korean War, I was caught up in military service. My middle years were passed in the era of the Viet Nam War. It came to seem the normal thing for young Americans to be going off to war. But mercifully this is an era that is now behind us, and sons in their young 20's are able to spend their youth in the pursuits of peace instead of serving their country in some deadly foreign field.

During the early 90's I continued to make various new friends through the mediation of Pitt's Center for Philosophy of Science. Here my contacts with Axel Wüstehube were especially close, both because of his interest in my work (he translated *Rationality* into German) and because he lived in our house in Verona during his Pittsburgh visit of 1990-91. Axel is one of the people who knows my philosophy well and has extended himself to make it more widely known in Germany.

The continuation of the study of Spanish that I commenced at age sixty also falls under his theme of internationalism. Embarked on an ongoing program of Spanish reading, I had, by the end of 1991, finished plowing my way through *Don Quijote*. At this point I began to subscribe to the weekly international edition of *El País*, and added this to my reading agenda. I also looked about for a conversation partner and found one in Mrs. Lidia Diáz, an Argentine doctoral student in Pitt's Department of Hispanic Languages who came to talk with me for a few hours each week during the 1991-92 academic year. In the spring of 1992 I also had a weekly conversation hour with Dr. Juan Alonzo Vásquez, a retired professor of this department who had taught philosophy in Argentina before emigrating to the USA, and since then various Spanish speaking Center fellows have helped to keep me in practice.

The payoff for my Spanish studies came in the spring of 1992, when the chance arose to spend a week in Spain, visiting with my friends Juan Carlos León in Murcia and Alfonso Perez de la Borda in Salamanca. First I gave some lectures at the University of Murcia, and then Alfonso drove me to Salamanca via a detour through Toledo where we spent four hours in unforgettably fascinating tourism (the cathedral, the old synagogues, the house of El Greco, etc.). I much enjoyed giving my lectures in Murcia and Salamanca—esp. the latter where we had some really good discussions. My impromptu report there on "The Present State of American Philosophy" led me to write substantial essays on that theme after my return to Pittsburgh, for I found it illuminating to go through the exercise of looking at U. S. Philosophy from the vantage point of an external perspective. Later on, in 1994, I gave a lecture in Madrid University's Summer Program at El Escorial, and in the summer of 1995 I gave a series of lectures at the El Ferrol campus of the University of La Coruña. This visit to Galicia—a distinctly different region of Spain—was arranged by my friend Wenceslao González, who also took Dorothy and myself on a mini-pilgrimage to the Cathedral at Santiago de Compostela.

The early 1990's saw a burgeoning of interest in my work in various European countries. This was attested not only by a steady stream of conference and lecture invitations but more emphatically by translation projects. In 1993, five translations of my works were in progress (German—1, French—1, Spanish—2, Italian—1), and by 1995 ten different books of mine had been published in translation, more than any other living American philosopher. Needless to say, I was much pleased by these indications that my philosophical work was well received abroad. Another indication was the award to me in the summer of 1990 of the Rector's Medal for Distinguished Scholarship at the University of Helsinki, where I was also gave the associated lecture. Dorothy and Cathy accompanied me on this occasion—my third visit to this lovely old Scandinavian port city, whose environs we now toured in the company of my old friends Timo Airaksinen and Arto Saarinen. In this regard too, the 1995 book entitled *The Primacy of Practice: A Study of The Philosophy of Nicholas Rescher* by my Italian friend Michele Marsonet was particularly notable. It gives a comprehensive picture of the system I have developed over the years, and one that is generally accurate—though it is only fair to admit that it seems to be part of human nature that we would rather be misrepresented then ignored.

Another highlight for me during this period was the Philosophy of Science Center's conference in Athens in the spring of 1992. The Acropolis and other antiquities were awesome, the setting Delphi sensational, the hospitality of our Greek colleagues delightful. It was possible for Mark to accompany me, and I much enjoyed his company. My Greek friend Aristides Baltas, whom I had also come to know through the Center, as well as my former student Dionysios Anapolitanos, helped to make our visit a memorable occasion.

In 1993 I made my first foray to Latin America with a visit to Argentina with Ezequiel de Olaso in Buenos Aires and my old friend Victor Rodríguez in Córdoba. The last visit was made particularly exciting for me because the Argentine National Autonomous University of Córdoba awarded me an honorary degree in the course of this visit. In 1994 Lehigh University, my old employer which had induced my return to philosophy teaching in 1956, also awarded me an honorary doctorate, enabling me to renew old contacts and to enjoy a trip down memory lane in Bethlehem. And in late 1994 the University of Konstanz in Germany, with which I had been closely connected over the years through mediation of Jürgen Mittelstrass and Gereon Wolters, bestowed honorary doctorates on Adolf Grünbaum and myself to recognize not only our work but also our role in the Center of Philosophy of Science. We live in a materialistic age and philosophy, as the saying has it, "bakes no bread," so that in the present day and age philosophers are not much honored in the wider society. But it is gratifying that in the world of academia itself, at least, the contributions of philosophers are occasionally appreciated.

On the occasion of the Konstanz award, Dorothy came along and we stayed once again in the Insel Hotel. We took a day off from academic activities and dissolved it to the progress of "getting in touch with one's roots." Dorothy's father's people came from Haigerloch and Ilmensee, only about 70-80 km from Konstanz in the Swabian sector of the of Hohenzollern domains. We rented a car and drove there to do a bit of sightseeing and on the spur of the moment called unannounced on Frau Elizabeth Beuter at Haigerloch with whom Dorothy's sister, Jackie Brown had been in touch in connection with her genealogical researches. Fortunately she was at home, and we had a nice visit with here and her children. Using the family tree that Jackie had made, Frau Beuter was able eventually to locate a remote Henle cousin many times removed and to identify other relatives, now dead, one of whom had been Bürgermeister at Ilmensee in the 1920's. It is interesting to think that Dorothy's people were also Swabians and came from places not all that far removed from Schrozberg, whence the Reschers hailed.

We received a bad fright in the matter of Dorothy's health in March of 1993. She had a heart attack—mercifully a small one occasioned by a blockage in one (non-major) artery, with the rest of her arterial system in good shape and able to make up for the lost circulation. With a regular regimen of exercise and physical activity to keep her circulatory system in good shape there is every expectation that Dorothy will continue in good health after as before. All the same these reminders of the frailties and vulnerabilities of our physical mechanisms are distinctly unwelcome—though they provide us with a "wake-up call" to concentrate on the things that are really rewarding and enriching in life and not waste our energies and resources on the things that are neither satisfying to oneself or important in the large scheme of things.

In the autumn of 1993, Dorothy was invited to join the Board of Directors of Gargaro Productions, a production company for musical theater performances. She had known Jane (Mrs. Kenneth) Gargaro since high school, and we had also known the Gargaros as fellow members of the University Oratory for many years. Dorothy now attended the board meetings very regularly and became involved as an idea source for matters of fund raising, advertising, and promotion. We also became regular attenders at opening nights, a duty made pleasant by the fact that Ken does an excellent job with his productions, and that the talent, while largely local, is generally first-rate and serves to draw young people into the theater.

I dedicated a good deal of time and effort at Pitt during the 1993-94 academic year to service on a search committee seeking a new provost to succeed my friend Don Henderson, who was taking early retirement. As usual, the committee was of complex composition (with representatives from the different schools, the administration, the students) and its personnel had very different interests and agendas. We held innumerable meeting to whittle several hundred prospects down to a final three. When all was at last said and done, the Chancellor picked Jim Maher—the chairman of our physics department—from our three finalists. This old and dear friend of mine quickly proved himself to be a superb choice for the provostship.

The mid 1990's saw my daily routine taking on a relatively rigid form. Arising at six AM I usually manage around an hours work before breakfast, during which I read several newspapers. By around 8:30 AM I arrive at the office, dedicating my mornings to University duties—teaching, correspondence, library work, etc. I frequently lunch with a colleague at some campus-proximate eatery—or else go home to eat. After an hour's post-luncheon rest and recreation, I proceed to my third floor study to work until the late afternoon. Then comes a walk with Pepper, followed by dinner and a period of relaxation. At around 7:30 PM I head for the study once more, but leave off working at around 9 for a mixture of activities (exercising on my stationary bicycle, reading Spanish, watching television). I retire around eleven but before actually going to bed generally spent another half hour at some work-disconnected reading—usually something biographical (including, for example, biographies of all US presidents until F.D.R.'s day). I generally find American political figures personally less interesting than British ones —perhaps because our biographical tradition focuses more extensively on external activities than on the inner person—but the overall story of the nation's development is a fascinating one. In particular the history of the Civil War— that crucially formative eventuation in American history—has increasingly enlisted my interest and I have become something of a "Civil War buff." All in all, I manage to read an average some three or four "general interest" books each month. As regards television watching, I favor a few sitcoms ("Newhart," "Seinfeld")—and of course the occasional British period dramatization. But with regard to films I am an utter Philistine, and go in search of entertainment pure and simple. (I dislike socially improving films and favor "mindless diversions.")

In early December of 1995 Dorothy and I took a short winter holiday in Charleston SC in connection with an academic visit. Staying at the King's Courtyard Inn in the historic section of town we visited various of the historic houses there, ranging in age from the Heyward-Washington House of 1772 to the Calhoun Mansion of 1876, as well as the Boone Plantation a short drive out of town. We also visited Mount Pleasant (lunching at Captain Guilde's Café) and inspected Daniel Island, whose projected development project has long interested me. This visit further whetted my growing appetite for a "winter escape" place in the South as a counterpart to our "summer escape" place in Oxford. (This may be one of the few "day dreams" I still allow myself at this late stage, though I begin to doubt that it will ever come to fruition.)

One new development of this period is that under Owen's influence Dorothy and I have been drawn into collaborative crossword puzzle solving. The N. Y. Times has a daily puzzle that increases in difficulty as the week moves along. Dorothy and I colaborately manage to solve the puzzle up to and including Wednesdays, get it about half done on Thursdays and Fridays, and are completely at sea by Saturday.

During my college years I was an ardent devotee of classical music, but this interest somehow got shifted onto the back burner over the subsequent decades, though during the first dozen years after our marriage Dorothy and I did attend the concert Season of the Pittsburgh Symphony (particularly in the years when William Steinberg was its music director). And in the 1990's I returned to this art form with renewed enthusiasm, often using tapes to provide "background music" while I worked, relying primarily on the work of "romantics" such as Bruckner, Mahler, and Rachmaninoff. (I cannot say that a background of music stimulates mental activity, but it does not seem to hamper it either.) Also, nowadays Dorothy and I enjoy the concerts given by the River City Brass Orchestra at Carnegie Music Hall.

In the summer of 1995 came my 67th birthday, and as I now draw within hailing distance of seventy it becomes possible to detect signs of decreasing physical and mental flexibility. I am also rather less sociable than heretofore, and note that I am becoming somewhat more selfcontained and taciturn on public occasions. All the same, the impetus to work still dwells within me. I continue to sense the inner stirrings of some useful book projects, and greatly hope that the health and energy needed for their production will yet be forthcoming.

But with the wisdom of passing years I have come to realize with increasing clarity that the most important part of myself that I will leave behind is not my books but my children. To be sure they do not really belong to me but to themselves, and they are destined, for better or worse, to make their way in the world by struggles in which I can help them but little, if at all. Yet I feel confident that those years of their childhood spent in familial communion have left as indelible a mark on them as on myself. And they may be sure that throughout the triumphs and turmoils of their lives my paternal eye will cast (however figuratively) its loving and caring glance upon them —eventually even from the other side of the great divide.

NOTES

1. For example:

> The lion and the unicorn were fighting for the crown.
> The lion eyed it greedily and said with a deep frown,
> "That crown I greatly covet,
> So, unicorn, my friend, If you will let me have it,
> Then I shall gladly send
> To you the whole world's stock of gold,
> Including both new and old."
> "Done," said the clever one-horned creature,
> "But please remember just this feature—
> That crown itself will also be
> One of the things you'll owe to me,
> For being made of gold, quite fine,
> It too will then come to be mine."
> The moral of this tale is clear:
> A bargain may be bought too dear.

Nineteen

RETROSPECT:
1995 (Age 67)

The past decade has flown by with astounding rapidity, presumably because I have kept very busy the whole while. I am one of those people who is never quite comfortable when idle, when not doing something or other—even if only thinking. And I have certainly kept busy. In the 1990-95 period I published over a dozen serious philosophical books—more than virtually any one of my professional colleagues has managed to produce in a lifetime.

In some ways my life nowadays is—mercifully—almost borringly routine in its externals, divided between work (at home or office), family life, and a series of forays (eg. to Oxford) whose structure also follows a pattern of sorts. But not only is this external dullness itself a benefit of sorts, but it is nowise at odds with an internal vibrancy that goes with new forays in the life of the mind. Moreover, life's tendency to run in established grooves is by no means unwelcome to a person of fundamentally conservative inclinations. A biographer of Charles Francis Adams remarked that in his later years this American statesman "chose to lead his own life free from involvement in any of the disquieting experiments of his age and amongst men who, like himself, preferred the older standards."[1] As I read this passage, it struck me how well this characterizes my own reaction to the turbulent America of the late 20th century, with its penchant for experimentation in matters of drugs, lifestyle, and political protest. I have long been content to be conservative in social matters, greatly preferring innovation in abstract matters of *thinking* to agitations in concrete matters of *living*, where, as I see it, the importance of "common sense" can hardly be exaggerated and much is to be said for heeding the guidance of well-established patterns.

Fate plays strange tricks on us all. Ten years ago I was considering the prospect of organizing some sort of gathering of those who staffed the Marine Corps Institute in the early 50's. However, it soon emerged that there was in train a more ambitious project by Wayne Pilny of North Royalton, Ohio to organize the alumni of the entire Marine Corps Barracks veterans of the 1951-54 period—not those of MCI alone, but also those of the Ceremonial Company stationed there. This apparently more feasible project resulted in a 40th anniversary reunion in 1994—which, ironically, I was forced to miss because of its timing in August, when we were away in Oxford, as usual. On a cognate note, I subsequently learned of the launching of an organization of RAND Corporation alumni, and I managed to establish contact with them in 1995. An inclination to take up the threads of the past is a part of my nature that is astir even when not working away at these autobiographical notes.

One aspect of this is an increasingly intensified interest in reading biographical works. Biography may be an acquired taste, but among English speakers it has become a fairly common one. Over a thousand such books are annually published nowadays in Britain alone and over two thousand in the US. There seems to be an insatiable desire to peer into the lives of other people. We want to look into the dark corners—to discover the clay feet of our idols and to learn the deep dark secrets which show that the rich and famous are even worse scoundrels than we ourselves. To be sure, an autobiographer is not likely to satisfy this craving—rare is the individual who sets out to debunk himself. Yet at least a biographical work—autobiography included—should not be grossly misleading, and I would be pleased to think that this is something I have managed to achieve in the present book.

I am well aware of how much I have to be thankful for. Not least of all, I have had the good fortune of finding both personal satisfaction and professional success in the pursuit of my philosophical interests. Those mid-journey hopes of mine (see p. 207-208) have been more than realized. As the following citations show, my philosophical work has secured its fair share of recognition: "Rescher's development of pragmatic idealism is characterized by an unusually wide range of sympathy and information" (*The Oxford Companion to Philosophy*). "Rescher's work is characterized by the extensiveness of his investigations and by its adoption of balanced points of view supported by a rigorous analysis of concepts" (*Diccionario de Filosofía*). "[His work is] unique in its scope within 20th century philosophy" (*Philosophie der Gegenwart*); "From his great energy, intellectual power, and restless curiosity has come a system of philosophy unsurpassed in our century" (*Routledge's Dictionary of Twentieth Century Philosophers*). With a reception like this, I clearly have nothing to complain about.

Then too, I am deeply grateful for the good fortune of my family life. No husband or parent has greater occasion than I to thank his luck stars for the gift of a loving spouse and engaging offspring.

The autobiography of an individual fortunate enough to have lived a life in which things have by and large gone well is likely to have an aura of smugness. I do not know how to avoid this, though would certainly like to do so. That self-satisfaction is unwarranted in these matters emerges from a recognition of the sheer contingency of things that comes vividly to view as I compare my life with that of my father, who had to sustain so many hard blows in life.

But the time is at hand for bringing this retrospect to a close. No one enjoys the company of someone whom one finds antipathetic. And so I feel entitled to regard the reader who had persevered so far as a friend. It is in this spirit that I pen these closing words. It would perhaps be premature to wish you farewell, o reader/friend. What the future will bring it is impossible to say. Who knows but that the occasion for yet another decennial supplement may still be forthcoming, so that we will meet again. But it is not likely. I am now 67 and only one of my immediate male forefathers reached 77—seeing that my father lived to 62, his father to 79, and his father to 57. My chances look to be on the order of one in three on this basis. But, ever hopeful, I choose to deem it premature to say a definitive good-bye, and so close with a more guarded —and somewhat equivocal—"til we meet again."

NOTES

1. Martin Duberman, *Charles Francis Adams* (Stanford, Stanford University Press, 1960), p. 338.

NAME INDEX